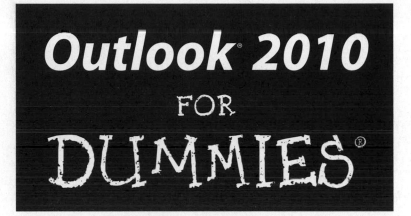

Outlook® 2010
FOR
DUMMIES®

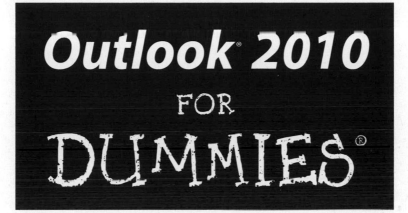

Outlook® 2010

FOR

DUMMIES®

by Bill Dyszel

WILEY

John Wiley & Sons, Inc.

Outlook® 2010 For Dummies®

Published by
John Wiley & Sons, Inc.
111 River Street
Hoboken, NJ 07030-5774

www.wiley.com

For general information on our other products and services, please contact our Customer Care Department within the U.S. at 877-762-2974, outside the U.S. at 317-572-3993, or fax 317-572-4002.

For technical support, please visit www.wiley.com/techsupport.

Wiley publishes in a variety of print and electronic formats and by print-on-demand. Some material included with standard print versions of this book may not be included in e-books or in print-on-demand. If this book refers to media such as a CD or DVD that is not included in the version you purchased, you may download this material at http://booksupport.wiley.com. For more information about Wiley products, visit www.wiley.com.

Wiley also publishes its books in a variety of electronic formats. Some content that appears in print may not be available in electronic books.

Library of Congress Control Number: 2010923567

ISBN 978-0-470-48771-6 (pbk); ISBN 978-0-470-63272-7 (ebk); ISBN 978-0-470-63273-4 (ebk); ISBN 978-0-470-63274-1 (ebk)

Manufactured in the United States of America

10 9 8 7 6 5 4 3

WILEY

About the Author

Bill Dyszel is the author of 19 books and a regular contributor to national publications including *PC Magazine*. Bill is also an award-winning filmmaker and an accomplished entertainer. He sang with the New York City Opera for 14 years and still appears regularly on the New York stage. He has produced scores of short films and currently ranks as the most prolific contributor to the 48-Hour Film Project, an international filmmaking competition. Many of his short, comedic films can be seen on YouTube.

About the Contributor

Daniel A. Begun is freelance technology journalist and consultant who has worked in the tech industry for nearly 20 years. He has written for CNET, *PC Magazine*, *Computerworld*, *Laptop* magazine, *Computer Shopper*, and the PC enthusiast site HotHardware.com, among others. Daniel is the former Labs Director for CNET, where he ran CNET's product testing labs.

Dedication

This book is dedicated to everyone with a love for lifelong learning.

Author's Acknowledgments

Thanks so much to the extraordinary team at Wiley that made this edition a reality — to Katie Mohr for her persistent focus on the project's outcome, to Mark Enochs for his wise editorial guidance, to John Edwards for his relentless attention to detail, and to Lee Musick for his enthusiastic focus on features.

Daniel Begun wins my endless gratitude for bringing his world-class technological expertise and experienced editorial judgment to the task of revising a significant portion of this edition for me in a period of unusually heavy deadlines. A first-rate technologist, crackerjack journalist, and veteran editor in his own right, Daniel's keen professional eye helped make this book more accurate, readable, and fun. He also helped keep the project on schedule through a complex and unpredictable process. Above all, Daniel is a wonderful colleague and a terrific guy in general, which turns a challenging task like this one into an absolute pleasure. Thank you, Daniel!

Publisher's Acknowledgments

We're proud of this book; please send us your comments through our online registration form located at http://dummies.custhelp.com. For other comments, please contact our Customer Care Department within the U.S. at 877-762-2974, outside the U.S. at 317-572-3993, or fax 317-572-4002.

Some of the people who helped bring this book to market include the following:

Acquisitions and Editorial

Senior Project Editor: Mark Enochs

Acquisitions Editor: Katie Mohr

Copy Editor: John Edwards

Technical Editor: Lee Musick

Editorial Manager: Leah Cameron

Editorial Assistant: Amanda Graham

Sr. Editorial Assistant: Cherie Case

Cartoons: Rich Tennant
(www.the5thwave.com)

Composition Services

Project Coordinator: Katherine Crocker

Layout and Graphics: Ashley Chamberlain, Christine Williams

Proofreader: The Well-Chosen Word

Indexer: Cheryl Duksta

Publishing and Editorial for Technology Dummies

    Richard Swadley, Vice President and Executive Group Publisher

    Andy Cummings, Vice President and Publisher

    Mary Bednarek, Executive Acquisitions Director

    Mary C. Corder, Editorial Director

Publishing for Consumer Dummies

    Kathleen Nebenhaus, Vice President and Executive Publisher

Composition Services

    Debbie Stailey, Director of Composition Services

Contents at a Glance

Table of Contents

Part VI: The Part of Tens... 313

Chapter 18: Ten Accessories for Outlook 315

Chapter 19: Ten Things You Can't Do with Outlook 319

Chapter 20: Ten Things You Can Do after You're Comfy 323

Introduction

....

Microsoft Outlook is now a teenager. I covered its first prerelease versions back in 1996, when nobody anywhere knew what it was. Today hundreds of millions of people use Microsoft Outlook every single day to send e-mail, make appointments, and speed up their work. Microsoft Outlook has become the world's principal tool for getting work done.

There's probably no program that's more essential to success in business today than Microsoft Outlook. I've had the pleasure of training literally thousands of people on all the different ways Outlook can improve their workflow and simplify their life. People are often surprised to discover how much faster they can work when they learn to use Outlook effectively.

Microsoft Outlook was designed to make organizing your daily information easy — almost automatic. You already have sophisticated programs for word processing and number crunching, but Outlook pulls together everything you need to know about your daily tasks, appointments, e-mail messages, and other details. More important, Outlook enables you to use the same methods to deal with many different kinds of information, so you have to understand only one program to deal with the many kinds of details that fill your life, such as

✔ Finding a customer's phone number

✔ Remembering that important meeting

✔ Planning your tasks for the day and checking them off after you're done

✔ Recording all the work you do so that you can find what you did and when you did it

Outlook is a Personal Information Manager that can act as your assistant in dealing with the flurry of small-but-important details that stand between you and the work you do. You can just as easily keep track of personal information that isn't business-related and keep both business and personal information in the same convenient location.

About This Book

As you read this book and work with Outlook, you discover how useful Outlook is, as well as find new ways to make it more useful for the things you do most. If you fit in any of the following categories, this book is for you:

✔ Your company just adopted Outlook as its e-mail program and you need to find out how to use it in a hurry.

✔ You've used Outlook for years just because "it was there," but you know you've only used a tenth of its power. Now you're overwhelmed with work and want to plow through that mountain of tasks faster by using Outlook better.

✔ You're planning to purchase (or have just purchased) Outlook and want to know what you can do with Outlook — as well as how to do your work more efficiently.

✔ You want an easier, faster tool for managing tasks, schedules, e-mail, and other details in your working life.

Even if you don't fall into one of these groups, this book gives you simple, clear explanations of how Outlook can work for you. It's hard to imagine any computer user who wouldn't benefit from understanding Outlook better.

If all you want is a quick, guided tour of Outlook, you can skim this book; it covers everything you need to get started. Getting a handle on most major Outlook features is fairly easy — that's how the program is designed. (You can also keep the book handy as a reference for the tricks that you may not need every day.)

The first part of this book gives you enough information to make sense of the whole program. Because Outlook is intended to be simple and consistent throughout, when you have the big picture, the details are fairly simple (usually).

Don't be fooled, though — you can find a great deal of power in Outlook if you want to dig deeply enough. Outlook links with your Microsoft Office applications, and it's programmable by anyone who wants to tackle some Visual Basic script writing (I don't get into that in this book). You may not want to do the programming yourself, but finding people who can do that for you isn't hard; just ask around.

Foolish Assumptions

I assume that you know how to turn on your computer and how to use a mouse and keyboard. In case you need a brush up on Windows, I throw in reminders as I go along. If Windows and Microsoft Office are strange to you,

I recommend picking up (respectively) Andy Rathbone's *Windows 7 For Dummies* or Wally Wang's *Microsoft Office 2010 For Dummies* (both published by Wiley).

If all you have is a copy of this book and a computer running Outlook 2010, you can certainly do basic, useful things right away (like send and receive e-mail), as well as a few fun things. And after some time, you'll be able to do *many* fun and useful things.

How This Book Is Organized

To make it easier to find out how to do what you want to do, this book is divided into parts. Each part covers a different aspect of using Outlook. Because you can use similar methods to do many different jobs with Outlook, the first parts of the book focus on *how* to use Outlook. The later parts concentrate on *what* you can use Outlook to do.

Part I: Getting the Competitive Edge with Outlook

I learn best by doing, so the first chapter is a quick guide to the things that most people do with Outlook on a typical day. You find out how to use Outlook for routine tasks such as handling messages, notes, and appointments. You can get quite a lot of mileage out of Outlook, even if you only check out the things I describe in the first chapter.

Because Outlook allows you to use similar methods to do many things, I go on to show you the things that stay pretty much the same throughout the program: how to create new items from old ones by using drag-and-drop; ways to view items that make your information easy to understand at a glance; and the features Outlook offers to make it easier to move, copy, and organize your files.

Part II: Taming the E-Mail Beast

E-mail is now the most popular function of computers. Tens of millions of people are hooked up to the Internet or an office network.

The problem is that e-mail can still be a little too complicated. As I show you in Part II, however, Outlook makes e-mail easier. Computers are notoriously finicky about the exact spelling of addresses, correctly connecting to the actual mail service, and making sure that the text and formatting of the message fit the software you're using. Outlook keeps track of the details involved in getting your message to its destination.

Outlook also allows you to receive e-mail from a variety of sources and manage the messages in one place. You can slice and dice your list of incoming and outgoing e-mail messages to help you keep track of what you send, to whom you send it, and the day and time you send it.

Part III: Managing Contacts, Dates, Tasks, and More

Outlook takes advantage of its special relationship with your computer and your office applications (Microsoft Outlook with Microsoft Office, Microsoft Internet Explorer, and Microsoft Windows — notice a pattern emerging here?) to tie your office tasks together more cleanly than other such programs — and to make it easier for you to deal with all the stuff you have to do. The chapters in Part III show you how to get the job done with Outlook.

In addition to planning and scheduling, you probably spend lots of time working with other people — you need to coordinate your tasks and schedules with theirs (unless you make your living doing something weird and antisocial, such as digging graves or writing computer books). Outlook allows you to share calendar and task information with other people, and also keep detailed information about the people with whom you collaborate. You can also assign tasks to other people if you don't want to do those tasks yourself (now *there's* a time saver). Be careful, though; other people can assign those tasks right back to you.

If you have yellow sticky notes covering your monitor, refrigerator, desktop, or bathroom door, Outlook's Notes feature might change your life. Notes are little yellow (or blue or green) squares that look just like those handy paper sticky notes that you stick everywhere as reminders and then lose. About the only thing that you can't do is set your coffee cup on one and mess up what you wrote.

Part IV: Beyond the Basics: Tips and Tricks You Won't Want to Miss

Some parts of Outlook are less famous than others, but no less useful. Part IV guides you through the sections of Outlook that the real power users exploit to stay ahead of the pack.

There are parts of Outlook that many people never discover. Some of those parts are obscure but powerful — others aren't part of Outlook at all (technically speaking). Maybe you want to know how to do things like create custom forms and set up Outlook to get e-mail from the Internet. If you use Outlook at home or in your own business, or if you just want to soup up your copy of Outlook for high-performance work, you'll find useful tips in Part IV.

Part V: Outlook at Work

Big organizations have different requirements than small businesses. Many large companies rely heavily on Outlook as a tool for improved teamwork and project management. Part V shows you the parts of Outlook that work best in the big leagues (or for people with big ambitions). You'll get all the info you need to collaborate using SharePoint and Microsoft Exchange, beef up your security, customize the way Outlook looks and works, and check your Outlook account when you're not in the office with Outlook Web Access.

Part VI: The Part of Tens

Why ten? Why not! If you must have a reason, ten is the highest number you can count to without taking off your shoes. A program as broad as Outlook leaves a great deal of flotsam and jetsam that doesn't quite fit into any category, so I sum up the best of that material in groups of ten.

Conventions Used in This Book

Outlook has many unique features, but it also has lots in common with other Windows programs — dialog boxes, pull-down menus, ribbons, and so on. To be productive with Outlook, you need to understand how these features work — and recognize the conventions I use for describing these features throughout this book.

Dialog boxes

Even if you're not new to Windows, you deal with dialog boxes more in Outlook than you do in many other Microsoft Office programs because so many items in Outlook are created with dialog boxes, which may also be called *forms*. E-mail message forms, appointments, name and address forms, and plenty of other common functions in Outlook use dialog boxes to ask you what you want to do. The following list summarizes the essential parts of a dialog box:

- ✔ **Title bar:** The title bar tells you the name of the dialog box.

- ✔ **Text boxes:** Text boxes are blank spaces into which you type information. When you click a text box, you see a blinking I-beam pointer, which means that you can type text there.

- ✔ **Control buttons:** In the upper-right corner of most dialog boxes, you find three control buttons:

  - The *Close button* looks like an X and makes the dialog box disappear.

  - The *Size button* toggles between maximizing the dialog box (making it take up the entire screen) and resizing it (making it take up less than the entire screen).

  - The *Minimize button* makes the dialog box seem to go away but really just hides it on the taskbar at the bottom of your screen until you click the taskbar to make the dialog box appear again.

- ✔ **Tabs:** Tabs look like little file-folder tabs. If you click one, you see a new page of the dialog box. Tabs are just like the divider tabs in a ring binder; click one to change sections.

The easiest way to move around a dialog box is to click the part that you want to use. If you're a real whiz on the keyboard, you may prefer to press the Tab key to move around the dialog box; this method is much faster if you're a touch typist. Otherwise, you're fine just mousing around.

Ribbons and tabs

Outlook 2010 features a colorful strip across the top called the Ribbon. It's adorned with festive-looking buttons. Many of those buttons are labeled with the names of the things that happen if you click them with your mouse, such as Save, Follow Up, or Delete. A row of tabs appears just above the Ribbon, each bearing a label such as Home, Send/Receive, or View. Clicking any of those words reveals an entirely different ribbon full of buttons for a different set of tasks.

This arrangement was a new feature with the release of Microsoft Office 2007 and was expanded in Outlook 2010, so even if you've used Microsoft Office or Microsoft Outlook for many years, it may be new to you. The idea is that people frequently call Microsoft and ask the company to add features to Outlook that don't need to be added because they've been there all along. The Ribbon is supposed to make those mysterious, hidden features more obvious. I think a better solution is to get more people to read this book. As a public service, I'm doing what I can to make that happen. I hope you'll join the cause.

Keyboard shortcuts

Normally, you can choose any Windows command in at least two different ways (and sometimes more):

- Click a button in the Ribbon or Navigation pane.
- Press a keyboard combination, such as Ctrl+B, which means holding down the Ctrl key and pressing the letter B (you use this command to make text bold).
- Press the F10 key to reveal a shortcut key, and then press that key (way too much trouble, but possible for those who love a challenge).

One rather confusing feature of Outlook is the way many commands are hidden within the tabs of the Ribbon. If you don't know which tab contains the button for the thing you want to do, you have to click every tab until you find the command you want. That's fine if you're a speed reader, but for most of us, hunting for rarely used commands slows us down a lot. Fortunately, after you've done a task once, you can usually find your way back to do it again.

Icons Used in This Book

Sometimes the fastest way to go through a book is to look at the pictures — in this case, icons that draw your attention to specific types of information that's useful to know. Here are the icons I use in this book:

The Remember icon points out helpful information. (Everything in this book is helpful, but this stuff is even *more* helpful.)

The Tip icon points out a hint or trick for saving time and effort, or something that makes Outlook easier to understand.

The Warning icon points to something that you may want to be careful about to prevent problems.

The Technical Stuff icon marks background information that you can skip, although it may make good conversation at a really dull party.

Part I

Getting the Competitive Edge with Outlook

The 5th Wave   By Rich Tennant

"Your mail program looks fine. I don't know why you're not receiving any personal e-mails. Have you explored the possibility that you may not have any friends?"

In this part . . .

Microsoft Outlook is the world's most popular tool for communication, collaboration, and personal productivity. In this first part, I show you the essential techniques for working smarter with the tools that Outlook offers. You'll also learn how Outlook's newest features can make you more productive than ever.

Chapter 1

The Outlook Features You Really Need to Know

I'm kicking off this book with Outlook's "Greatest Hits," the things you'll want to do with Outlook every single day. The list sounds simple enough: sending e-mail, making appointments, and so on. But even if you use only about 10 percent of Outlook's features, you'll be amazed at how this little program can streamline your life and spiff up your communications. People get pretty excited about Outlook — even if they take advantage of only a tiny fraction of what the package can do. But there's more here than meets the eye; Outlook does ordinary things extraordinarily well. I know you want to do the same, so read on.

Why Do So Many People Use Outlook?

Millions of people use Outlook because millions of people use Outlook. That's not redundant — Outlook is the standard tool for communicating, collaborating, and organizing for hundreds of millions of people around the world. When so many people use the same tool for organizing the things they do individually, it becomes vastly easier for everyone to organize the things they do together by using that tool. That's the case with Outlook. It's a powerful tool even if you work all alone, but that power gets magnified when you use it to collaborate with others.

What's new in Microsoft Outlook 2010

Every version of Outlook adds some new nips and tucks, but this time, Outlook got its most extensive facelift ever. The Ribbon is the most prominent change, bringing a new look to the main Outlook screen. Ribbons in the various Outlook modules are also more powerful and flexible than ever. Some other improvements include:

✔ Quick Steps automate and streamline the tasks that you perform frequently.

✔ Threaded e-mail conversations make it easier for you follow an ongoing conversation, or ignore it if you want.

✔ Faster searches and better search tools

✔ Richer text-editing tools and better handling of images

✔ You can connect to your favorite social media services and track the online activities of people you know well.

✔ You can customize the Ribbon to suit your needs.

But the main benefit of using Outlook remains the same — it offers a single tool that unifies your communications with all of your daily activities and helps you get more done with less effort.

Easy Ways to Do Anything in Outlook

Well, okay, maybe you can't use Outlook to decipher hieroglyphics — but if you learn a little about some basic techniques, you can do a lot in Outlook — click an icon to do something, view something, or complete something.

Using Outlook is so easy, I can sum it up in just a few simple sentences to cover the most common tasks:

✔ **Open an item and read it:** Double-click the item.

✔ **Create a new item:** Click an icon in the Navigation pane, click a New button in the Ribbon at the top of the screen, and fill out the form that appears. When you're done, click the Send button — or alternatively, the Save and Close buttons.

✔ **Delete an item:** Click the item once to select it, and then click the Delete icon in the Ribbon at the top of the screen. The Delete icon contains a black X.

✔ **Move an item:** Use your mouse to drag the item to where you want it.

Does that seem too simple? No problem. If you have an itch to complicate things, you *could* try to use Outlook while hopping on a pogo stick or flying the space shuttle. But why? These four tricks can take you a long way.

Outlook can also do some sophisticated tricks, such as automatically sorting your e-mail or creating automated form letters, but you'll need to understand a few details to take advantage of those tricks. The other 300 pages of this book cover the finer points of Outlook. If you only wanted the basics, I could've sent you a postcard.

The figures you see in this book and the instructions you read assume that you're using Outlook 2010 the way it comes out of the box from Microsoft — with all the standard options installed. If you don't like the way the program looks (or how things are named) when you install Outlook, you can change many of the things you see. If you change too much, however, some instructions and examples I give you won't make sense, because then the parts of the program that I talk about may have names you gave them, rather than the ones Microsoft originally assigned. The Microsoft people went to great lengths to make Outlook's features easy to find. I suggest leaving the general arrangement alone until you're comfortable using Outlook.

E-Mail: Basic Delivery

E-mail is Outlook's most popular feature. I've run across people who didn't know Outlook could do anything but exchange e-mail messages. It's a good thing that Outlook makes it so easy to read your e-mail, although it's too bad that so many people stop there.

Reading e-mail

When you start Outlook, you normally see a screen with four columns. The leftmost column is the Navigation pane, which lets you switch between different modules in Outlook to perform different tasks. The second column from the left is your list of messages; the third column (called the Reading pane) contains the text of one of those messages. If the message is short enough, you may see its entire text in the Reading pane, as shown in Figure 1-1. If the message is longer, you'll have to open it to see the whole thing.

Here's how to see the entire message:

1. **Click the Mail button in the Navigation pane.**

   You don't need this step if you can already see the messages.

2. **Double-click the title of the message.**

   Now you can see the entire message.

3. **Press Esc to close the message.**

   The message form closes.

Figure 1-1:
Double-
click the
message
you want to
read.

Mail button

Navigation pane

Reading pane

A quick way to skim the messages in your Inbox is to click a message and then press the up-arrow or down-arrow key. You can move through your message list as you read the text of your messages in the Reading pane.

If you feel overwhelmed by the number of e-mail messages you get each day, you're not alone. Billions and billions of e-mail messages fly around the Internet each day, and lots of people are feeling buried in messages. In Chapter 6 I'll show you the secrets of sorting and managing your messages, along with the brand-spanking new Conversations feature that makes it easy to deal with extended email discussions.

Answering e-mail

Anytime you're reading an e-mail message in Outlook, buttons labeled Reply and Reply All appear somewhere near the top of the screen. That's a hint. When you want to reply to a message you're reading, click the Reply button. A new message form opens, already addressed to the person who sent the original message. If you're reading a message sent to several people besides you, you also have the option of sending a reply to everyone involved by clicking the Reply All button.

Some people get carried away with the Reply All button and live to regret it. If you receive a message addressed to lots of other people and click the Reply All button to fire back a snide response, you could instantly offend dozens of clients, bosses, or other bigwigs. Use Reply All when you need it, but make sure that you really know who's getting your message before you click the Send button.

When you reply to a message, the text of the message that was sent to you is automatically included. Some people like to include original text in their replies, and some don't. In Chapter 5, I show you how to change what Outlook automatically includes in replies.

Creating new e-mail messages

At its easiest, the process of creating a new e-mail message in Outlook is ridiculously simple. Even a child can do it. If you can't get a child to create a new e-mail message for you, you can even do it yourself.

If you see a button labeled New E-Mail in the upper-left corner of the screen, just click it, fill out the form, and click the Send button. How's that for simple? If you don't see the New E-Mail button, follow these steps instead:

1. **Click the Mail button in the Navigation pane.**

   Your message list appears.

2. **Click the New E-Mail button in the Ribbon.**

   The New Message form appears.

3. **Fill out the New Message form.**

   Put the address of your recipient in the To box and a subject in the Subject box, and type a message in the main message box.

4. **Click the Send button.**

   Your message is on its way.

If you want to send a plain e-mail message, that's all you have to do. If you prefer to send a fancy e-mail, Outlook provides the bells and whistles — some of which are actually useful. You might (for example) send a High Priority message to impress some big shots, or send a Confidential message about a hush-hush topic. (Discover the mysteries of confidential e-mail in Chapter 4.)

Sending a File

Some people swear that they do nothing but exchange e-mail all day. Swearing is exactly what I'd do if I were in their shoes, believe me. If you're lucky, you probably do lots of things other than exchange e-mail; you probably do most of your daily work in programs other than Outlook. You might create documents in Microsoft Word or build elaborate spreadsheets with Excel. When you want to send a file by e-mail, Outlook gets involved, although sometimes it works in the background.

To e-mail a document you created in Microsoft Word, for example, follow these steps:

1. **Open the document in Microsoft Word.**

   The document appears on-screen.

2. **Click the File tab in the upper-left corner of the screen.**

   The Backstage view appears.

3. **Choose Share.**

   The Share page appears. Yes, I know you learned how to share in kindergarten, but this is different.

4. **Choose Send Using Email.**

   A list appears, detailing different ways to send your file via e-mail.

5. **Click the Send as Attachment button.**

   The New Message form appears with your document listed on the Attached line (as pictured in Figure 1-2). If you want to type a message in the main part of the screen you can, but it isn't necessary.

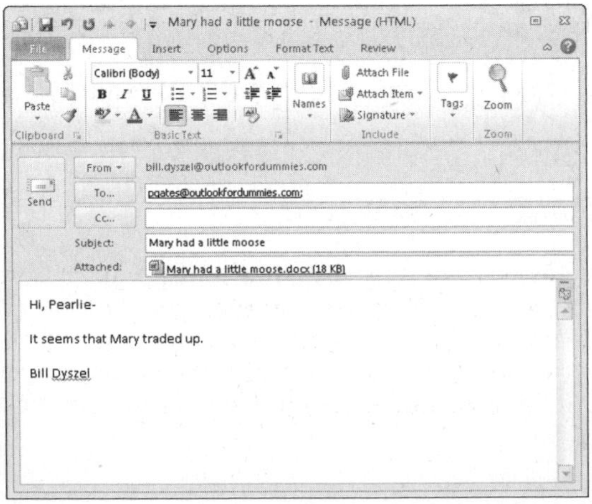

Figure 1-2:
You can
e-mail a
document
right from
Microsoft
Word.

6. **Type the e-mail address of your recipient in the To field.**

   The address you enter appears in the To field.

7. **Click the Send button.**

   Your file is now en route.

Whew! When you're just sending one Word file, these steps seem like a long way to go, but they'll always get your document on its way. For some reason, the folks at Microsoft made this task more laborious as the years have passed. But don't be discouraged. If you e-mail documents frequently, I describe a more powerful way to attach files in Chapter 5.

Quick Calendar Keeping

Time management is a myth. You can't get more than 24 hours in a day, no matter how well you manage it. But you can get more done in a 24-hour day if you conscientiously keep your calendar current. Outlook can help you with that.

Entering an appointment

If you've ever used an old-fashioned paper planner, the Outlook Calendar will look familiar to you. When you click the Calendar icon and then click the Day tab, you see a grid in the middle of the screen with lines representing each segment of the day. You can adjust the length of the segments from as little as five minutes to as much as an hour (as in Figure 1-3). To enter an appointment at a certain time, just click the line next to the time you want your appointment to begin, type a name for your appointment, and press Enter.

If you want to enter more detailed information about your appointment — such as ending time, location, category, and so on — see Chapter 8 for the nitty-gritty on keeping track of all the details in your calendar.

Managing your schedule

Time management involves more than just entering appointments. If you're really busy, you want to manage your time by slicing and dicing your list of appointments to see when you're free to add even more appointments. You can choose from several different views of your Calendar by clicking the Day, Work Week, Week, Month, and Schedule View buttons at the top of the

Calendar screen. If you need a more elaborate collection of Calendar views, choose one of the views listed under the Change View button in the View tab in the Ribbon. To really master time management, see Chapter 8 to see the different ways you can view your Outlook Calendar.

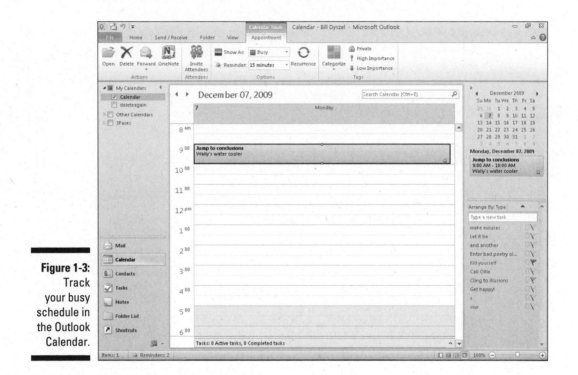

Figure 1-3:
Track your busy schedule in the Outlook Calendar.

Adding a Contact

When it's not *what* you know but *who* you know, you need a good tool for keeping track of who's who. Outlook is a great tool for managing your list of names and addresses, and it's just as easy to use as your Little Black Book. To enter a new contact, click the Contacts button in the Navigation pane; then click the New Contact icon in the Ribbon to open the New Contact entry form. Fill in the blanks on the form (an example appears in Figure 1-4), and then click the Save & Close button. Presto — you have a Contacts list.

Outlook's Contacts feature can be a lot more than your Little Black Book — if you know the ropes. Chapter 7 reveals the secrets of searching, sorting, and grouping the names in your list — and of using e-mail to keep in touch with all the important people in your life.

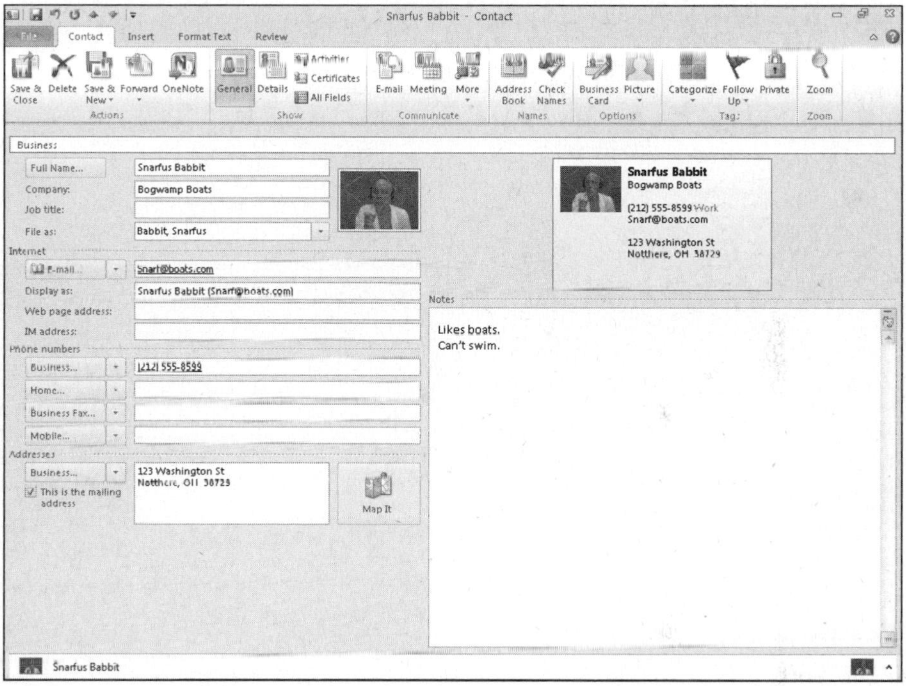

Figure 1-4:
Keep
detailed
informa-
tion about
everyone
you know in
the Contacts
list.

Entering a Task

Knowing what you need to do isn't enough: you need to know what to do next. When you're juggling a thousand competing demands all at once, you need a tool that shows you, at a glance, what you need to do next to keep your work moving forward.

Outlook 2010 has several task management tools that help you organize your lengthy To-Do list for peak performance. Those tools include the Tasks module, the To-Do List, and the Daily Task List. Chapter 9 describes all of them, but here's the quick way to get started in a jiffy.

To enter a new task, follow these steps:

1. **Click the text that says** Click Here to Add a New Task.

   The words disappear, and you see the insertion point (a blinking line).

2. **Type the name of your task.**

   Your task appears in the block under the Subject line in the Task list (which in turn appears in Figure 1-5).

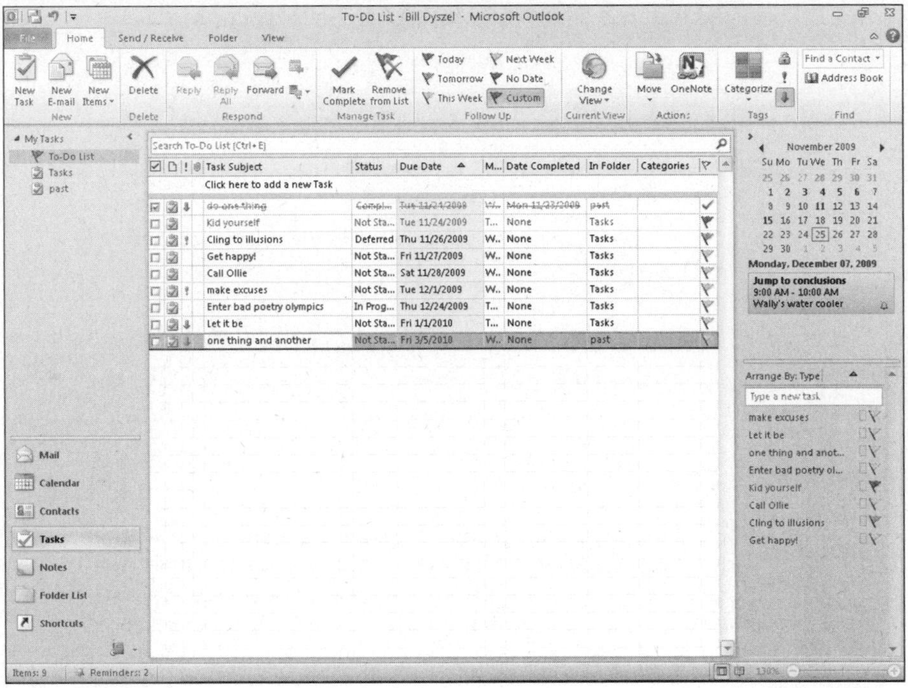

Figure 1-5:
Entering
your task
in the
Task list.

3. Press Enter.

Your new task moves down to the Task list with your other tasks.

Outlook can help you manage anything from a simple shopping list to a complex business project. In Chapter 9, I show you how to deal with recurring tasks, how to regenerate tasks, and how to mark tasks as complete (and earn the right to brag about how much you've accomplished).

Taking Notes

I have hundreds of little scraps of information that I need to keep somewhere, but until Outlook came along, I didn't have a place to put them. Now all the written flotsam and jetsam I've decided I need goes into my Outlook Notes collection — where I can find it all again when I need it.

To create a new note, follow these steps:

1. Click the Notes button in the Navigation pane (or press Ctrl+5).

Your list of notes appears.

2. **Click the New Note button in the Ribbon.**

   A blank note appears.

3. **Type the text you want to save.**

   The text you type appears in the note (see Figure 1-6).

4. **Press Esc.**

   The note you created appears in your list of notes.

An even quicker way to enter a note is to press Ctrl+Shift+N and type your note text. You can see how easy it is to amass a large collection of small notes. Chapter 10 tells you everything you need to know about notes, including how to find the notes you've saved as well as how to sort, categorize, and organize your collection of notes and even how to delete the ones you don't need anymore.

After you're in the habit of using Outlook to organize your life, I'm sure that you'll want to move beyond the basics. That's what the rest of this book shows you. When you're ready to share your work with other people, send e-mail like a pro, or just finish your workday by 5:00 p.m. and get home, you'll find ways to use Outlook to make your job — and your life — easier to manage.

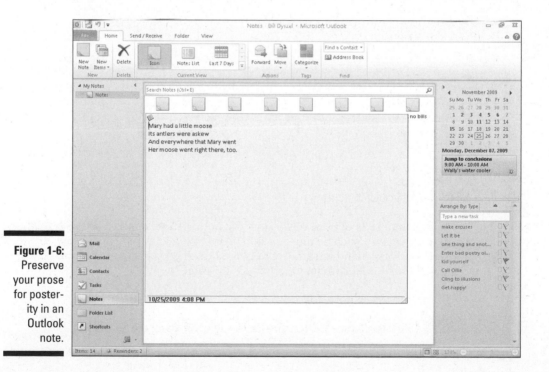

Figure 1-6:
Preserve
your prose
for poster-
ity in an
Outlook
note.

Chapter 2

Inside Outlook: Mixing, Matching, and Managing Information

. . . .

In This Chapter

▶ Examining the many faces of Outlook

▶ Choosing menus

▶ Getting the big picture from the Information Viewer

▶ Using the tools of the trade

▶ Fine-tuning with the Folder list

. . . .

*Y*ou have too much to do. I know that even if I've never even met you. We're now a decade into the 21st century, and if you can read this book, there's a good chance you have more things to do than time to do them. Welcome to the future — it's already here and it's already booked solid.

When I wrote the first edition of this book in 1996, few people had either sent or received an e-mail message. Now many people are slaves to e-mail messages, online appointments, and other electronically generated demands. That means we have more stuff to do than we ever imagined possible — even in the 1990s.

Fortunately, we all get more done now than we did in the past, partly because of tools like Microsoft Outlook. In fact, hundreds of millions of people worldwide use Outlook to get more done every day. But most of those people only use a fraction of Outlook's power, so they work harder than necessary while getting less done. The people I've trained find that knowing even a tiny fraction more about what the program can do for them makes their lives noticeably easier. Let's hear it for making your life easier!

Outlook and Other Programs

Outlook is a part of Microsoft Office. It's called an Office *suite,* which means it's a collection of programs that includes everything you need to complete most office tasks. Ideally, the programs in a suite work together, enabling you to create documents that you couldn't create as easily with any of the individual programs. For example, you can copy a chart from a spreadsheet and paste it into a sales letter that you're creating in your word processor. You can also keep a list of mailing addresses in Outlook and use the list as a mailing list to address form letters (see Chapter 13).

Microsoft Office includes a group of programs that cost less to buy together than you would pay to buy them separately. The concept is a little like buying an encyclopedia: It's cheaper to buy the entire set than it is to buy one book at a time. Besides, who wants just one volume of an encyclopedia (unless you're interested only in aardvarks)?

Outlook turns up in connection with several other Microsoft products, as well. Microsoft Exchange Server is the backbone of the e-mail system in many corporations, and Outlook is often the program that employees of those corporations use to read their company e-mail. Another program, called SharePoint, connects to Outlook to help streamline the work of a group the way Outlook speeds up the work of an individual. Outlook's first cousin, Outlook Express (a.k.a. Windows Mail), is included free when you install Internet Explorer and as a part of all versions of Windows. Outlook is also linked strongly to Internet Explorer, although technically they're separate programs. You don't need to worry about all this, though. You can start Outlook and use it the same way no matter which other programs it's bundled with.

About Personal Information Management

When it comes to the basic work of managing names, addresses, appointments, and e-mail, the word processing and spreadsheet programs just don't get it. If you're planning a meeting, you need to know with whom you're meeting, what the other person's phone number is, and when you can find time to meet.

In designing Outlook, Microsoft took advantage of the fact that many people use Microsoft products for most of the work they do. The company created something called a *Personal Information Management (PIM)* program that speaks a common language with Microsoft Word, Excel, and the rest of the Microsoft Office suite. Microsoft also studied what kind of information people use most often, and tried to make sure that Outlook could handle most of it. The program also has scads of *customizability* (a tongue-twister of a buzzword that just means you can set it up however you need, after you know what you're doing).

Whatever the terminology, Outlook is — above all — easy to understand and hard to mess up. If you've used any version of Windows, you can just look at the screen and click a few icons to see what Outlook does. You won't break anything. If you get lost, going back to where you came from is easy. Even if you have no experience with Windows, Outlook is fairly straightforward to use.

There's No Place Like Home: Outlook's Main Screen

Outlook's appearance is very different from the other Microsoft Office applications. Instead of confronting you with a blank screen, Outlook begins by offering you a screen filled with information that's easy to use and understand. If you've spent much time surfing the Web, you'll find the Outlook layout pretty similar to most Web pages. Just select what you want to see by clicking an icon on the left side of the screen, and the information you selected appears on the right side of the screen.

Feeling at home when you work is nice. (Sometimes, when I'm at work, I'd rather *be* at home, but that's something else entirely.) Outlook makes a home for all your different types of information: names, addresses, schedules, to-do lists, and even a list to remind you of all the stuff you have to do today (or didn't get done yesterday). You can move around the main screen as easily as you move around the rooms of your home. Even so, to make it easier to get your bearings at first, I recommend waiting until you feel entirely at home with Outlook before you start rearranging the screen.

The Outlook main screen — which looks remarkably like Figure 2-1 — has all the usual parts of a Windows screen (see the Introduction of this book if you're unfamiliar with how Windows looks), with a few important additions. At the left side of the screen, you see the Navigation pane. Next to the Navigation pane is the Information Viewer, the part of the screen that takes up most of the space.

Looking at modules

All the work you do in Outlook is organized into *modules,* or sections. Each module performs a specific job for you: The calendar stores appointments and manages your schedule, the Tasks module stores and manages your To-Do list, and so on. Outlook is always showing you one of its modules on the main screen (also known as the Information Viewer). Whenever you're running Outlook, you're always using a module, even if the module contains no information — the same way your television can be tuned to a channel even if nothing is showing on that channel. The name of the module you're currently using is displayed in large type at the top of the Information Viewer, so you can easily tell which module is showing.

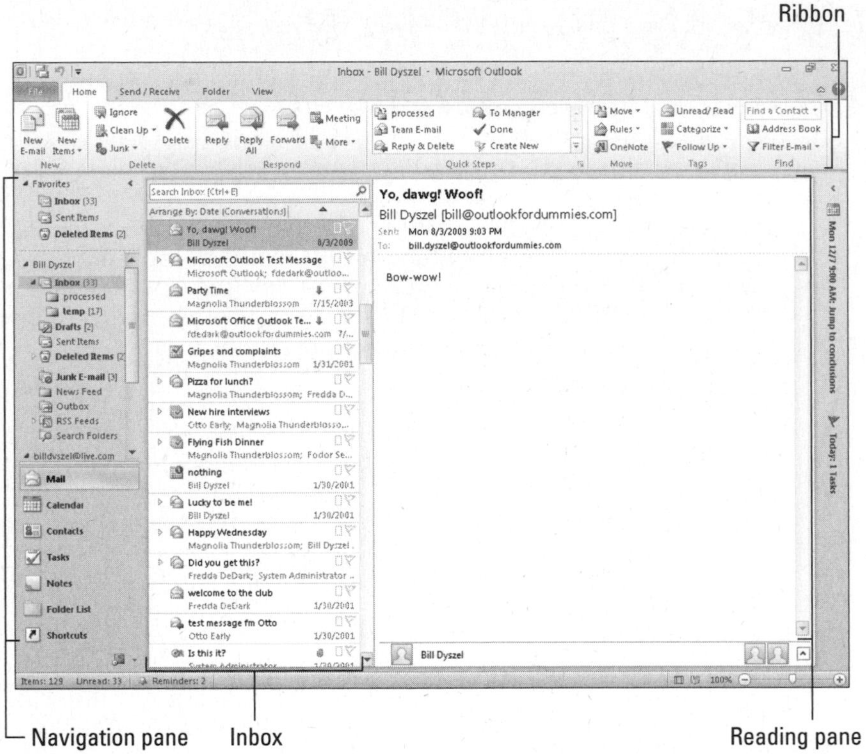

Ribbon

Figure 2-1:
The Outlook
main
screen.

Navigation pane   Inbox   Reading pane

Each module is represented by a button in the Navigation pane on the left side of the screen. Clicking any button takes you to a different module of Outlook:

- ✔ The **Mail button** takes you to the Inbox, which collects your incoming e-mail.

- ✔ The **Calendar button** shows your schedule and all your appointments.

- ✔ The **Contacts button** calls up a module that stores names and addresses for you.

- ✔ The **Tasks button** displays your To-Do list.

- ✔ The **Notes button** takes you to a module you can use to keep track of random tidbits of information that don't quite fit anywhere else.

- ✔ The **Folder List button** displays the entire collection of Outlook folders, allowing you to click and see the contents of a folder.

To change Outlook modules, simply click the module's button in the Navigation pane.

Your Outlook screen might not always look exactly like this one looks, but buttons and icons with the same names typically do the same things.

Finding your way with the Navigation pane

Navigating your way through some computer programs can be a pain, but Outlook can ease your discomfort somewhat with the help of the Navigation pane. You're probably so accustomed to making choices by clicking something on the left side of your computer screen that you don't need a name for that thingy over there. But in this case, that thingamajig has an official, Microsoft-certified name, so by gosh, I'm going to use it.

The Navigation pane usually occupies the first few inches on the left side of the Outlook screen. I say *usually* because you can collapse it into a tiny, almost invisible sliver on the left edge of the page by clicking the little chevron in the upper-right corner of the Navigation pane. That gives you more workspace on the screen. When you want to expand the Navigation pane again, click the chevron, and the pane returns to its original size. When It's fully expanded, the Navigation pane contains several buttons with names such as Mail, Calendar, Contacts, Tasks, and Notes — the basic Outlook modules. I explain these modules later, but the names alone already tell you the story.

The Navigation pane is made up of two sections: an upper window section and a bottom section made up of buttons. Each button in the bottom section is connected to one of Outlook's main modules — Mail, Calendar, Contacts, Tasks, and so on. Just click a button, any button, and you'll see what it sets in motion. Clicking the button changes the stuff on the main screen to fit what that button describes. Click the Calendar button, for example, and a calendar screen shows up. Click Contacts, and you get a screen for names and addresses. The process is like changing the channels on the TV set. If you switch to a channel you don't want, switch to another — no problem.

The top section of the Navigation pane displays different kinds of information at different times. Sometimes the top half of the Navigation pane shows the Folder list, sometimes it shows a list of available calendars, and sometimes it displays folders you've designated as favorites. You can right-click a folder and choose Show in Favorites if you want that folder to appear in this top window section.

Just above the Mail icon in the Navigation pane, you see a gray border that separates buttons on the bottom from the top part of the bar. If you drag that gray borderline downward with your mouse, the buttons in the Navigation pane disappear one by one. That's something you might want to do to get a better view of your Folder list. You can make those buttons reappear by simply dragging the gray border upward again.

The Information Viewer: Outlook's hotspot

The Information Viewer is where most of the action happens in Outlook. If the Navigation pane is like the channel selector on your TV set, the Information Viewer is like the TV screen. When you're reading e-mail, you look in the Information Viewer to read your messages; if you're adding or searching for contacts, you see contact names here. The Information Viewer is also where you can do all sorts of fancy sorting tricks that each module in Outlook lets you perform. (I talk about sorting Contacts, Tasks, and so forth in the chapters that apply to those modules.)

Because you can store more information in Outlook than you can see at any one time, the Information Viewer shows you only a slice of the information available. The calendar, for example, can store dates as far back as the year 1601 and as far ahead as 4500. I used to use that to see the day when my credit card bills would finally be paid off, but in this economy, I may need to take a longer view. In any case, the Information Viewer displays information in manageable slices. The smallest calendar slice you can look at is one day; the largest slice is a month.

The Information Viewer organizes the items it shows you into units called *views.* You can use the views that are included with Outlook when you install it, or you can create your own views and save them. (I go into more details about views in Chapter 16.)

You can navigate among the slices of information that Outlook shows you by clicking different parts of the Information Viewer. Some people use the word *browsing* for the process of moving around the Information Viewer — it's a little like thumbing through the pages of your pocket datebook (that is, if you have a million-page datebook). To see an example of how to use the Information Viewer, look at the Calendar module in Figure 2-2.

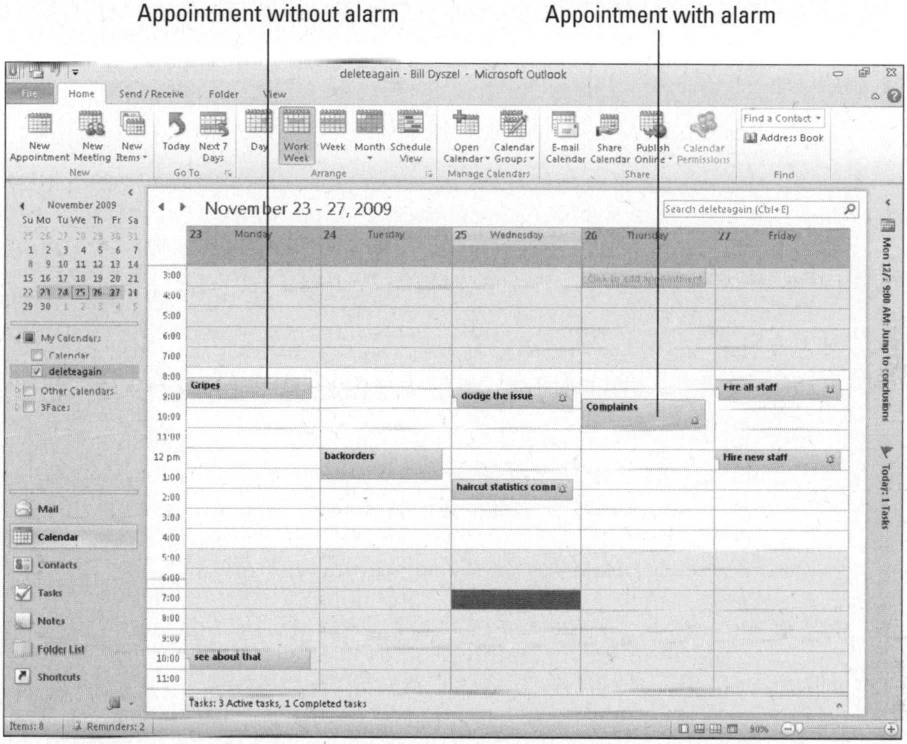

Appointment without alarm   Appointment with alarm

Figure 2-2:
The calendar in the Information Viewer.

To browse the calendar data in the Information Viewer, follow these steps:

1. **Click the Calendar button in the Navigation pane (or press Ctrl+2).**

   The calendar appears.

2. **Click the word *Week* at the top of the Calendar screen.**

   The weekly view of the calendar appears.

Try these tricks to see how the Information Viewer behaves:

✔ Click a date in the small calendar in the Navigation pane. The large calendar changes to a view that includes that date.

✔ Click the W for Wednesday at the top of one of the small calendars in the Navigation pane. The large calendar changes to a monthly view.

You can change the appearance of the Information Viewer in an infinite number of ways to make the work you do in Outlook make sense to you. For example, you may need to see the appointments for a single day, or only the items you've assigned to a certain category. Views can help you get a quick look at exactly the slice of information you need.

When you choose the Day or Week view, a row at the bottom of the Calendar screen shows all the tasks scheduled for completion that day, as well as any e-mail messages you've flagged for that day. That's to help you manage your time better. After all, if you have too many meetings on a certain day, you may not have time to finish a lot of tasks; the Outlook calendar makes that easy to see. You can drag a task from one day to another to balance your schedule a bit.

The To-Do bar

Outlook 2010 features a region called the To-Do bar, the place to go to manage everything you need to do. Outlook has always had a Task list, which offers a tool for tracking all the projects and errands that you think to enter. But now that we all live and work in a 24/7 world of e-mail and instant digital communications, you probably have things to do that you don't think to add to your Task list — particularly items that come to you via e-mail.

The To-Do bar, shown in Figure 2-3, takes up the rightmost column of the Outlook screen (unless you click the arrow at the top of the To-Do bar, which makes the bar collapse against the side of the screen). The To-Do bar ties together your tasks, flagged e-mail messages, and calendar appointments so that you can see what you need to do at a glance. You can open the To-Do bar in any Outlook module: Mail, Calendar, Contacts, Tasks, or Notes.

Productivity experts say that a neat, well-organized Task list can help you get more done with less effort and even make more money in less time. Who doesn't want that? Unfortunately, the Outlook 2010 To-Do bar has a maddening way of cluttering itself up automatically, which makes it nearly useless unless you actively manage it. To find out more about taming the To-Do bar and the Task list, see Chapter 9.

Navigating the Folder list

If you want to navigate Outlook in a more detailed way than you can with the Navigation pane, you can use the Folder list. If you think of the Navigation pane buttons as being like a car's radio buttons for picking favorite stations, the Folder list is like the fine-tuning button that tunes in the stations between your favorite ones. The Folder list simply shows your Outlook folders — both the usual folders you see when Outlook is new and any folders you might create, if you create any. Most people don't create extra folders in Outlook, so folder navigation isn't important for most people — the buttons in the Navigation pane do everything most people need. On the other hand, I know people who create elaborate filing systems by creating dozens of Outlook folders for their e-mails and even their tasks. It's personal; some people are filers, some are pilers. Take your pick.

To-Do bar

Figure 2-3:
The To-Do
bar.

A tale of two folders

Folders can seem more confusing than they need to be because, once again, Microsoft gave two different things the same name. Just as two kinds of Explorer (Windows and Internet) exist, more than two kinds of Outlook exist, and way too many kinds of Windows exist. You may run across two different kinds of folders when you use Outlook — and each behaves differently.

You may be used to folders in Windows XP, Vista, or Windows 7, which are the things you use to organize files. You can copy, move, and delete files to and from folders on your hard drive. Outlook doesn't deal with that kind of folder. If you need to manage the files you've created on your computer, click the Windows Start button and then choose Documents.

Outlook has its own special folders for storing items (calendar items, contact names, tasks, and so on) that you create in the various Outlook modules. Each module has its own folder, and the Folder list gives you immediate access to any of them.

If you're looking at an Outlook module, such as the Inbox for example, and you turn on the Folder list by clicking the Folder List button in the Navigation pane, you see a list of folders that represent the other standard Outlook modules, such as the Task list, Contacts, Calendar, and so on.

Using the Folder list

The only time you absolutely must use the Folder list is when you want to create a new folder for a separate type of item (such as a special Contact list or a folder for filing e-mail) or find that folder again to use the items you've stored there.

You may quite possibly never use the Folder list. The Navigation pane includes the folder choices that most people use most of the time. You may never need to get a different one. Fortunately, the Folder list appears all by itself when you're likely to need it.

If you don't see the Folder list but want to, click the Folder List button in the Navigation pane (or press Ctrl+6). It's a matter of taste, so take your pick.

Tying It All Together: The Ribbon

The most controversial aspect of the last two releases of Microsoft Office has been the introduction of the Ribbon. You either love it or hate it. Either way, we're all stuck with it for the time being. Microsoft representatives have told me that they designed the Ribbon in response to the flood of requests they received year after year to add features to Office that were already there. People simply couldn't find some of the more useful features of the programs. Unfortunately, revamping the whole suite baffled millions of experienced users. Most of us have learned our way around the new territory, and now we feel better. But the Ribbon, despite all the bellyaching, explains itself fairly well.

As you can tell from first glance, the Ribbon is organized into tabs, groups, and buttons. Each tab contains a different set of groups, and each group contains a different set of buttons. In Outlook, each module has its own

Ribbon, which is organized suitably for the purposes of its module. Most of the buttons are clearly labeled with the name of the thing they do, such as Reply, New Appointment, Business Card, and so on. At the lower right corner of some groups there's a tiny icon called the Properties button that you can click to view more detailed choices than you see in the Ribbon. When you get used to the Ribbon, it's really not that bad. It's like eating your spinach: It's good for you.

Viewing ScreenTips

Each button in the Ribbon displays a little popup tag when you hover the mouse pointer over it. The shadow tells you that if you click there, the button will do what it's there to do: paste, save, launch missiles (just kidding) — whatever.

Another slick thing about buttons is that when you rest the mouse pointer on any of them for a second or so, a little tag pops up to tell you the button's name (see Figure 2-4). Tags of this sort, called *ScreenTips,* are very handy for deciphering exactly what those buttons are supposed to do.

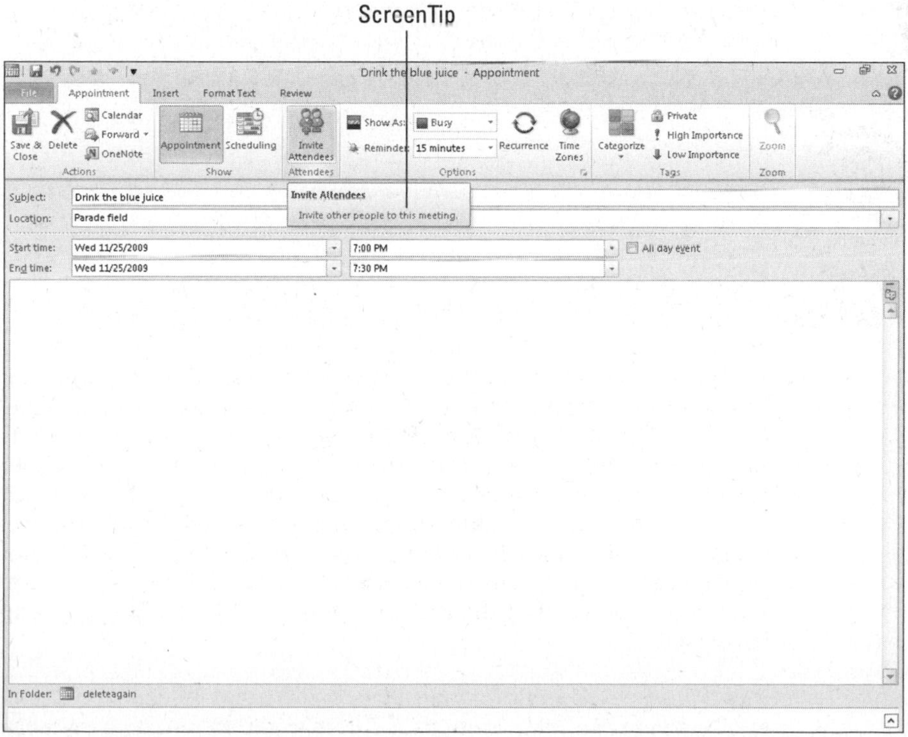

ScreenTip

Figure 2-4:
A ScreenTip tells you the name of the tool you're using.

Some buttons have a little triangle at the bottom. This triangle means that the button offers a pull-down menu. Most Outlook modules contain a button called Move. Click the button to pull down its menu and see all the different places to which you can send an Outlook item.

Using the New Items button

Every Outlook module includes a New Items button, which allows you to create an item in any other module. Perhaps you're entering the name and address of a new customer who is also mentioned in an interesting article in today's paper. You want to remember the article, but it doesn't belong in the customer's address record. Although you're still in the Calendar module (see Figure 2-5), you can pull down the New Items button's menu and create a quick note, which gets filed in the Notes section. Using the New Items button to create a new note when you're looking at the Calendar screen can get confusing. At first, you may think the note isn't entered, but it is. Outlook just files it in the Notes module, where it belongs.

New Items menu   New Items button

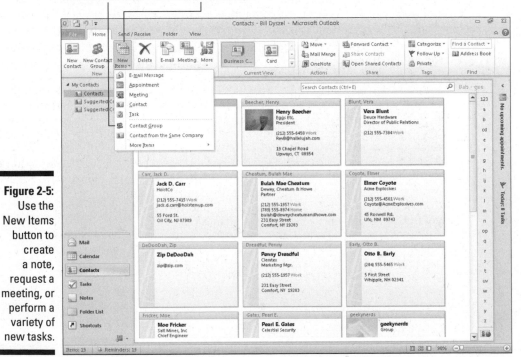

Figure 2-5:
Use the New Items button to create a note, request a meeting, or perform a variety of new tasks.

Finding Things in a Flash with Instant Search

Outlook makes it incredibly easy to accumulate dribs and drabs of data. That quickly becomes a problem because it's tough finding things when you have so much to find. Outlook has always had a Search feature, but it was painfully slow. By the time it found what you were looking for, you no longer needed what it found. Fortunately, the people at Google scared Microsoft by inventing a tool that could search Outlook data in a jiffy. After ten years of offering the same crummy Search tool, the people at Microsoft cooked up a new tool for Outlook that was worth using. The new tool is called Instant Search, and it's pretty slick. I hope Google scares Microsoft this way more often.

Near the top of the Information Viewer pane, in the center of the screen, you see the Instant Search box. It's a box with a little magnifying glass on the right and some text on the left. Click that box and type the first few letters of a word that you want to find. Almost immediately, the Information Viewer screen goes blank, then shows only the items that contain the text you entered (see Figure 2-6). For example, if you're in the Contacts module and you type **jon**, you see only the records that contain names like Jones, Jonas, and Jonquil — any word that contains the letters *jon*. While Outlook is displaying the items it found, the magnifying glass is replaced by an X. Clear the search results by clicking the X.

In some cases, searching for a certain group of letters isn't specific enough. For example, you may want Outlook to just show the people named Jones *and* who work for XYZ Company. You can create a more detailed search by clicking the More button in the Ribbon. That reveals a group of labeled boxes that you can select to search for specific types of information (see Figure 2-7). The exact collection of boxes varies according to which Outlook module you're searching. If you're in the Contacts module, you have choices such as Name, Company, Business Phone, and so on. To find all the Joneses at XYZ Corporation, search for the name Jones and the XYZ Company; instantly you'll be keeping up with the Joneses at XYZ.

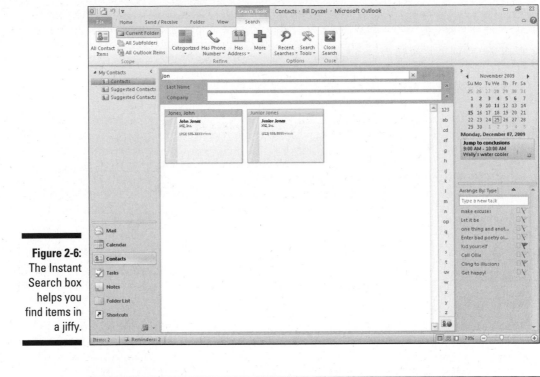

Figure 2-6:
The Instant
Search box
helps you
find items in
a jiffy.

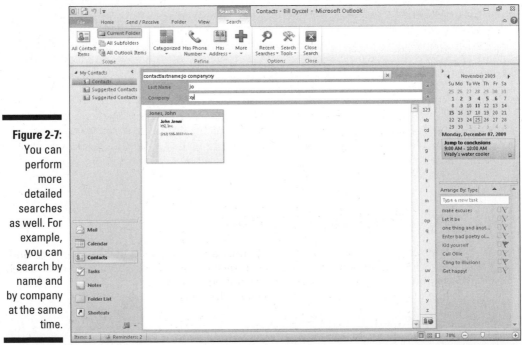

Figure 2-7:
You can
perform
more
detailed
searches
as well. For
example,
you can
search by
name and
by company
at the same
time.

If the items Outlook offers don't meet your needs, you can make different choices by clicking the label for each type of information; then you can see a list of other kinds of information to search for (see Figure 2-8). For example, when you're searching your Contacts List, you can pick City or State to find people in a certain location.

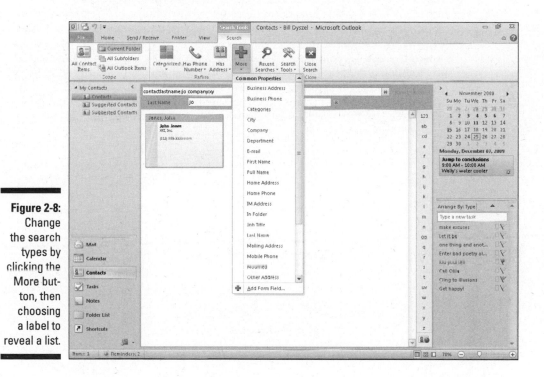

Figure 2-8:
Change the search types by clicking the More button, then choosing a label to reveal a list.

The best way to understand the Instant Search feature is to try it out. Just type some information into the box to see what you get, and then click the X to create a new search. If you get a lot of results, try using the More button to narrow the list.

Getting Help in Outlook

Even though Outlook is as user-friendly a program as you could hope to find, at times you may want to take advantage of the efficient Windows online Help system when you're temporarily stumped (of course, you can turn to this book for help, but sometimes online help is faster).

The Windows Outlook Help system appears as a separate pop-up window whenever you press F1. You can also launch Outlook Help by clicking the itsy-bitsy blue question mark near the upper-right corner of the Outlook screen. I can only guess why Microsoft gave other functions giant, circus-colored buttons but relegated the Help button to an area slightly smaller than a gnat's navel. Maybe they want us all to go blind so we'll need to buy Microsoft's marvelous computer speech programs. In any case, if you manage to get the Windows Help system open, it finds answers to any question you type in the text box at the top of the screen. When you type a question in the text box and press Enter, a list of possible answers appears in the box following the text box. Click the answer that seems best related to your question, and a full explanation appears in a new window. The Help system includes lots of blue text, just like you see in your Web browser, which you can click to make the Help system show you more information about the blue-lettered topic.

Chapter 3

On the Fast Track: Drag 'til You Drop

In This Chapter

▶ Finding rapid response techniques

▶ Getting in control of your tasks

▶ Creating Contact records

▶ Creating and sending e-mail messages

▶ Deleting information

Typing — ugh! Who needs it? It's amazing to think that we still use a 19th-century device — the typewriter keyboard — to control our computers in the 21st century. We appear to be stuck with the QWERTY keyboard (the standard we all know and, uh, *love*) for a while longer, but we can give our carpal tunnels a rest now and then: By using the mouse, trackball, or touch-pad, we can drag and drop rather than hunt and peck.

Most people recognize that a tool like Outlook can dramatically improve your productivity, but many ignore Outlook's most powerful productivity tools, including Tasks, the Calendar, and the ability to seamlessly connect all of your information together. Some of those tools can be powerful weapons in your battle to conquer your time.

Dragging

If you want to work quickly in Outlook, a trick called *drag and drop* gives you the fastest and easiest way to get things done. From what I've seen, most people don't take advantage of Outlook's drag-and-drop talents.

When I say *drag*, I'm not referring to Monty Python's men in women's cloth-ing. I mean the process of zipping items from one place to another with quick, easy mouse moves, which is by far the fastest way to complete many tasks in Outlook.

The drag-and drop-technique keeps all the different elements of your daily workload connected to each other. Outlook treats all items equally. An e-mail message, a task, an appointment, and an address book record are all the same to Outlook — each is just a slightly different way to organize the same information.

Before you can drag an item, you have to *select* it, which simply means to click the item once. Then the rest of the process is straightforward:

- ✔ *Dragging* means clicking your mouse on something and moving the mouse to another location while holding the mouse button down at the same time. The item you're dragging moves with the mouse pointer.

- ✔ *Dropping* means letting go of the mouse button. The mouse pointer detaches from the object you dragged and leaves it in its new location.

When you drag an item, you see an icon hanging from the tail of the mouse pointer as you move the pointer across the screen. The icon makes the pointer look like it's carrying baggage, and to some degree, that's true. Dragging your mouse between Outlook modules "carries" information from one type of item to another.

When you drag and drop items between different Outlook modules, you can keep creating new types of items from the old information, depending on what you drag and where you drop it. For example, when you make an airline reservation and the airline sends you a summary of your itinerary by e-mail, the most useful place for that information is in your calendar, on the day of your flight. You could enter an appointment and type in all the information, but it's much faster to drag the airline's e-mail message straight to your calendar. You not only save time, but all the information is absolutely accurate because it's the same information.

Everything you can do by using the drag-and-drop method can also be done through Ribbon choices or keystroke shortcuts, but you lose the advantage of having the information from one item flow into the new item, so you have to retype information. I don't have time for that, so I just drag and drop.

After you've tried drag and drop, you'll see how much it helps you. And because I'm using this chapter to show you how to get everything done faster, I describe every action in terms of a drag-and-drop movement rather than through Ribbon choices or keyboard shortcuts. However, throughout the rest of the book, I describe how to do things using the Ribbon, which is a more intuitive way to explain most Outlook features, but trust me, drag and drop is usually faster. So when you read other parts of the book, don't think I'm discouraging you from trying drag and drop; I'm just trying to offer you the clearest explanation I can. (Whew! I'm glad that's off my chest.)

Dispatching Tasks in a Flash

Nobody in business talks anymore — everybody sends e-mail. When your boss wants you to do something, you usually find out via e-mail. But all those messages clutter your e-mail Inbox so quickly that you can easily lose track of what you need to do. That's why most productivity experts suggest that you convert e-mailed instructions into a to-do list item right away and avoid losing track of important details.

You can create tasks from e-mail messages by dragging the message to the To-Do bar. You can add other information later, such as due date and category, but a single drag and drop is all you really need — and 25 hours in the day.

The Outlook 2010 Calendar module features a strip at the bottom called the Daily Task List that lets you drag each task to a particular day, which helps you deal with the fact that many tasks take time. When your schedule is crowded and your e-mail Inbox is cluttered, knowing what you need to do isn't enough — you also need to figure out when you'll have time to do it.

Your one-page productivity system

High-priced productivity gurus crank out over-stuffed guidebooks like sausages. What's so productive about slogging through 400-page productivity books? Every productivity book says pretty much the same thing, and the stuff that matters fits on one page. So I'll spare you 399 pages of jargon and gibberish — you're too busy for that.

Respond to every task *immediately* in one of four ways:

- ✓ **Do it** (if you can finish it in under two minutes).

- ✓ **Delete it** (after you've done it or determined that no action is required).

- ✓ **Defer it** (by dragging it immediately to your Outlook Task list or Calendar).

- ✓ **Delegate it** (if you have someone to whom you can delegate things . . . you lucky thing).

To reach peak productivity, you should constantly seek ways to do the following:

- ✓ **Centralize:** Store all your information in a single location. Outlook is a good place to do that.

- ✓ **Streamline:** Strive to touch any item no more than once.

- ✓ **Simplify:** A simple system that you actually follow is better than a complex one that you don't follow.

You should also strive to automate as many routine tasks as you can. Outlook offers powerful task-automation tools to help you zip through busy work. Some of my favorite tools are Rules and Quick Steps, both of which I discuss in Chapter 6. I'm also fond of Quick Parts, which I cover in Chapter 21. Even if you only use a fraction of Outlook's power to streamline your work, you'll find that you get better results faster with less effort.

Only the Day, Workweek, and Week views of your calendar offer this feature. You can open the Daily Task list by clicking the View tab in the Calendar Ribbon; then click the Daily Task List button and choose Normal. A tiny chevron in the lower-right corner of the calendar screen also opens the Daily Task list when you click it.

You can't drag an e-mail message directly to the Daily Task list, but you can drag tasks into the Daily Task list from the To-Do bar, as shown in Figure 3-1. Open the To-Do bar the same way you open the Daily Task list: by going to the Ribbon and clicking the To-Do Bar button and choosing Normal.

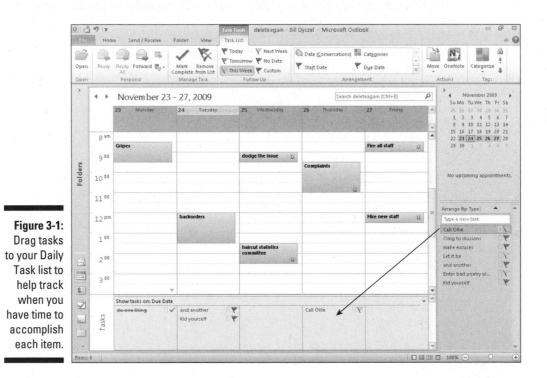

Figure 3-1: Drag tasks to your Daily Task list to help track when you have time to accomplish each item.

The most productive thing about the Daily Task list is that you can drag unfinished tasks from one day to the next. That way you don't lose track of tasks when your schedule gets interrupted.

Making Time Stand Still with Calendar Wizardry

The most popular way to make plans with other people is through e-mail; it's cheap, fast, and complete. Whether you are asking people to lunch, hosting a party, putting on a show, or organizing an exhibition, you probably already know how convenient e-mail can be for organizing get-togethers.

When you receive a plain e-mail announcement about an event and you want to plug its details into your calendar, you can do that in Outlook by following these steps:

1. **Click the Mail button in the Navigation pane (or press Ctrl+1).**

   A list of your current incoming e-mail messages appears.

2. **Select the message from which you want to make an appointment.**

3. **Drag the selected message to the Calendar button.**

   The New Appointment form opens with the text from the message you dragged in the note section of the New Appointment form. Figure 3-2 shows an appointment created in this way.

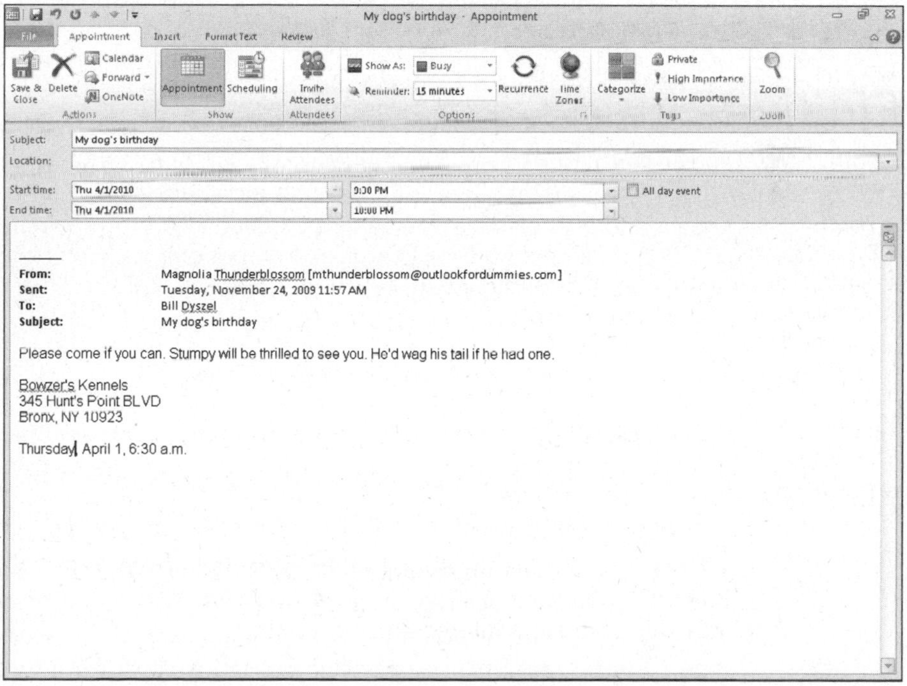

Figure 3-2:
When you drag an e-mail message to your calendar, the message text is stored with your new appointment.

4. **If you want to include more information about the event, type that information in the appropriate box on the New Appointment form.**

   You probably want to fill in the Start Time and End Time boxes to reflect the actual time of your appointment.

5. **Click the Save & Close button.**

   You now have all the event information stored right in your calendar for future reference.

The great thing about creating an appointment from an e-mail message is that all the details included in your message end up right in your calendar. If you need driving directions, agenda details, or other information that was included in the message, just double-click the appointment in your calendar to get the lowdown. And if you use a BlackBerry or smartphone with Outlook, all the information from your Outlook calendar ends up on your mobile device. As a result, you'll have your appointment details handy wherever you go.

 If you work in an office that uses Microsoft Exchange for e-mail, you can take advantage of much more powerful features for organizing meetings. I cover those features in Chapter 14.

Keeping Friends Close and Enemies Closer Quicker

You can drag an item from any other Outlook module to the Contacts button, but the only item that makes sense to drag there is an e-mail message. That is, you can drag an e-mail message to the Contacts button to create a contact record that includes the e-mail address. You not only save work by dragging a message to the Contacts button, but you also eliminate the risk of misspelling the e-mail address.

To create a new contact record, follow these steps:

1. **Click the Mail button in the Navigation pane (or press Ctrl+1).**

   A list of your current incoming e-mail messages appears.

2. **Select the message for which you want to make a contact record.**

3. **Drag the selected message to the Contacts button in the Navigation pane.**

   The New Contact form opens, with the name and e-mail address of the person who sent the message filled in. Figure 3-3 shows a New Contact form created this way.

4. **If you want to include more information, type it into the appropriate box on the New Contact form.**

You can change existing information or add information — the company for whom the person works, the postal mail address, other phone numbers, personal details (say, whether to send a complimentary gift of freeze-dried ants for the person's pet aardvark), and so on.

If the body of the e-mail message contains information you want to use as contact information, select that information and drag it to the appropriate box of the New Contact form.

5. **Click the Save & Close button.**

   You now have the e-mail address and any other information for the new contact stored for future reference.

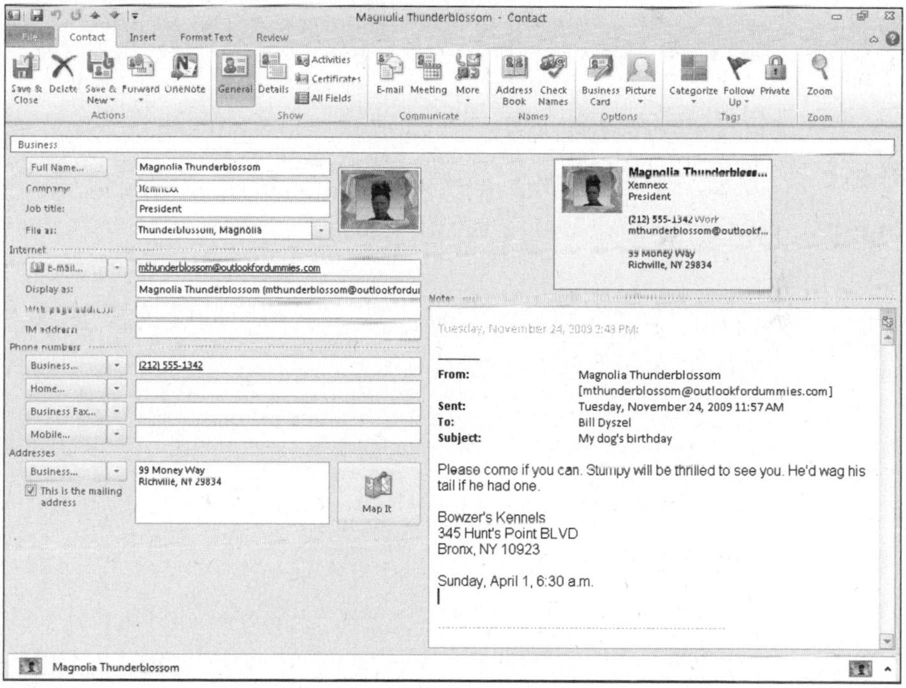

Figure 3-3: Somebody is about to create a contact record.

Another quick way to capture an e-mail address from an incoming message is to right-click the name of the sender in the From field of the incoming message block. The From field is not a normal text box, so you may not think that right-clicking it would do anything, but it does: A shortcut menu appears. Choose Add to Contacts to open the New Contact form, and then follow the last two steps of the preceding list.

Creating Instant E-Mail Messages

When you drag an item to the Inbox, Outlook automatically converts it into an outgoing e-mail message:

- ✔ If the item you drag to the Inbox contains an e-mail address (for example, a contact), Outlook automatically creates the message with that person's e-mail address filled in.
- ✔ If the item you drag to the Inbox contains a subject (for example, a task), Outlook automatically creates the message with that subject filled in.

Creating from a name in your Contacts list

Addressing messages is one of the most productive drag-and-drop techniques in Outlook. E-mail addresses can be cumbersome and difficult to remember, and if your spelling of an e-mail address is off by even one letter, your message won't go through. It's best to just keep the e-mail addresses of the people to whom you sent messages in your Contacts list and use those addresses to create new messages.

Create an e-mail message from your Contacts list this way:

1. **Click the Contacts button in the Navigation pane (or press Ctrl+3).**

   The Contacts list appears, as shown in Figure 3-4. You can use any view, but Address Cards view is easiest; you can click the first letter of the person's name to see that person's card. (For more about viewing your Contacts list, see Chapter 7.)

2. **Drag a name from your Contacts list to the Mail button in the Navigation pane.**

   The Message form appears, with the address of the contact filled in.

3. **Type a subject for your message.**

   Keep it simple; a few words will do.

4. **Click in the text box and type your message.**

   You can also format text with bold type, italics, and other effects by clicking the appropriate buttons on the toolbar.

5. **Click the Send button.**

   The display returns to the Contacts list, and your message is sent.

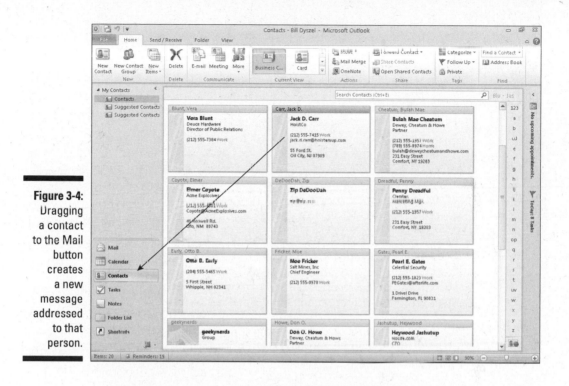

Figure 3-4:
Dragging
a contact
to the Mail
button
creates
a new
message
addressed
to that
person.

Creating from an appointment

After you enter the particulars about an appointment, you may want to send
that information to someone to tell that person what the appointment is
about, where it occurs, and when it occurs.

To send an e-mail message with information about an appointment, follow
these steps:

1. **Click the Calendar button in the Navigation pane (or press Ctrl+2).**

   The calendar appears, as shown in Figure 3-5.

2. **Drag the appointment you're interested in from the calendar to the
   Mail button.**

   The Message form appears. The subject of the message is already
   filled in.

3. **In the To text box, type the name of the person to whom you want to
   send a copy of the appointment.**

   Alternatively, you can click the To button and choose the person's name
   from the Address Book. If you use the Address Book, you have to click
   To again and then click the OK button.

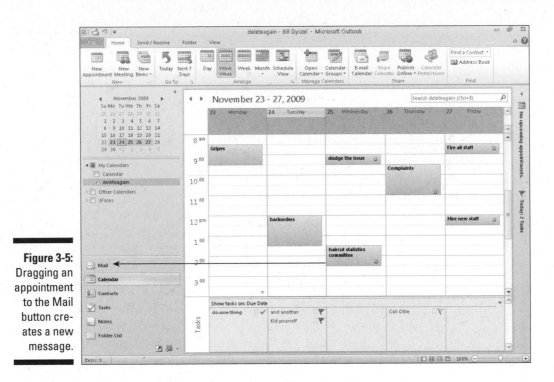

Figure 3-5:
Dragging an
appointment
to the Mail
button cre-
ates a new
message.

4. **Click the Send button.**

   Your recipient gets an e-mail message with details about the meeting. You can add additional comments in the text box.

If you plan to invite other people in your organization to a meeting and you want to check their schedules to plan the meeting, you can also click the Schedule button in the Ribbon.

Expanding Your Outlook Workspace

The Outlook screen packs a lot of information into a small space. That seems efficient at first, but it's also distracting, and distraction is the enemy of productivity. You can minimize parts of the Outlook screen to make space when you're not using them. By doing that, you'll be more focused on the tasks that require your concentration.

If you look closely, you'll see several little caret figures on the Outlook screen. They look like this: >; see Figure 3-6. Clicking the caret figure toggles one part of the screen between being collapsed and expanded. You'll see that figure on the Ribbon, the Navigation pane, the To-Do bar, the Social

Connector, and the Daily Task list. Click the caret once to make a section disappear, and then click it again to make it reappear.

This caret collapses or expands the Ribbon

This caret collapses or expands the To-Do bar.

This caret collapses or expands the Navigation pane.

Figure 3-6:
You can
expand and
collapse
parts of the
Outlook
screen by
clicking
the carets
on each of
the major
screen
elements.

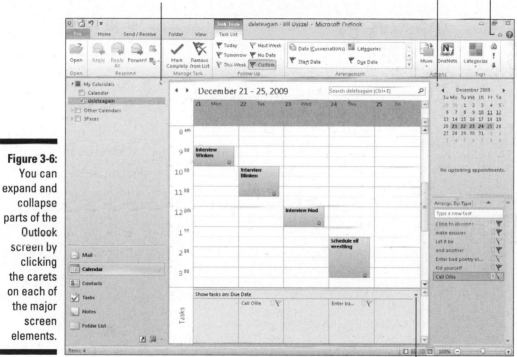

This caret collapses or expands the Daily Task list.

Zen of the Right Button

So far I've talked about holding down your mouse button as if your mouse has only one button. But most PC mice have two buttons; some have even more. Many people use only the left button and they get along just fine.

When you *right-drag* an item (drag it by holding down the right mouse button instead of the left button), something different happens when you drop the item off: A menu asks what result you want. I don't always remember what's going to happen when I drag an item and drop it off, so I like to use the right-drag feature just to be sure.

For example, if you right-drag a contact to the Mail button, a menu with a half-dozen choices appears. The choices include

✔ Address New Message

✔ Copy here as message with text

✔ Copy here as message with shortcut

✔ Copy here as message with attachment

✔ Move here as message with attachment

Part II
Taming the E-Mail Beast

The 5th Wave   By Rich Tennant

"I like getting complaint letters by e-mail. It's easier to delete than to shred."

In this part . . .

The double-edged sword of e-mail can be a weapon that gives you an important advantage. If you manage e-mail wisely, you can get more done more quickly than anyone else you know. If you let a flood of e-mail engulf you, you'll feel constantly overwhelmed. In this part, you'll learn more about e-mail than most people ever know, and I also describe tools that can keep you on top of that e-mail tsunami.

Chapter 4

The Essential Secrets of E-Mail

In This Chapter

▶ Creating, sending, and replying to messages

▶ Previewing, forwarding, and deleting messages

▶ Saving messages as files

*W*hen I wrote the first edition of *Outlook For Dummies* some 13 years ago, many readers had yet to celebrate the sending of their very first e-mail. After this much time, e-mail isn't something to celebrate anymore — not unless you celebrate washing the dishes or changing the litter box. (Woo-hoo!) E-mail has become every working person's biggest chore. I find that many of the people I train put a lot more effort into e-mail than is really necessary, especially if they have a tool as powerful as Outlook to speed things up.

Front Ends and Back Ends

You need two things to send and receive e-mail:

✔ A program that helps you create, save, and manage your messages

✔ A program that actually transports the messages to and from the other people with whom you exchange messages

Some technical people call these two parts the front end and the back end, respectively. Outlook is a *front end* for e-mail. It helps you create, format, store, and manage your messages, but it has little to do with actually getting your messages to your destination. That work is done by a *back-end* service (such as Microsoft Exchange Server in your office), by your *Internet service provider (ISP),* or by an online e-mail service (such as Gmail or Yahoo! Mail).

You can't send e-mail anywhere without an Internet connection. Computer manufacturers make it fiendishly simple to sign up for several online services through the Windows desktop. Remember, though, that your easiest choice isn't always your best choice. Literally hundreds of companies are out there ready to give you Internet access, so it pays to shop around. (I tell you more about connecting Outlook to an e-mail system in Chapter 12.)

Creating Messages

In many ways, electronic mail is better than regular paper mail (sneeringly referred to as *snail mail*). E-mail is delivered much faster than paper mail — almost instantaneously. I find that speedy delivery is really handy for last-minute birthday greetings. E-mail is also incredibly cheap; in fact, it's free most of the time.

The quick-and-dirty way

Creating a new message is insanely easy. Start Outlook, click the New E-Mail button, enter an address in the To text box, enter a subject in the Subject box, enter a message in the Message box, and click the Send button. (Nailed that one, didn't you? Was that easy or what?)

The slow, complete way

You may prefer a more detailed approach to creating an e-mail message. If you have a yen for fancy e-mail — especially if you want to take advantage of every bell and whistle Outlook can add to your message — follow these steps:

1. **Click the Mail button in the Navigation pane (or press Ctrl+Shift+I).**

   The Mail module appears.

2. **Click the New E-Mail button in the Ribbon (or press Ctrl+N).**

   The New Message form appears (as shown in Figure 4-1).

3. **Click the To text box and type the e-mail addresses of the people to whom you're sending your message.**

   If you're sending messages to multiple people, separate their addresses; you can use either commas or semicolons.

   You can also click the To button itself, find the names of the people to whom you're sending the message in the Address Book, double-click their names to add them to the To text box, and then click the OK button. (Or, you can use the AutoName feature, which I describe in the "What's in an AutoName?" sidebar, later in this chapter.)

4. **Click the Cc text box and type the e-mail addresses of the people to whom you want to send a copy of your message.**

   You can also click the Cc button to add people from the Address Book.

5. **Click the Check Names button in the New Message form's Ribbon (or press Ctrl+K).**

If you haven't memorized the exact e-mail address of everyone you know (gasp!), the Check Names feature lets you enter a part of an address and then looks up the exact address in your Address Book so that you don't have to be bothered. Double-check what Check Names enters; sometimes it automatically enters the wrong address, which can yield embarrassing results if you don't realize it and send the message.

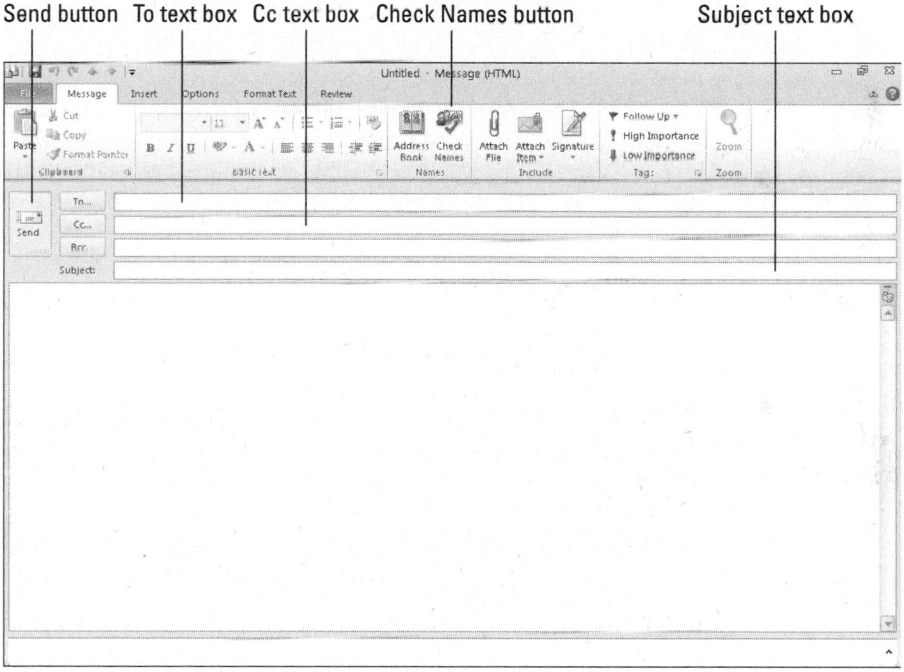

Send button   To text box   Cc text box   Check Names button   Subject text box

Figure 4-1:
The New
Message
form.

6. **Type the subject of the message in the Subject text box.**

   You should keep your subject line brief. A snappy, relevant subject line makes someone want to read your message; a long or weird subject line doesn't.

   If you forget to add a subject and try to send a message, Outlook opens a window that asks whether you really meant to send the message without a subject. Click the Don't Send button to go back to the message and add a subject. If you want to send your message without a subject, just click the Send Anyway button (but not before you've written your message).

7. **Type the text of your message in the Message box.**

   If you use Microsoft Word as your word processor, you're probably familiar with the formatting, graphics, tables, and all the tricks available in Word to make your e-mail more attractive. Those same tricks are available in Outlook by using the tools at the top of the message form.

There may be times when you don't need to put anything in the Message text box, such as when you are forwarding a message or sending an attachment. If that is the case, simply skip this and move onto the next step.

I've listed a few message-formatting tricks you can use in Chapter 20. You can also read Dan Gookin's *Word 2010 For Dummies* (published by Wiley) for more complete information about using Microsoft Word. If you're completely at home with Word, you'll be happy to know that your word processing skills are just as useful in Outlook, too. You can type a message using nearly all the formatting you'd use in any other document (including italics, bold, and bullets) and then click the Send button.

Be careful how you format e-mail to send to people on the Internet. Not all e-mail systems can handle graphics or formatted text, such as boldface or italics, so the masterpiece of correspondence art that you send to your client may arrive as gibberish. If you don't know what the other person has on his or her computer, go light on the graphics. When you're sending e-mail to your colleagues in the same office, or if you're sure that the person you're sending to also has Outlook, the formatting and graphics should look fine.

8. **Select the Review tab and click the Spelling & Grammar button at the top of the message screen (or press F7).**

   Outlook runs a spell check to make sure that your message makes you look as smart as you actually are.

9. **Click the Send button (or press Ctrl+Enter or Alt+S).**

   Your mail is moved to the Outbox. If your computer is online, Outlook immediately sends any messages from the Outbox. If Outlook is configured to not immediately send messages (as might be the case in some offices), you can press F9 (or select Send/Receive and click the Send/Receive All Folders button in the Ribbon) to send any e-mail messages that are queued up in the Outbox. If you composed messages while your computer was offline, when it is again connected to the Internet, you can press F9 to send your messages. When a message is sent, it is automatically moved to the Sent Items folder.

What's my e-mail address?

Your e-mail address appears as different versions for different people, depending on how much of the address they share with you. For instance, if you use Yahoo! Mail and your account name is Jane_Doe, your e-mail address appears to the world at large as `Jane_Doe@yahoo.com`. The same is true if you're on an office e-mail system. If you work for International Widgets Corporation, you may be `Jdoe@widgets.com`. (Check with your company's computer guru about your corporate e-mail address.) Your coworkers can probably send you messages at simply `Jdoe`.

Yet another way to tell Outlook to send messages from the Outbox is to click the small button that looks like two overlapping envelopes located in the upper-left corner of the Outlook window — which is visible from any screen within Outlook. If you hover the mouse pointer over this button, a window appears telling you that this is the Send/Receive All Folders button. Whenever you send messages by clicking the Send button in a message, by clicking the Send/Receive All Folders button, or by pressing F9, you are also telling Outlook to retrieve all incoming messages as well — so don't be surprised if you receive some messages whenever you tell Outlook to send messages.

Setting priorities

Some messages are more important than others. The momentous report that you're sending to your boss demands the kind of attention that wouldn't be appropriate for the wisecrack you send to your friend in the sales department. Setting the importance level to High tells the recipient that your message requires some serious attention.

You can choose from three importance levels:

- ✔ Low
- ✔ Normal
- ✔ High

What's in an AutoName?

One neat Outlook feature is that you can avoid memorizing long, confusing e-mail addresses of people to whom you send mail frequently. If the person to whom you're sending a message is entered as a contact in your Address Book (see Chapter 7 for more information about contacts) and you've included an e-mail address in the Address Book record, all you have to type in the To text box of the New Message form is the person's name — or even just a part of the person's name. Outlook helps you fill in the rest of the person's name and figures out the e-mail address. You know you got it right when Outlook underlines the name with a solid black line after you press Enter or Tab or click outside the To box. If Outlook underlines the name with a wavy red line, that means Outlook thinks it knows the name you're entering but the name isn't spelled quite right — so you have to correct the spelling. Or, you can right-click the name to see a list of e-mail addresses that Outlook thinks might include the correct one. If Outlook doesn't put an underline below the name, it's telling you that it has no idea to whom you're sending the message — but it will still use the name you typed as the literal e-mail address. Making doubly sure that the name is correct is a good habit to cultivate.

Here's how you set the priority of a message:

1. **While composing your message, select the Message tab in the Ribbon and click the small arrow to the right of the word *Tags*.**

   The Properties dialog box appears, as shown in Figure 4-2. This dialog box enables you to define a number of optional qualities about your message.

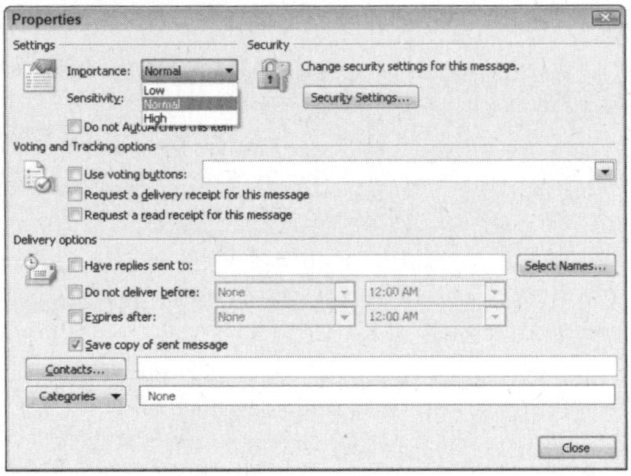

Figure 4-2:
Use the
Properties
dialog box
to set the
priority
of your
message.

2. **Click the triangle at the right end of the Importance box.**

   A menu of choices drops down.

3. **Choose Low, Normal, or High.**

   Usually Importance is set to Normal, so you don't have to do anything. Putting a Low Importance on your own messages seems silly, but you can also assign importance to messages received in your Inbox, to tell yourself which messages can be dealt with later, if at all.

4. **Click the Close button (or press Esc) to close the Properties dialog box.**

An even quicker way to set the priority of a message is to use the buttons in the Message tab of the Ribbon. The button with the red exclamation point marks your message as a High Importance message. The button with the blue arrow pointing downward marks your message as a Low Importance message. You might wonder why anyone would mark a message Low Importance. After all, if it's so unimportant, why send the message in the first place? Apparently, some bosses like their employees to send in routine reports with a Low Importance marking so that the bosses know to read that stuff *after* all those exciting new e-mail messages they get to read every day.

Setting sensitivity

Sensitivity isn't just something Oprah talks about. You may want your message to be seen by only one person, or you may want to prevent your message from being changed by anyone after you send it. *Sensitivity* settings enable you to restrict what someone else can do to your message after you send it and who that someone else can be — even Oprah.

Follow these steps to set the sensitivity of a message:

1. **While composing your message, select the Message tab in the Ribbon and click the small arrow to the right of the word *Tags*.**

   The Properties dialog box appears.

2. **Click the triangle at the right end of the Sensitivity box.**

   A menu drops down, showing the Normal, Personal, Private, and Confidential choices (as shown in Figure 4-3). Most messages you send will have Normal sensitivity, so that's what Outlook uses if you don't say otherwise. The Personal, Private, and Confidential settings only notify the people getting the message that they may want to handle the message differently from a Normal message. (Some organizations even have special rules for dealing with Confidential messages.)

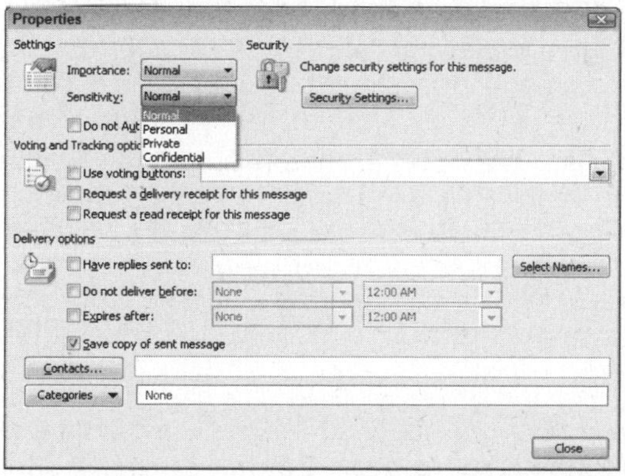

Figure 4-3:
Set the sensitivity of your message from the Properties dialog box.

3. **Choose Normal, Personal, Private, or Confidential.**

4. **To close the Properties dialog box, click the Close button (or press Esc).**

5. **When you finish composing your message, click the Send button (or press Alt+S).**

   Outlook sends your message.

Sensitivity means nothing, as a practical matter. Setting the sensitivity of a message to Private or Confidential doesn't make it any more private or confidential than any other message; it just notifies the recipient that the message contains particularly sensitive information. Many corporations are very careful about what kind of information can be sent by e-mail outside the company. If you use Outlook at work, check with your system administrators before presuming that the information you send by e-mail is secure.

Another feature you'll notice on the Message form is Permission (on the Options tab of the Ribbon), which actually has the potential to prevent certain things from happening to your message, such as having someone forward your message to everyone you know. (How embarrassing.) However, both you and your recipient have to be set up on a compatible e-mail system with something called an *Information Rights Management Service* to make that work. You also can't be sure that it will work with some e-mail services, such as Hotmail or Yahoo! Mail. You can find out more about Information Rights Management at `http://office.microsoft.com/en-us/help/HP062208591033.aspx`.

Setting other message options

When you open the Properties dialog box the way I describe in the previous section, you may notice a number of strange-sounding options. Some of these other options include Request a Read Receipt for This Message (which notifies you when your recipient reads your message) and Expires After (which marks a message as expired if your recipient doesn't open it before a time that you designate). Those are handy options, but if you want to use them, there's a catch: Both your e-mail system and your recipient's e-mail system must support those features or they probably won't work. If you and your recipient are both on the same network using Microsoft Exchange Server, everything should work just fine. If you're not both using Outlook or on an Exchange Network, (frankly) it's a gamble. (See Chapter 14 for more about how to use the features of Outlook that work only on Exchange Server.)

Adding an Internet link to an e-mail message

All Microsoft Office programs automatically recognize the addresses of items on the Internet. If you type the name of a Web page, such as `www.outlookfordummies.com`, Outlook changes the text color to blue and underlines the address, making it look just like the hypertext you click to jump among different pages on the Web. That makes it easy to send someone information about an exciting Web site; just type or copy the address into your message. If the Web page address doesn't start with www, Outlook might not recognize it as a Web address; if that happens, just put `http://` in front of it. Depending on what the recipient uses to read e-mail, he or she should be able to just click the text to make a Web browser pop up and open the page you mention in your message.

Reading and Replying to E-Mail Messages

Outlook has a couple of ways to tell you when you receive an e-mail message. The status bar in the lower-left corner of the Outlook screen tells you how many e-mail messages you have overall in your Inbox and how many of those are unread. The word *Inbox* in the Folder list changes to boldface type when you have unread e-mail, and when you look in the Inbox, you see titles of unread messages in boldface as well; see Figure 4-4.

Number of unread messages

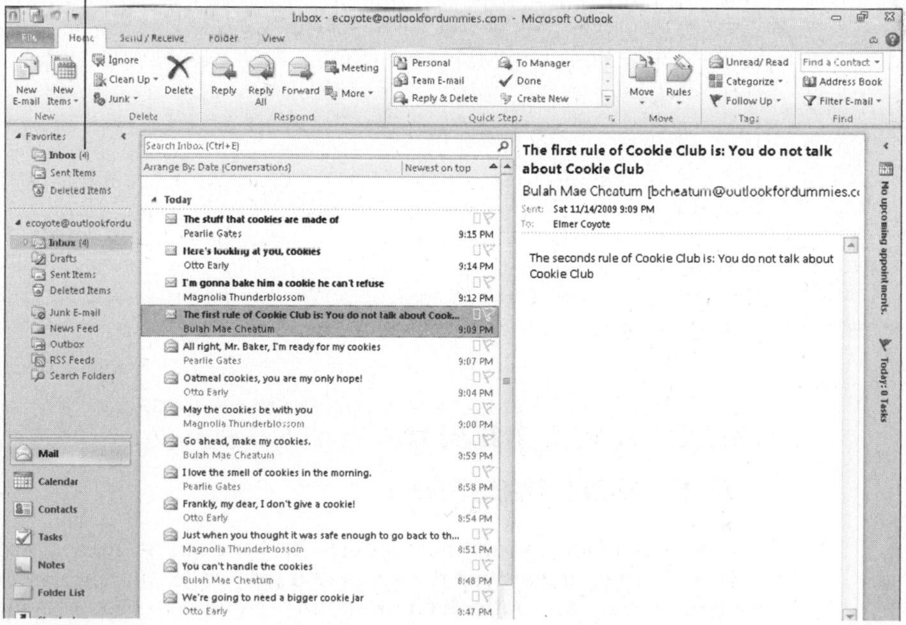

Figure 4-4: Numbers next to your Inbox icon tell you how many unread messages you have.

To open and read an e-mail message, follow these steps:

1. **Click the Mail button in the Navigation pane (or press Ctrl+Shift+I).**

   The Inbox screen opens, showing your incoming mail.

2. **Double-click the title of the message you want to read.**

   The message opens, and you can see the text of the message (as shown in Figure 4-5). If the message is really long, press the down-arrow key or the Page Down key to scroll through the text.

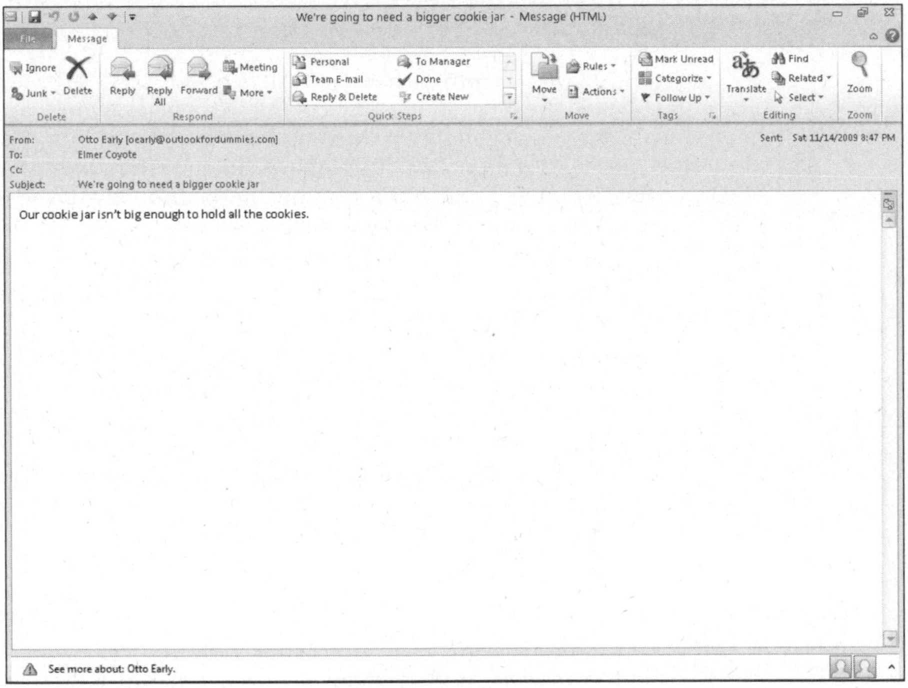

Figure 4-5:
Double-click
a message
to open it
and read the
contents.

3. **To close the Message screen, press Esc (or press Alt+F4).**

   The Message screen closes, and you see the list of messages in your Inbox.

Previewing message text

When you start getting lots of e-mail, some of it will be important, but some of it will be relatively unimportant — if not downright useless. When you first see the mail in your Inbox, it's nice to know which messages are important and which are not so that you can focus on the important stuff. You can't count on the people who send you e-mail to say "Don't read this; it's unimportant" (although a Low Importance rating is a good clue). Outlook tries to help by enabling you to peek at the first few lines of a message so that you know immediately whether it's worth reading.

To see previews of your unread messages, follow these steps:

1. **Click the Mail button in the Navigation pane (or press Ctrl+Shift+I).**

   The Inbox screen opens, showing your incoming mail.

2. **Select the View tab in the Ribbon, click the Change View button, and choose Preview.**

   The list of messages in your Inbox appears, with the first few lines of each *unread* message displayed in blue. See Figure 4-6.

Change View button

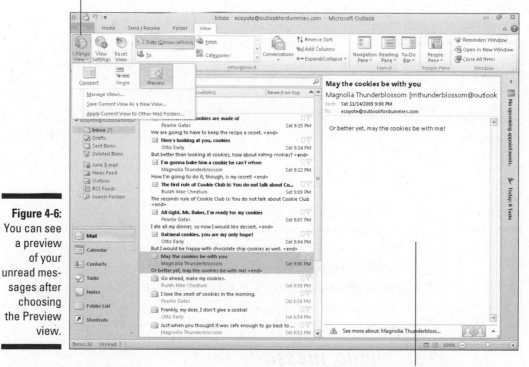

Figure 4-6:
You can see a preview of your unread messages after choosing the Preview view.

Preview of unread mail

Every module in Outlook has a collection of views that you can use to make your information easier to use. The Preview view is the best way to look at your incoming e-mail. In Chapter 16, I show you some other views that can make your collection of e-mail messages more useful.

An even better way to zoom through your Inbox is to open the Reading pane, an area of the Outlook screen that displays the contents of any message you select. To set up your Reading pane, select the View tab in the Ribbon, click the Reading Pane button, and then choose either Right, Bottom, or Off. You can't go wrong with any of the three choices; if you don't like one, change to another. When you've turned on the Reading pane, you can skim through your messages by pressing either the up-arrow or down-arrow key.

Sending a reply

The thing I love about e-mail is that sending a reply is so easy. You don't even need to know the person's address when you're sending a reply; just click the Reply button and Outlook takes care of it for you.

Here's how you reply to a message:

1. **Click the Mail button in the Navigation pane (or press Ctrl+Shift+I).**

   The Inbox screen opens, showing your incoming mail.

2. **Double-click the title of the message to which you want to reply.**

   The message you double-clicked opens, and you can see the contents of the message.

   If the message is already open, you can skip the first two steps and go directly to Step 3.

3. **Choose one of these options:**

   - To reply to the people in the From field, click the Reply button.
   - To reply to the people in the Cc field *and* the From field, click the Reply All button.

   The Reply screen appears (as shown in Figure 4-7).

   You may get (or send) e-mail that's addressed to a whole bunch of people all at one time. Ideally, at least one person should be named in the To field; more than one person can also be in the Cc field, which is for people to whom you're sending only a copy. Little difference exists between what happens to mail that's going to people in the To field and mail that's going to the people in the Cc field — all of them can reply to, forward, or ignore the message. You don't always need to reply to the people in the Cc field, or you may want to reply to only some of them. If you do, click the Reply button and add them again to the Cc field. Or, you could click the Reply All button and delete the users from the Cc field who you don't want to include.

4. **Type your reply in the Message box.**

   Don't be alarmed when you discover some text already in the text box — it's part of the message to which you're replying. Your blinking cursor is at the top of the screen, so anything that you type precedes the other person's message. (This arrangement means that the person who gets your message can review the original message as a memory-jogger when you get your reply.)

5. **Click the Send button.**

   The Message form disappears and the message you replied to reappears.

6. **Press Esc to close the Message screen.**

   The message you replied to disappears and your Inbox reappears.

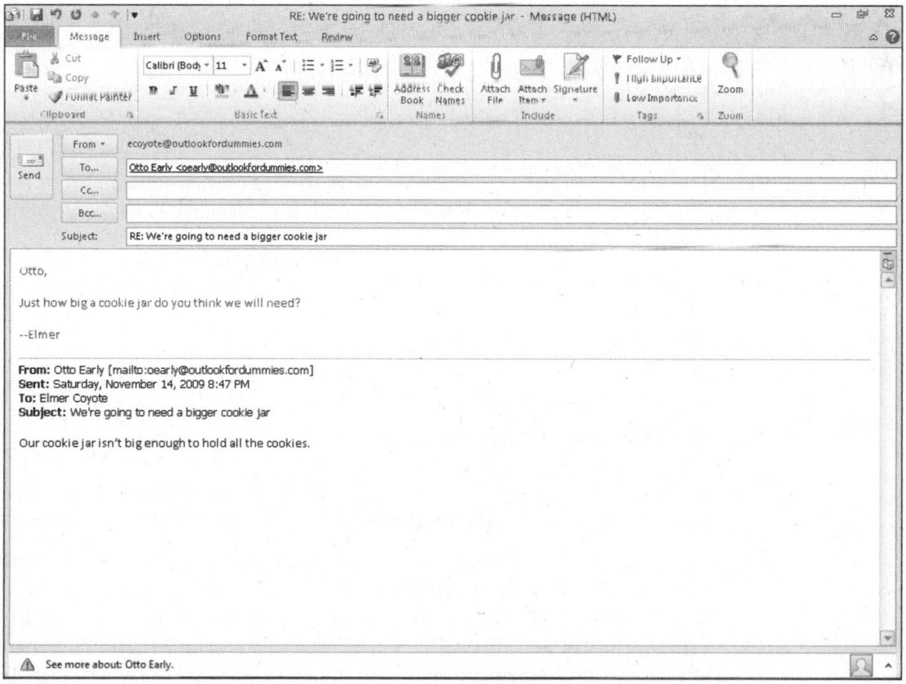

Figure 4-7:
The Reply
screen.

Using a Web link from your e-mail

When you open a message, sometimes you see blue, underlined text with the name of a Web page or e-mail address. If you want to look at the Web page, just click the underlined text of the Web page. If everything is installed correctly, your Web browser pops up and opens the Web page whose name you've clicked. If you want to send a message to the e-mail address, just click the underlined text and a New Message form opens with the e-mail address already in the To field.

Don't get caught by phishing

Sneaky people are always looking for new ways to trick you, especially on the Internet. In recent years, a common scam called *phishing* has cost people time, money, and grief after they responded to an e-mail by an impostor who claimed to represent a bank or other financial institution.

If you get an e-mail that purports to be from a bank or other business and asks you to click a link to log on to "verify" personal information, especially passwords, don't fall for it. The link will probably direct you to a Web site that might *look* legitimate — but the personal information you are asked to enter can then be used for fraud or identity theft. Contact the business directly, preferably by phone, to make sure that the e-mail isn't a fake. One way to confirm that an e-mail is phony is to hover your mouse over a link in the message until the URL or Internet address pops up. If the address it links to isn't the same as the address of the institution that claims to be sending the message, it's a phishing scam. Just delete it.

That's Not My Department: Forwarding E-Mail

You may not always have the answer to every e-mail message you get. You may need to send a message along to somebody else to answer, so pass it on.

To forward a message, follow these steps:

1. **Click the Mail button in the Navigation pane (or press Ctrl+Shift+I).**

   The Inbox screen opens, showing your incoming mail.

2. **Click the title of the message you want to forward.**

   The message you selected appears in the Reading pane; see Figure 4-8. You can forward the message as soon as you read it. If you've already opened the message, you can skip the first two steps.

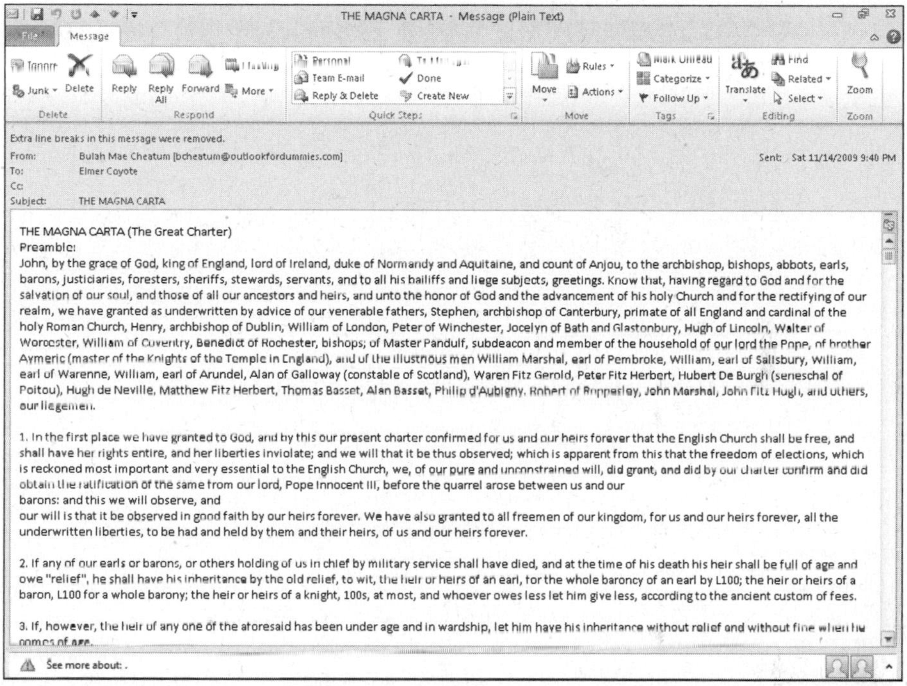

Figure 4-8:
The message you want to forward is opened.

[Screenshot shows an Outlook message window titled "THE MAGNA CARTA · Message (Plain Text)" with the following content:]

Extra line breaks in this message were removed.

From: Bulah Mae Cheatum [bcheatum@outlookfordummies.com]   Sent: Sat 11/14/2009 9:40 PM
To: Elmer Coyote
Cc:
Subject: THE MAGNA CARTA

THE MAGNA CARTA (The Great Charter)
Preamble:
John, by the grace of God, king of England, lord of Ireland, duke of Normandy and Aquitaine, and count of Anjou, to the archbishop, bishops, abbots, earls, barons, justiciaries, foresters, sheriffs, stewards, servants, and to all his bailiffs and liege subjects, greetings. Know that, having regard to God and for the salvation of our soul, and those of all our ancestors and heirs, and unto the honor of God and the advancement of his holy Church and for the rectifying of our realm, we have granted as underwritten by advice of our venerable fathers, Stephen, archbishop of Canterbury, primate of all England and cardinal of the holy Roman Church, Henry, archbishop of Dublin, William of London, Peter of Winchester, Jocelyn of Bath and Glastonbury, Hugh of Lincoln, Walter of Worcester, William of Coventry, Benedict of Rochester, bishops; of Master Pandulf, subdeacon and member of the household of our lord the Pope, of brother Aymeric (master of the Knights of the Temple in England), and of the illustrious men William Marshal, earl of Pembroke, William, earl of Salisbury, William, earl of Warenne, William, earl of Arundel, Alan of Galloway (constable of Scotland), Waren Fitz Gerold, Peter Fitz Herbert, Hubert De Burgh (seneschal of Poitou), Hugh de Neville, Matthew Fitz Herbert, Thomas Basset, Alan Basset, Philip d'Aubigny, Robert of Ropperley, John Marshal, John Fitz Hugh, and others, our liegemen.

1. In the first place we have granted to God, and by this our present charter confirmed for us and our heirs forever that the English Church shall be free, and shall have her rights entire, and her liberties inviolate; and we will that it be thus observed; which is apparent from this that the freedom of elections, which is reckoned most important and very essential to the English Church, we, of our pure and unconstrained will, did grant, and did by our charter confirm and did obtain the ratification of the same from our lord, Pope Innocent III, before the quarrel arose between us and our barons: and this we will observe, and
our will is that it be observed in good faith by our heirs forever. We have also granted to all freemen of our kingdom, for us and our heirs forever, all the underwritten liberties, to be had and held by them and their heirs, of us and our heirs forever.

2. If any of our earls or barons, or others holding of us in chief by military service shall have died, and at the time of his death his heir shall be full of age and owe "relief," he shall have his inheritance by the old relief, to wit, the heir or heirs of an earl, for the whole barony of an earl by L100; the heir or heirs of a baron, L100 for a whole barony; the heir or heirs of a knight, 100s, at most, and whoever owes less let him give less, according to the ancient custom of fees.

3. If, however, the heir of any one of the aforesaid has been under age and in wardship, let him have his inheritance without relief and without fine when he comes of age.

See more about: .

3. **Click the Forward button.**

   The Forward screen appears; see Figure 4-9. The subject of the original message is now the subject of the new message, except the letters FW: (for Forward) are inserted at the beginning.

4. **Click the To text box and type the e-mail address of the person to whom you're forwarding the message.**

   If the person to whom you're forwarding the message is already entered in your Address Book, just start typing the person's name — Outlook figures out the e-mail address for you.

5. **Click the Cc text box and type the e-mail addresses of the people to whom you also want to forward a copy of your message.**

   Many people forward trivia (such as jokes of the day) to scads of their friends by e-mail. Most recipients are included as Cc addresses.

   Remember, business e-mail etiquette is different from home e-mail etiquette. Many employers have strict policies about appropriate use of their corporate e-mail systems. If you work for such a company, be aware of your company's policies.

   If you want to pester your friends by sending silly trivia from your home computer to their home computers (as I do), that's your own business.

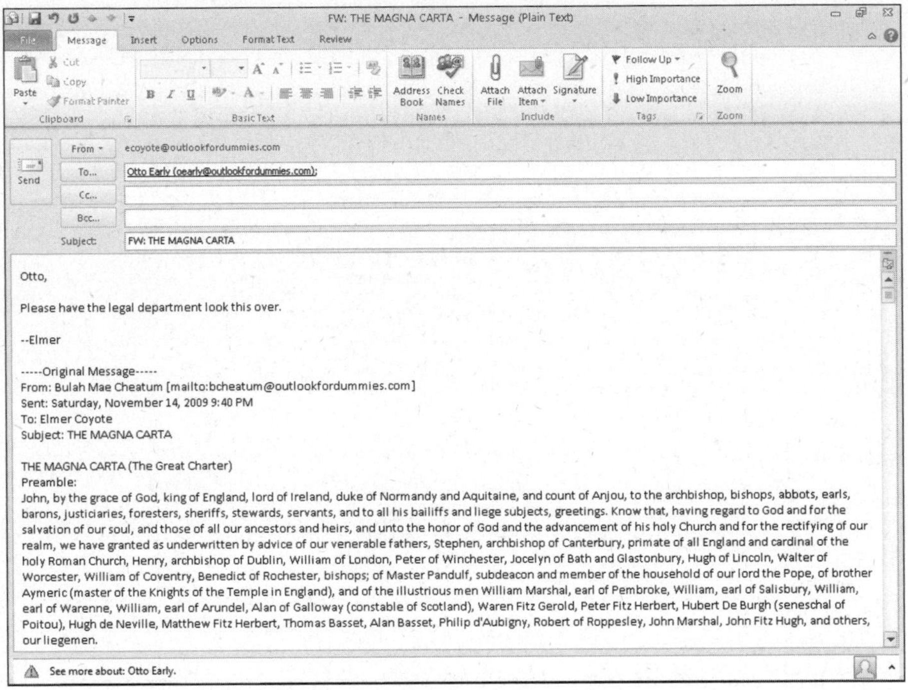

Figure 4-9:
The Forward
screen.

6. **In the text box, type any comments you want to add to the message.**

   The text of the original message appears in the text box. You can preface the message that you're forwarding if you want to give that person a bit of explanation — for example, **This is the 99th message I've had from this person; somebody needs to get a life.**

7. **Click the Send button.**

   Your message is on its way.

Blind Copying for Privacy

When you send a message to a large group, everyone who receives the message can see the e-mail addresses in the To and Cc fields, which means that you've just given out e-mail addresses that some people might rather keep private. Everybody already gets way too many weird, unsolicited e-mails, and many people get peeved when you broadcast their address without permission.

Blind copies give you the best of both worlds. If you put all the e-mail addresses in the Bcc field, nobody's privacy is compromised. By using *BCCs* (an old abbreviation for blind carbon copy, a quaint reminder to those who'll admit that they're old enough to remember carbon paper), you can keep secret addresses secret.

The Bcc field isn't always displayed when you create a message in Outlook. If you don't see a box labeled Bcc right below the Cc box, click the Options tab in the Ribbon and then click the Bcc button.

Deleting Messages

You can zap an e-mail message without a second thought; you don't even have to read the thing. As soon as you see the Inbox list, you know who's sending the message and what it's about, so you don't have to waste time reading Burt's Bad Joke of the Day. Just zap it.

If you accidentally delete a message you didn't want to lose, click the Deleted Items folder. You'll find all the messages you've deleted in the last few months (unless you've emptied the Deleted Items folder). To recover a deleted message, just drag it from the Deleted Items list to the icon for whichever folder you want to put it in.

Here's how you delete a message:

1. **Click the Mail button in the Navigation pane (or press Ctrl+Shift+I).**

   The Inbox screen opens, showing your incoming mail.

2. **Click the title of the message that you want to delete.**

   You don't have to read the message; you can just delete it from the list.

3. **Click the Delete button on the Home tab in the Ribbon (or just press the Delete key on your keyboard).**

Another quick way to delete a message is to click the Delete button that appears at the top of the message you're reading (or press Ctrl+D). It's easy to recognize the Delete button; it's marked with a huge, black X. You know it doesn't mean buried pirate treasure — it means "make this message walk the plank."

When you delete messages, Outlook doesn't actually eliminate deleted items; it moves them to the Deleted Items folder. If you have unread items in your Deleted Items folder, the words *Deleted Items* change to boldface type, followed by the number of unread items — the same way Outlook annotates the

Inbox with the number of unread items. You can get rid of the annotation by first selecting the Deleted Items icon in the Folder list, choosing the Folder tab in the Ribbon, and then clicking the Empty Folder button. Or, you can just ignore the annotation. After you empty your Deleted Items folder, the messages that were in it disappear forever.

Saving Interrupted Messages

If you get interrupted while writing an e-mail message, all is not lost. You can just save the work you've done and return to it later. Just click the Save button — the small icon that looks like a blue floppy disk in the upper-left corner of the New Message form — (or press Ctrl+S), and your message is saved to the Drafts folder, as shown in Figure 4-10 (unless you had reopened the message from the Outbox, in which case Outlook saves the unfinished message back to the Outbox). Alternatively, you can select the File tab and click the Save button.

Drafts folder

Figure 4-10:
You can
save
incomplete
messages
and return
to finish
them later.

When a message is ready to be sent, its name appears in the Outbox in italics. If you've saved it to work on later, its name appears in normal text, not italics. If you're not finished with the message and plan to return to it later, save it (press Ctrl+S). If the message is ready for prime time, send it by pressing Alt+S.

Saving a Message as a File

You may create or receive an e-mail message that's so wonderful (or terrible) that you just have to save it. You may need to print the message and show it to someone else, save it to disk, or export it to a desktop-publishing program.

To save a message as a file, follow these steps:

1. **With the message already open, select the File tab from the Ribbon and then choose Save As (or press F12).**

   The Save As dialog box appears.

2. **Use the Navigation pane on the left side of the Save As dialog box to choose the drive and folder in which you want to save the file.**

   By default, Outlook initially chooses your Documents folder, but you can save the message on any drive and in any folder you want.

3. **Click the File Name text box and type the name you want to give the file.**

   Type any name you want — if you type a filename that Outlook can't use, it opens a window telling you that the filename is not valid.

4. **Click the triangle at the end of the Save as Type box and choose Text as your file type (as shown in Figure 4-11).**

   There are several file types to choose from, but the Text file format is most easily read by other applications. The different file type options are:

   - **Text Only (*.txt):** A very simple file format that removes all of the message's formatting. As the name implies, it saves only the text of the message.

   - **Outlook Template (*.oft):** This format is for saving a message that you want to use repeatedly in Outlook. It saves the message's formatting as well as any attachments.

   - **Outlook Message Format (*.msg):** This format keeps all of the message's formatting and attachments; but it can only be read by Outlook.

- **Outlook Message Format - Unicode (*.msg):** This is the same as the previous file format, but it uses "international" characters that can be read by versions of Outlook that use different languages. This is Outlook's default setting.

- **HTML (*.htm or *.html):** This saves a message in a file format that can be displayed using a Web browser (such as Internet Explorer or Firefox) or any other application that can display HTM or HTML files (such as Word). File attachments are not saved, but the formatting of the message is maintained. In addition to saving a copy of a message with the HTM file extension, a separate folder is also created, which contains supporting files that the HTM file needs.

- **MHT files (*.mht):** This is the same as the HTM file format, except that an additional folder isn't created. Applications that can display HTM and HTML file should also be able to display MHT files.

5. **Click the Save button (or press Enter).**

   The message is saved to the file and folder you specified in Step 2.

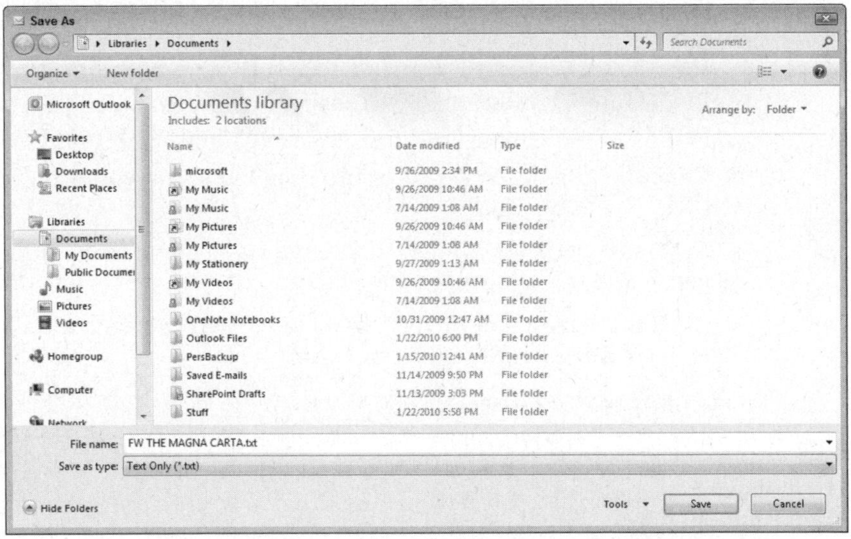

Figure 4-11:
The Save As
dialog box.

Chapter 5

E-Mail Tools You Can't Do Without

*O*utlook can do all sorts of tricks with the mail you send out, as well as with the messages you receive. You can flag messages with reminders, customize your messages with a signature, or add special formatting to the messages you send as replies.

Some Outlook features work only if the system that's backing it up supports those same features, and some Outlook features work only if the person to whom you're mailing uses a system that supports the same features you're using. Microsoft Exchange Server is a program that runs on many corporate networks — which adds a number of features to Outlook, such as accessing someone else's Inbox or diverting messages to someone else. If you want to know more about the features you may have on a corporate network with Microsoft Exchange Server, see Chapter 14. If you're not among the fortunate ones who have Exchange Server, don't worry — Outlook can still do plenty all by itself.

Nagging by Flagging

Over time, *flags* have become one of my favorite Outlook features. I get thousands of messages each week, and I need help remembering to get back to important messages that otherwise might get lost in the shuffle. If I can't respond to an important message right away, I like to flag that message as soon as I read it. Then I'm sure to get back to it. You can also plant a flag in a message you send to others to remind them of a task they have to do if both you and the other person are using Microsoft Outlook.

One-click flagging

Why flag a message? To help get your work done faster! So you need to know the fastest possible way to flag a message, right? Of course.

When you look at the list of messages in your Inbox, you see a little box at the right end of each subject line that contains a little, gray outline of a flag, sort of a shadow flag. When you click that little shadow, it changes from gray to red to show that you've flagged it. Now, whenever you look at your list of messages, you know which messages need further attention. Those you've flagged also appear in the To-Do bar on the right side of the Outlook screen so that you can see flagged messages even after they've slipped below the bottom of the screen. See Figure 5-1.

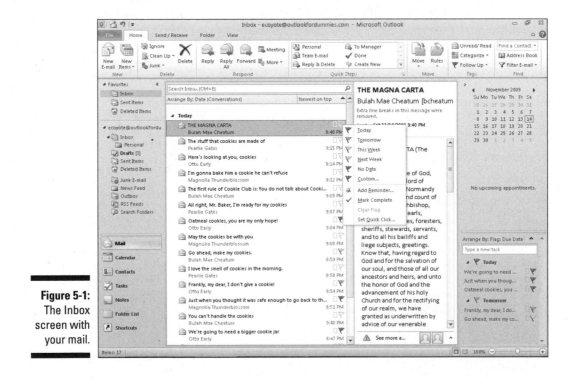

Figure 5-1:
The Inbox screen with your mail.

After you've attended to your flagged message, click the flag again. That replaces the flag with a check mark to show that you've taken care of that message.

Setting flags for different days

If you only click once on a message to add a flag, a copy of the message appears in your To-Do bar, along with the list of things you're scheduled to do today. You might not be ready to deal with a certain message today; you might prefer to put it off until tomorrow or next week. If you right-click the flag icon on the Message form (shown in Figure 5-1), you see a list of possible due dates for a flag, including Today, Tomorrow, This Week, Next Week, No Date, and Custom. (The 12th of Never remains unavailable. Sorry.) After you've picked a due date, you can always change it by dragging the item from one due date to another in the To-Do bar. For example, you can drag an item from the Today group to the Next Week group (if both groups are visible). You can also double-click the item to reopen it and choose a different due date. If the due date comes and goes without making a change to a flag (such as marking it complete or updating the due date), the message heading in your Inbox and To-Do bar turns red.

Changing the default flag date

For unusually busy people and compulsive procrastinators, you can change the default due dates of your flags by following these steps:

1. **Right-click any flag.**

   The flag shortcut menu appears.

2. **Choose Set Quick Click.**

   Another shortcut menu appears, offering several choices of due date; see Figure 5-2.

Figure 5-2:
Choose from a lovely assortment of default flag choices.

3. **Pick the date that suits you.**

   The date you choose becomes the default flag due date.

If you have trouble committing to a date (you're so fickle), you can choose No Date and just wait until someone complains. I call that the Squeaky Wheel school of time management: Put everything off until somebody yells about something, then just do that. It's a popular approach with people who work for the government.

Adding a flag with a customized reminder

Of course, flags can do a lot more than stand there looking pretty for a week or so. Outlook flags can pop up and remind you to do something at any time you choose. They can also pop up and pester someone *else* when you put a reminder on a message you send. (Who could resist that?) Adding a reminder to a flag takes more than one click — but not much more. To attach a flag to your e-mail messages (those you send and those you receive), follow these steps:

1. **Click the Mail button in the Navigation pane (or press Ctrl+Shift+I).**

   The Inbox screen opens, showing your incoming mail.

2. **Right-click the flag on the message you want to flag.**

   The flag shortcut menu appears.

3. **Choose Add Reminder.**

   The Custom dialog box appears. At this point, if you click the OK button (or press Enter), your message is flagged and set to remind you at 4:00 p.m. today. That may be a wee bit too soon — especially if it's already after 4:00 p.m. — so you can set more detailed options by using the remaining steps.

4. **Click the triangle at the right end of the Flag To text box and choose one of the menu items (or type your own choice).**

   One handy flag is Follow Up, which reminds you to confirm an appointment or other arrangement.

5. **Enter dates in the Start Date box, Due Date box, Reminder box, or all the boxes.**

   The date and time you type in the Reminder box indicate when a reminder will pop up to jog your memory. The other two dates help you keep track of how many tasks you're juggling at once. You can be pretty loose about how you enter dates in Outlook. You can type the date **3/2/11**; Outlook understands. You can type **first wednesday of march**; Outlook understands. You can type **week from Wednesday**; Outlook understands that to mean "seven days after the Wednesday that comes after today." You don't even have to worry about capitalization. (Don't type **I hate mondays**, though — Outlook doesn't understand that. But I do.)

If you'd rather just pick a date from a calendar, you can click the arrow at the right end of any of the date boxes to reveal a calendar and then just click the date you want.

6. **Click the OK button.**

When the reminder date you entered in the Custom dialog box arrives, a reminder dialog box helps give you a gentle nudge.

Changing the date on a reminder

Procrastination used to be an art; Outlook makes it a science. When someone nags you with reminder, you can still put it off. Yes, dear, you *can* do it later.

To change the date on a reminder that someone sent you, follow these steps:

1. **Click the Mail button in the Navigation pane (or press Ctrl+Shift+I).**

   The Inbox screen opens, showing your incoming mail.

2. **Click the message that has a reminder you want to change.**

   The message appears highlighted to show that you've selected it.

   You can right click the message's flag icon to open the Custom dialog box or can you can access the Custom dialog box as described in the next step.

3. **Select the Home tab, choose Follow Up in the Ribbon, and then click Add Reminder (or press Ctrl+Shift+G).**

   The Custom dialog box appears; see Figure 5-3.

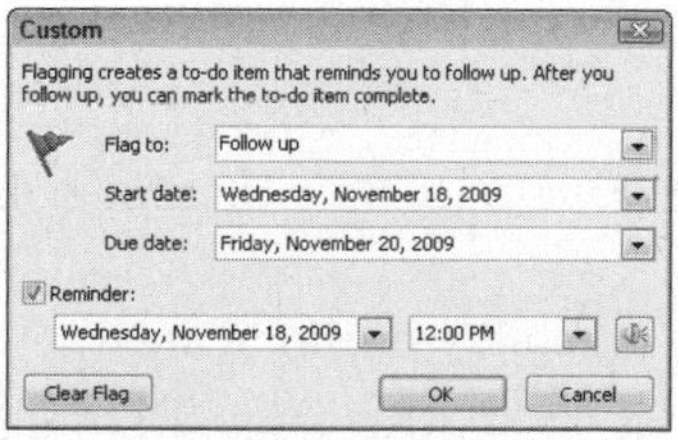

Figure 5-3:
The Custom dialog box for setting reminders.

4. **Select the Reminder check box and select the new date when you want the reminder flag to appear.**

   If the check box is already selected, don't click it; doing so would deselect it. Enter the date and time when you think you'll feel ready to be flagged again. Typing **999 years from now** will work — really!

5. **Click the OK button.**

Of course, you can always put something off if you really try. When a flag reminder pops up, click the Snooze button to put it off for a while, just as you do with your alarm clock.

Saving Copies of Your Messages

Nothing is handier than knowing what you've sent and when you sent it. You can save all your outgoing mail in Outlook so that you can go back and look up the messages you've sent. Outlook starts saving sent items when you first install the program, but you can turn this feature on and off. So before you go changing your options, look in your Sent Messages folder to see whether it contains messages.

To save copies of your messages, follow these steps:

1. **Select the File tab and click the Options button.**

   The Outlook Options dialog box appears.

2. **Click the Mail button in the navigation window on the left.**

   The Mail settings appear, as shown in Figure 5-4.

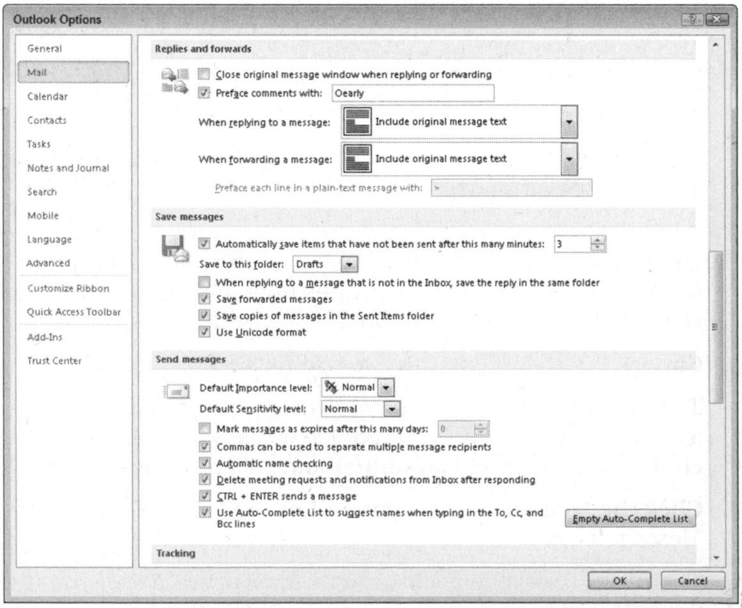

Figure 5-4:
You can decide whether to save copies of the messages you send by using the Outlook Options dialog box.

3. **Scroll down to the Save Messages section and select the Save Copies of Messages in the Sent Items Folder check box.**

   If the box already contains a check mark, leave it alone. (That's the way Outlook is set up when you first install it.) If you click the box when it's already checked, you turn off your option for saving messages. Don't worry if you make a mistake; you can always change it back. Just make sure that a check mark appears in the box if you want to save messages.

4. **Click the OK button.**

Setting Your Reply and Forward Options

You can control the appearance of the messages you forward, as well as your replies. If your office uses Microsoft Outlook, you can make your text look pretty incredible in messages you send to one another by adding graphics, wild-looking fonts, or special effects, such as blinking text. If you're sending mail to recipients who use programs other than Microsoft Outlook or to people to who use Web-based e-mail services, such as Gmail (see Chapter 12 for more about online services and Internet service providers), some of the customizations might not translate well.

To set your options, follow these steps:

1. **Select the File tab in the Ribbon and click the Options button.**

   The Outlook Options dialog box appears.

2. **Click the Mail button in the navigation window on the left.**

   The Mail settings window appears.

3. **Scroll down to the Replies and Forwards section and click the triangle at the right end of the When Replying to a Message box.**

   A menu of options drops down. When Outlook is first installed, Include Original Message Text is the default option. The diagram on the left side of the scroll-down menu illustrates how the message will be laid out when you choose each option; see Figure 5-5.

4. **Choose the style you prefer to use for replies.**

   The little diagram on the left side of the menu changes when you make a choice to show what your choice will look like. If you don't like the choice you've made, try another and see how it looks in the diagram.

5. **Click the triangle at the right end of the When Forwarding a Message box.**

   The When Forwarding a Message box has one fewer choice than the When Replying to a Message box does, but the two menus work the same way. Also, they both have that little diagram of the page layout off to the left.

6. **Choose the style you prefer to use for forwarding messages.**

   Just pick one; you can always change it.

7. **Click the OK button.**

   The Outlook Options dialog box closes.

You can do all sorts of fancy, exciting, and even useful tricks with e-mail by taking advantage of Outlook's options. If the advanced options seem confusing, you can easily ignore them. Just click the Reply button and type your answer.

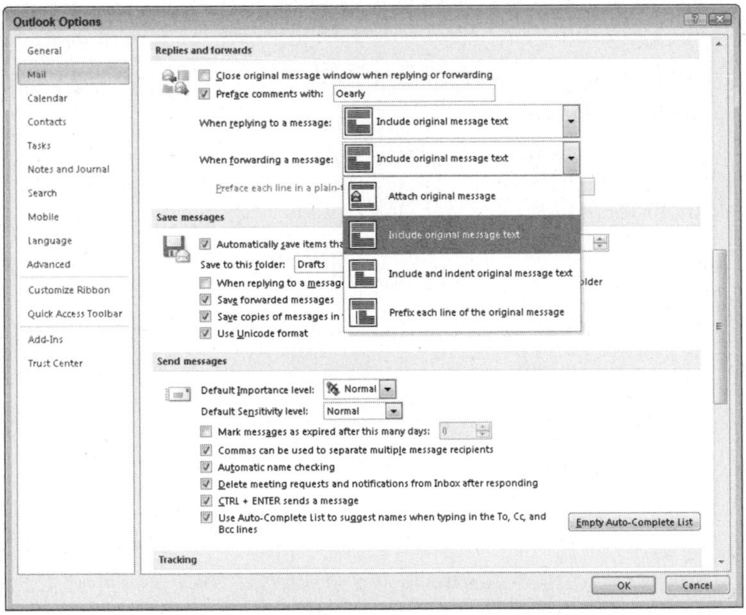

Figure 5-5: Change the appearance of your replies and forwards in the Mail settings dialog box.

Adding Comments to a Reply or Forward

When you forward or reply to a message, it helps to include parts of the original message that you're forwarding or replying to so that the person reading your message knows exactly what you're responding to. The question is, how will the reader know which comments are from the original e-mail and which are yours?

Outlook lets you preface your comments with your name or any text you choose. It's always best to use your name, but if you want to confuse the issue, you could always use a phrase such as "Simon says."

To tag your replies with your name, follow these steps:

1. **Select the File tab in the Ribbon and click the Options button.**

   The Outlook Options dialog box appears.

2. **Click the Mail button in the navigation window on the left.**

   The Mail settings appear.

3. **Scroll down to the Replies and Forwards section and select the Preface Comments With check box.**

   If the check box is already selected, don't click it; doing so would deselect it.

4. **In the Preface Comments With text box, type the text you want to accompany your annotations.**

   Your best bet is to enter your name here. Whatever you enter will be used as the prefix to all the text you type when you reply to messages; see Figure 5-6.

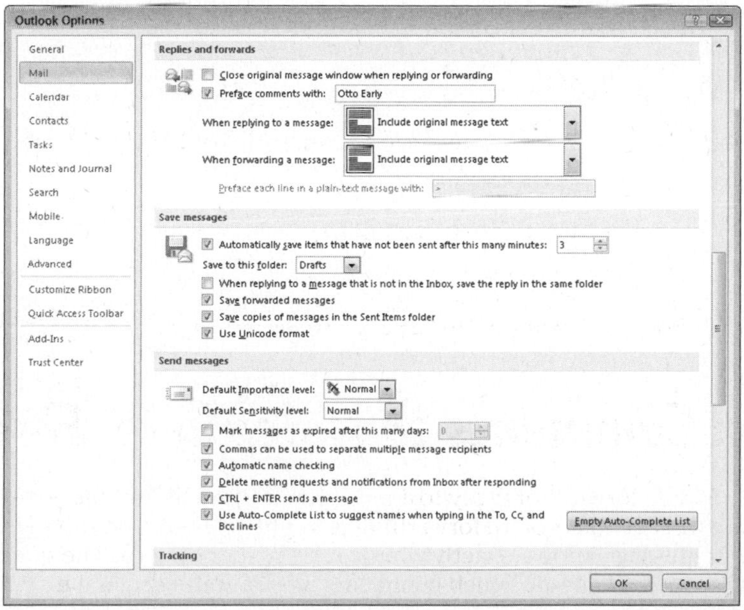

Figure 5-6: Preface your comments in replies and forwards with your name.

5. Click the OK button.

You can select and delete the text of the original message when you create a forward or reply, but including at least a part of the original message makes your response easier to understand. You also have the option of selecting and deleting the parts of the original text that aren't relevant to your reply.

Sending Attachments

If you've already created a document in another application that you want to send, you don't have to type the document all over again in Outlook; just send the document as an *attachment* to an e-mail message. You can attach any kind of file — word processing documents, spreadsheets, and presentations from programs, such as PowerPoint. You can even send pictures or music. Any kind of file can be sent as an attachment.

The easiest way to send a file from a Microsoft Office program (such as Microsoft Word 2010) is to open that file in the Microsoft Office program it was created in, select the File tab in the Ribbon, click the Share button, select Send Using E-Mail from the Share menu, and then click the Send as Attachment button. If you'd rather not do that, you can send a file attachment straight from Outlook by following these steps:

1. **Click the Mail button in the Navigation pane (or press Ctrl+Shift+I).**

   The Mail module opens.

2. **Click the New E-Mail button in the Ribbon (or press Ctrl+N).**

   The New Message form appears.

3. **Click the Attach File button in the New Message form's Ribbon.**

   The Insert File dialog box appears; see Figure 5-7. It looks like the dialog box you use for opening files in most Windows programs, and it works like opening a file, too. Just click the name of the file you want to send and click the Insert button.

   If the format of your e-mail is either HTML or Plain Text, the name of the file appears in the Attached box in the Message form's message header. If the format of your e-mail is Rich Text, an icon appears in the text of your message, representing the file you attached to your message. When you send this e-mail message, a copy of the file you selected goes to your recipient.

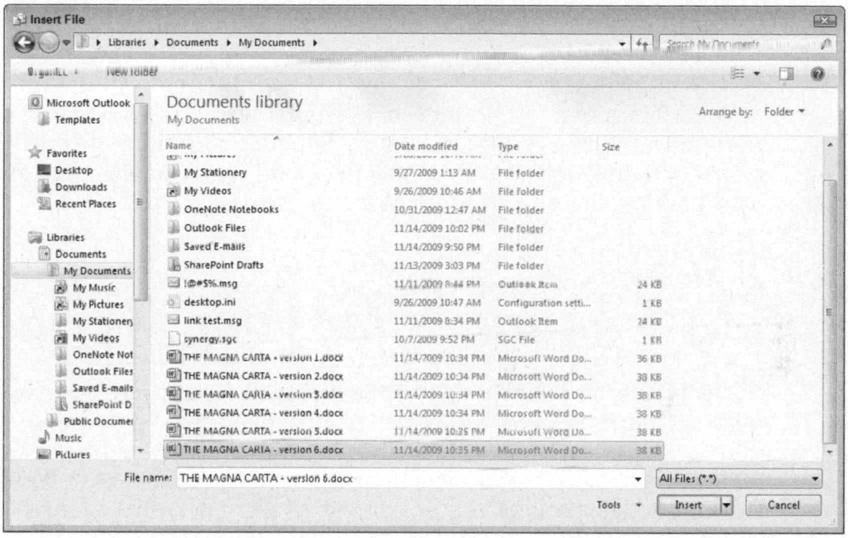

Figure 5-7:
The Insert
File dialog
box.

4. **Type your message (if you have a message to send).**

   You may not have a message; perhaps you want to send only the attachment. If what you want to say is in the attachment, that's fine, but
   remember that the contents of an attachment don't show up on the
   recipient's screen until he or she actually opens the attachment.

5. **Click the To button in your Message form.**

   The Select Names dialog box appears.

6. **Select a name from your Address Book and click the To button in the
   Select Names dialog box.**

   The name of the selected person appears in the To box of the Select
   Names dialog box. If the name of the person to whom you want to send
   your message isn't in the list, you can select Suggested Contacts from
   the Address Book drop-down list. (If the name of the person still doesn't
   appear in the list, click the Cancel button and return to the Message
   form. Then just type the person's e-mail address in the To text box and
   skip ahead to Step 8.)

7. **Click the OK button.**

   The name of the selected person is now in the To box of the message.

8. **Click the Subject text box and type a subject for your message.**

   A subject is optional, but if you want somebody to read what you send,
   including a subject helps.

9. **Click the Send button.**

   Your message and its attachment are sent.

 Another approach for sending an attachment is to find the file on your computer using Windows Explorer, right-click that file, choose Send To from the shortcut menu, and then click Mail Recipient. You can also drag and drop attachments directly into Outlook's New Message form.

Creating Signatures for Your Messages

Many people like to add a signature to the end of every message they send. A *signature* is usually a small portion of text that identifies you to everyone who reads your message and tells something you want everyone to know. Many people include their name, the name of their business, their business's Web address, their motto, a little sales slogan, or some squib of personal information.

You can tell Outlook to add a signature automatically to all your outgoing messages, but you must first create a signature file. Here's how to create your signature file:

1. **Select the File tab in the Ribbon and click the Options button.**

   The Outlook Options dialog box appears.

2. **Click the Mail button in the navigation window on the left.**

   The Mail settings windows appear.

3. **In the Compose Messages section, click the Signatures button.**

   The Signatures and Stationery dialog box appears, as shown in Figure 5-8.

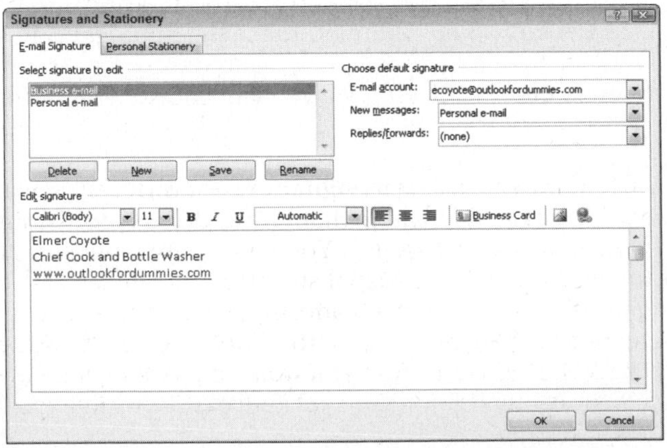

Figure 5-8:
The Signatures and Stationery dialog box.

4. **Click the New button.**

   The New Signature dialog box appears.

5. **Type a name for your new signature.**

   The name you type appears in the New Signature box. You can name a signature anything you want.

6. **Click the OK button.**

   The New Signature dialog box closes.

7. **Type the text of the signature you want in the Edit Signature box, and add any formatting you want.**

   To change the font, size, color, or other text characteristics, use the buttons just above the text box. If you're more comfortable creating highly formatted text in Microsoft Word, you can create your signature in Word and then select and copy it to the Edit Signature box.

   Many people receive e-mail on cell phones and other kinds of devices that don't know what to do with fancy formatting, so you may be best off with a fairly plain signature. Also, try to be brief. You don't want your signature to be longer than the message to which it's attached.

8. **Click the OK button.**

   Your new signature is now saved, and the Signatures and Stationery dialog box closes.

9. **Click the OK button in the Outlook Options window.**

   The Outlook Options window closes.

   Your new signature will now appear on every new message you send. If you create more than one signature, you can switch to a different default signature by following Steps 1 through 3 and then choosing the signature you want from the New Messages scroll-down menu in the Choose Default Signature section. If you want to include a signature in your replies and forwards, choose the signature you want from the Replies/Forwards scroll-down menu in the Choose Default Signature section.

If you use more than one e-mail address, you can choose your signatures in a couple ways:

  ✔ **Set up Outlook to use different signatures on different e-mail addresses.** For example, assume that one address is for business and another is for personal messages. You can create a businesslike signature for the first and a more casual signature for the latter. To designate which signature goes with which address, select the address from the E-Mail Account drop-down menu in the Choose Default Signature section and then pick the signature that you want to use for that e-mail address. Repeat this for each additional e-mail address for which you want to include a signature.

✔ **Choose signatures one at a time.** When you finish writing the body of an e-mail message, click the Insert tab in the New Message form's Ribbon and then click the Signature button to see the list of signatures you've created. Clicking the name of the signature that you want to use makes that signature appear in your message.

One of my favorite timesavers is to create a signature that contains a message that I send out frequently. For example, when I'm working on a book like this, I often contact many different people asking for information about products that improve or work with Outlook. Instead of typing the same message over and over, I turn that message into a signature and then insert that "signature" each time I send the message. It's sneaky, because that's not what signatures were designed to do, but it saves a lot of typing.

Chapter 6

Conquering Your Mountain of Messages

In This Chapter

▶ Setting up a new mail folder

▶ Filing messages in folders

▶ Looking at your messages

▶ Using the Rules Wizard

▶ Dealing with junk e-mail

▶ Archiving e-mail

*Y*ou spend too much time on e-mail. I know you do. Everybody does. Some experts estimate that the average business employee spends up to two hours each day on e-mail, and it's getting worse every year. Pretty soon, you'll spend more time on e-mail than you spend working. (Some people already do.) Then you'll spend more time on e-mail than you spend awake. After that . . . I don't want to think about it. I'd rather get Outlook to cut down the time I spend wrestling with e-mail.

Outlook has some handy tools for coping with the flood of electronic flotsam and jetsam that finds its way into your Inbox. You can create separate folders for filing your mail, and you can use Outlook's View feature to help you slice and dice your incoming messages into manageable groups. You can even archive old messages to keep your Inbox from getting too bloated.

Even better than the View feature is the Rules Wizard, which automatically responds to incoming messages according to your wishes. You can move all messages from certain senders to the folder of your choice — for instance, consigning everything from Spam-O-Rama.com to oblivion — send automatic replies to messages about certain subjects, or delete messages containing words that offend you.

Speaking of spam, an even more effective way to deal with offensive or aggressively useless messages is to use the junk e-mail filters built into

Outlook. The filters should already be turned on — but you can crank up the settings to have even less junk mail cluttering up your Inbox.

Organizing Folders

You're probably familiar with organizing items into folders. Windows organizes all your other documents into folders, so why should Outlook be any different? Well, Outlook *is* a little different than Windows regarding folders. But the idea is the same: create a folder and drag stuff to it.

Creating a new mail folder

The simplest way to manage incoming mail is just to file it. Before you file a message, you need to create at least one folder in which to file your messages. You only need to create a folder once; it's there for good after you create it (unless, of course, you later decide to delete it). You can create as many folders as you want; you may have dozens or just one or two.

I have folders for filing mail from specific clients, for example. All the e-mail I've received in connection with this book is in a folder called `Outlook For Dummies`. (Clever title, eh?) Another folder called `Personal` contains messages that aren't business related.

To create a folder for new mail, follow these steps:

1. **Click the Mail button in the Navigation pane (or press Ctrl+Shift+I).**

   The Mail module appears.

2. **Select the word *Inbox* in the Folder list.**

   The word *Inbox* is highlighted.

3. **Select the Folder tab in the Ribbon, and click the New Folder button.**

   The Create New Folder dialog box appears (as shown in Figure 6-1).

4. **In the Name text box, type a name for your new folder, such as** *Personal.*

   You can name the folder anything you like. You can also create many folders for saving and sorting your incoming e-mail. Leaving all your mail in your Inbox gets confusing. On the other hand, if you create too many folders, you may be just as confused as if you had only one.

5. **Click the OK button.**

   Your new folder appears in the Folder list.

You now have a new folder named Personal (or whatever name you entered) for filing messages that you want to save for future reference. I like to use three or four mail folders for different types of mail to make finding what I'm looking for easier.

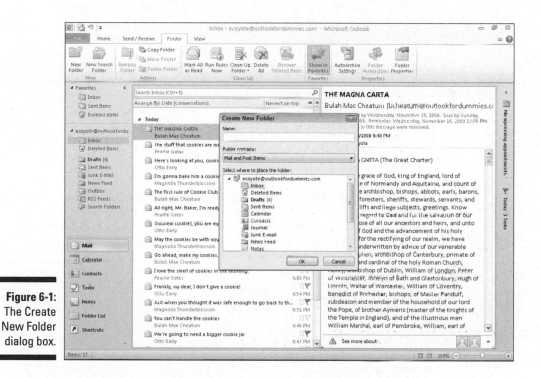

Figure 6-1:
The Create New Folder dialog box.

Moving messages to another folder

Filing your messages is as easy as dragging them from the folder they're in to the folder where you want them. Just click the Inbox to look at your messages when they arrive, and then drag each message to the folder where you want your messages to stay.

For a different way to move messages to another folder, follow these steps:

1. **Click the Mail button in the Navigation pane (or press Ctrl+Shift+I).**

   Your list of incoming mail messages appears.

2. **Click the title of the message you want to move.**

   The message is highlighted.

3. **Select the Home tab in the Ribbon, and click the Move button.**

   The Move drop-down list appears.

4. **Select the name of the folder to which you want to move your message.**

   As soon as you click the folder name, your message is moved to the folder you chose. If you created a folder named `Personal` (or anything else) in the preceding section of this chapter, you can move the message there.

 The Outlook toolbar has a button called Move that you can click to move or copy a selected message to the folder of your choice. The best thing about the button is that it remembers the last ten folders to which you moved messages. That feature makes it easy to move messages to folders that may be tricky to find in the Folder list. Sometimes its memory is a little too good: If you delete a folder and it is one of the ten most recent folders Outlook moved a message to, that folder will still appear in the list. If you try to move a message to a non-existent folder, Outlook warns you that the folder is not available and doesn't move the message.

 If you created many folders, the folder you want to move the message to might not appear in the list of available folders when you click the Move button. If the folder you want isn't listed, click the Other Folder button at the bottom of this Folder list. The Move Items dialog box opens, displaying all folders.

Organizing Your E-Mail with Search Folders

The Search Folders feature in Outlook is designed to help you organize the messages in your Inbox and other folders. Search Folders provide a single place where you can always look to find a certain kind of message. A search folder doesn't actually move your messages; it's really a kind of imaginary location for your messages so that you only have to look at one type of message at a time.

When you first start Outlook, no search folders are in the Navigation pane, so if you want to use Search Folders, you'll need to add one of the default Outlook search folders or create your own custom search folder.

Setting up a search folder

To set up a search folder, follow these steps:

1. **Click the Mail button in the Navigation pane (or press Ctrl+Shift+I).**

   The Mail module appears.

2. **Select the Folder tab in the Ribbon, and then click the New Search Folder button (or press Ctrl+Shift+P).**

   The New Search Folder dialog box appears; see Figure 6-2.

3. **Select the type of search folder you'd like to add from the list in the New Search Folder dialog box.**

   More than a dozen different kinds of folders are available. You can either use a predefined folder or create your own type of search folder (by choosing Create a Custom Search Folder at the bottom of the list).

4. **If a Choose button appears at the bottom of the New Search Folder dialog box when you select a search folder, click the button and fill in the requested information.**

   When you click some of the search folder types to select them, the bottom of the New Search Folder dialog box changes, offering you a choice suitable to the type of folder you're creating.

5. **Click the OK button.**

   The New Search Folder dialog box closes and your new search folder appears in the Navigation pane.

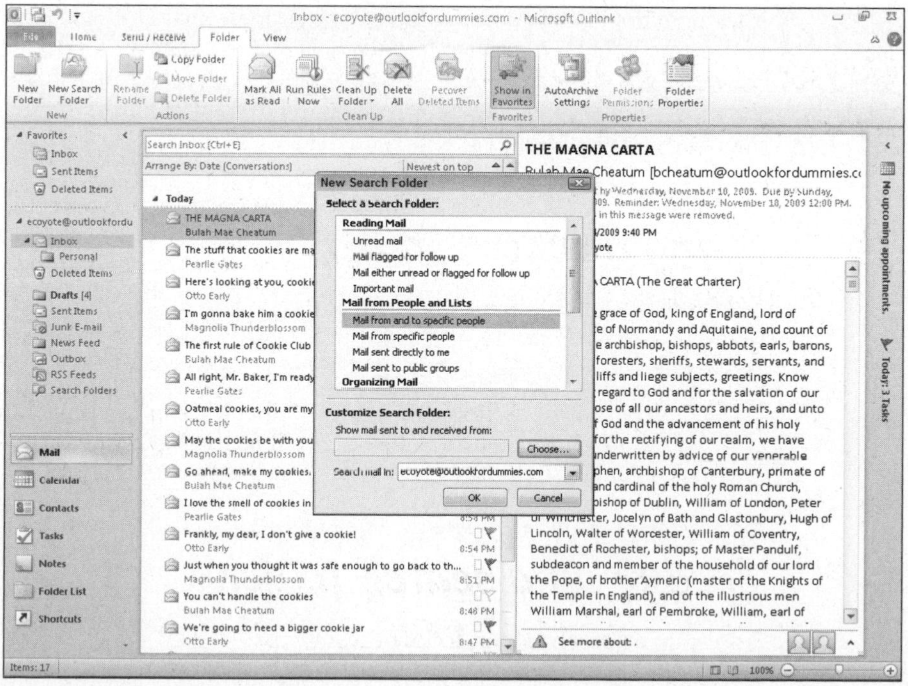

Figure 6-2: The New Search Folder dialog box.

Some useful predefined search folders are as follows:

- ✔ **Mail flagged for follow up:** This folder shows only the messages you've flagged. When you remove the flag from a message, you'll no longer see it in this search folder, but you can still find it in the Inbox or folder in which it actually resides.

- ✔ **Large mail:** This search folder organizes your messages in order of how much storage space they require. Normally, you're probably not too concerned with the size of the messages you receive — but don't be surprised if the system administrators where you work ask you not to store too much mail in your Inbox. If you have lots of messages with attachments (or messages in which friends include their photographs), you may find your Inbox filling up quickly.

  You can use the Large mail search folder to figure out which messages are taking up the most space — and eliminate the largest ones. The messages you'll see in this folder are categorized by size, starting with Large and moving up to Huge and Enormous.

- ✔ **Unread mail:** This folder shows you only the messages you haven't read yet. When you read a message in this folder, it disappears from the folder, but you'll still be able to find it in your Inbox.

You need not limit yourself to the search folders that Outlook provides. You can create your own custom folders as well. For example, if you receive regular messages about sales in a certain region, you can set up a custom search folder that automatically shows you all the messages you've received containing that information.

Using a search folder

You don't need to do anything special to use a search folder. Just click the name of the search folder you want to look at in the Folder list, and a list of those messages appears. When you're ready to go back to your Inbox, just click the Inbox button in the Folder list to see your whole collection of messages again.

Deleting a search folder

After your search folder has served its purpose, there's no reason for you to keep it. Remember, the contents of the search folder are really just imaginary; deleting this folder does not delete the messages it contains. Just click the search folder you want to delete to highlight it, select the Folder tab in the Ribbon, and click the Delete Folder button to make your search folder disappear.

Using the Reading Pane

If you want to skim through a whole bunch of messages quickly, the Reading pane can help. The Reading pane is normally open when you first install Outlook. If it got closed somehow, select the View tab in the Ribbon, click the Reading Pane button, and click the Right option to open it.

When you do, the Inbox screen divides into two sections:

- ✔ The left shows your list of messages.
- ✔ The right shows the contents of the message you've selected; see Figure 6-3.

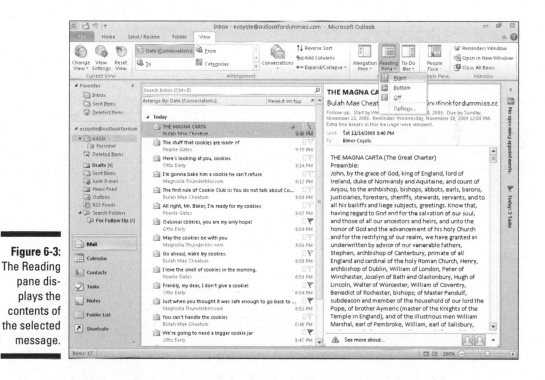

Figure 6-3: The Reading pane displays the contents of the selected message.

To move from one message to the next, just press the ↓ or ↑ key. You can also view any message in your Inbox by clicking the message title. If you prefer to see the text of your messages on the bottom of the screen, you can also select the View tab in the Ribbon, click the Reading Pane button, and click the Bottom option — but you can't see as much of your message this way. I generally prefer setting the Reading pane to appear on the right, although sometimes the To-Do bar cramps the Reading pane. You can make more room for the Reading pane by clicking the little right-facing arrow at the top of the To-Do bar, which squeezes the bar into a skinny little ribbon on the right edge of the screen. You can click the left-facing arrow in the squeezed ribbon to reopen the To-Do bar.

The Reading pane displays quite a lot more of a message's contents than using the Preview view (see Chapter 4). If your friends send messages that use text formatting or contain images, you can fully appreciate their graphic genius much better by viewing their messages in the Reading pane.

Playing by the Rules

Rules are another of my favorite features in Outlook. The Rules feature lets you make Outlook act on certain kinds of e-mail messages automatically. For example, I get tons of e-mail messages, and I can easily waste the whole day sorting through them. I have much more entertaining ways to waste my time, such as pasting sticky notes to my forehead and having imaginary conversations with Donald Trump. ("Oh, yeah? Well, you're fired too, ya jerk!") That's why I set up rules in Outlook to automatically sort my incoming mail into different folders; it lets me spend a little less time wading through all those messages and more time on my overactive fantasy life.

The question of how many different rules you can create with the Rules Wizard may be one of those vast cosmic mysteries, but I'm sure that you can create more rules than you or I will ever need.

Creating a rule

You usually discover the need to create a rule right after getting a message that ticks you off. Your first impulse may be to kick your computer, but don't do that. You might hurt yourself, especially if the computer is on top of the desk. By creating a rule, you'll never have to read another message from that so-and-so again — unless that so-and-so is your boss. Then you may have to make another kind of rule.

The Rules Wizard is called a *wizard* because of the way the program leads you step by step to create each rule. The process is pretty simple. To create a simple rule to move an incoming message from a certain person to a certain folder, follow these steps:

1. **Click the Inbox icon in the Navigation pane (or press Ctrl+Shift+I).**

   The Mail module appears.

2. **Select the Home tab in the Ribbon, click the Rules button, and then click Manage Rules & Alerts.**

   Don't click Create Rule — it only gives you a limited number of options based on whichever message is currently selected. Selecting Manage Rules & Alerts opens the Rules and Alerts dialog box; but you're still one click away from the Rules Wizard.

3. **Click the New Rule button.**

   The Rules Wizard dialog box appears. The dialog box contains a list of the types of rules you can create; see Figure 6-4.

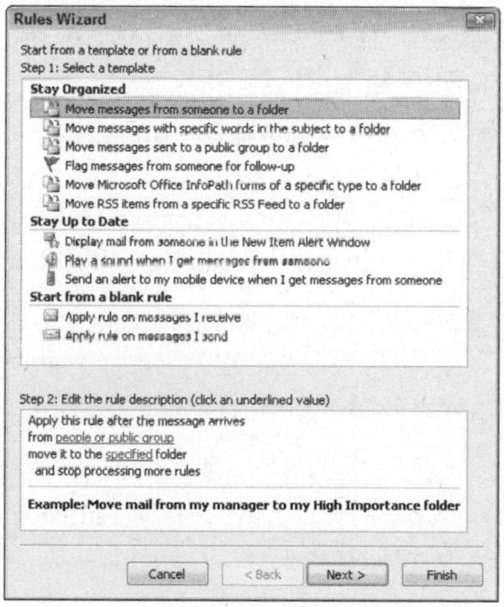

Figure 6-4: The Rules Wizard dialog box enables you to make the rules.

4. **Choose the type of rule you want to create.**

   The Rules Wizard offers several common types of rules you may want to create, such as

   - Move messages from someone to a folder

   - Move messages with specific words in the subject to a folder

   - Move messages sent to a public group to a folder

   The collection of suggested rules is divided into useful categories such as Stay Organized and Stay Up to Date. I'm disappointed that the list doesn't include Stay Sane, Stay Employed, or even Stay Home but Still Get Paid. I'm sure that those will be available in a future version of Outlook. For this example, I suggest choosing Move Messages from Someone to a Folder. Click the Next button, and after doing so, you see, in the rule description box at the bottom of the dialog box, the message

    Apply this rule after the message arrives from people
    or public group move it to the specified folder and
    stop processing more rules. (That's a mouthful, but Outlook
    understands.)

5. **In the Select conditions box, make sure that the from people or public group selection has check mark in front of it; then click the first piece of underlined text in the rule description box, which says** people or public group.

    The Rule Address dialog box appears.

6. **Double-click the name of each person whose messages you want to move to a new folder.**

    The e-mail address of each person you choose appears in the From text box at the bottom of the Rule Address dialog box.

7. **Click the OK button when you've chosen all the people whose messages you want to move.**

    The Rule Address dialog box closes, and the names you've selected replace the words people or public group in the rule description box.

8. **Click the next piece of underlined text in the rule description box, which says** specified.

    Another dialog box opens, offering you a choice of folders to which you can move the message (as shown in Figure 6-5).

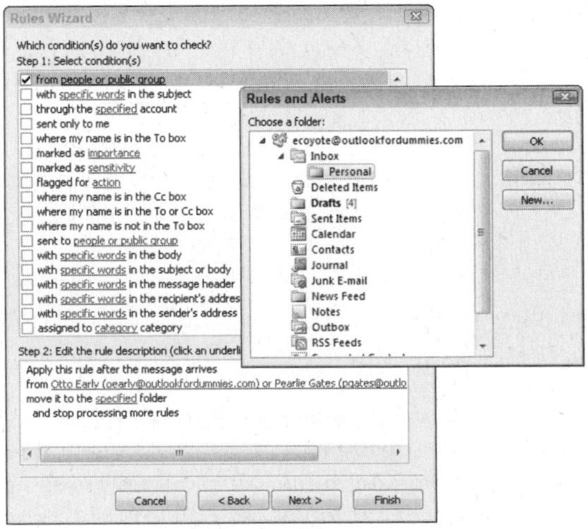

Figure 6-5:
Choose the
folder to
which your
messages
will go.

9. **Double-click the name of the folder to which you want to move messages.**

   The dialog box closes, and the name of the folder you chose appears in the sentence in the rule description box. You can add more conditions to the rule if you want (such as `where my name is in the Cc box`) by selecting them from the Select conditions box. If you press the Next button a couple more times, you can also add actions (such as `clear the message flag`) and exceptions (such as `except if sent only to me`) to your rule.

10. **Click the Finish button.**

    The Rules and Alerts dialog box appears, providing a list of all your rules. Each rule has a check box next to it. You can turn rules on and off by selecting or deselecting the check boxes. If a check mark appears next to a rule, it's turned on; otherwise, the rule is turned off.

11. **Click the OK button to close the Rules and Alerts dialog box.**

Rules can do much more than just sort incoming messages. You can create rules that automatically reply to certain messages, flag messages with a particular word in the subject, delete messages from specific people . . . the sky's the limit.

Running a rule

Normally, rules go into action when messages arrive in your Inbox. When you create a rule to move messages from a certain person to a certain folder, the messages that arrive after you create the rule get moved, but the messages sitting in your Inbox keep sitting there. If you want to apply a rule to the messages already sitting in your Inbox, use the Run Rules Now button at the top of the Rules and Alerts dialog box. Select the rule that you want to run and then click the Run Rules Now button at the top of the dialog box.

Filtering Junk E-Mail

If you feel overwhelmed by junk e-mail, you're not alone; more junk e-mail messages are now sent over the Internet than legitimate ones. It's now safe to assume that if you get e-mail, you get junk e-mail, also known as *spam.* Outlook includes a filtering system that looks over all your incoming mail and automatically moves anything that looks like junk e-mail to a special folder. You can delete everything that gets moved to your Junk E-Mail folder now and again — after checking to make sure that Outlook didn't mistakenly move real e-mail to your Junk E-Mail folder.

No machine is perfect, and no program that runs on a machine is perfect. I don't entirely know how Outlook figures out which messages are junk and which are real. I find that some junk e-mail still gets through, but Outlook catches more than half the junk messages I get. Once or twice I've seen it dump items from real people into the Junk E-Mail folder. (Outlook once sent a message from my father to the Junk E-Mail folder; I've been checking the Junk E-Mail folder regularly ever since.) Some folks prefer to use software that integrates with Outlook to filter out junk mail. If you don't think Outlook is up to the job, you'll want to invest in what is commonly referred to as *antispam software,* which is often part of a larger *security suite* of applications that protects your entire computer.

Fine-tuning the filter's sensitivity

You don't need to do anything to turn on junk e-mail filtering in Outlook. The program already guards against junk e-mail the first time you start it up; however, the protection level is set to Low.

Whether you feel that Outlook moves too many incoming messages — or too few — to the Junk E-Mail folder, you can adjust Outlook's sensitivity to suit your taste by changing the junk e-mail settings.

To adjust Outlook's junk e-mail settings, follow these steps:

1. **Click the Mail button in the Navigation pane (or press Ctrl+Shift+I).**

   The Mail module appears.

2. **Select the Home tab in the Ribbon, click the Junk button, and then click Junk E-Mail Options.**

   The Junk E-Mail Options dialog box appears (as shown in Figure 6-6) with the Options tab on top.

3. **Click the option you prefer.**

   The circle next to the option you click darkens to show what you've selected. The options that Outlook offers you include the following:

   - *No Automatic Filtering:* At this setting, every sleazy message goes right to your Inbox, unchallenged. If that's your cup of tea, fine. Most people want a little more filtering.

   - *Low:* The junkiest of the junk gets moved, but a lot of nasty stuff still gets through.

   - *High:* This setting is aggressive enough that you can expect to see a certain amount of legitimate e-mail end up in the Junk E-Mail folder. If you choose this setting, be sure to check your Junk E-Mail folder from time to time to be sure that important messages don't get trashed by mistake.

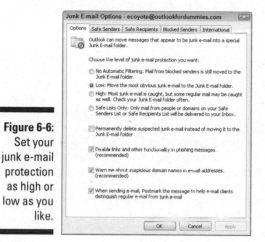

Figure 6-6:
Set your
junk e-mail
protection
as high or
low as you
like.

- *Safe Lists Only:* This setting moves all messages out of your Inbox except for the ones from people or companies that you've designated in your Safe Senders lists.

Also, the check boxes at the bottom of the Options tab offer you a range of other choices:

- *Permanently delete suspected junk e-mail instead of moving it to the Junk E-Mail folder:* I think this might be a bit too aggressive, but it's your choice. I haven't seen a perfect Junk E-Mail filter yet, so it's probably better to push junk messages over to the Junk E-Mail folder and manually empty the folder occasionally. On the other hand, you may work in a company that limits the amount of e-mail you're allowed to store, and the messages in your Junk E-Mail folder count against your limit. So zapping junk e-mail may be the best option.

- *Disable links and other functionality in phishing messages:* Phishing isn't just an incorrectly spelled pastime; it's a way of doing something very wrong to lots of unsuspecting e-mail recipients. Phishing is the term used for an e-mail message that tries to impersonate a bank or financial institution in an effort to steal your personal information. It's the first step in an identity theft operation, so Outlook tries to detect false e-mails and disable the Web links they contain. Even so, you should never give personal financial information or passwords to anyone in response to an e-mail message. Go straight to your financial institution by phone or log on to its Web site directly (not by clicking the links in an e-mail). You could be the victim of all kinds of bad stuff if you're not careful. Let Outlook provide you with some added protection and turn this option on.

- *Warn me about suspicious domain names in e-mail addresses:* Some places have a bad reputation, both on the Web and off. If you receive an e-mail from a suspicious location, Outlook will warn you so that you don't get yourself into trouble. Mother told you there'd be Web sites like this. She also told you to eat your vegetables. Did you? I didn't think so. Well, I'm telling you to turn this option on too.

- *When sending e-mail, postmark the message to help e-mail clients distinguish regular e-mail from junk e-mail:* If you turn this on, all the messages you send will include an "electronic postmark" that some e-mail programs, such as Outlook, can read and interpret to mean that your message probably isn't spam. E-mail programs think postmarked messages probably aren't spam because creating the postmark for each message slows Outlook a bit momentarily — not enough for the average e-mailer to notice, but enough to signifi-cantly slow down a spammer who is trying to send out thousands of messages as quickly as possible. Therefore spammers are less likely to include an electronic postmark in their messages. You won't suffer any adverse effects from using this feature — and it might even help you — so you have nothing to lose by turning it on.

4. **Click the OK button.**

   The Junk E-Mail Options dialog box closes.

There you are! With any luck, you'll no longer need to wade through mes-sages about get-rich-quick schemes or pills that enlarge body parts you don't even have.

Filtering your e-mail with sender and recipient lists

Outlook's junk e-mail handling feature includes an option that you can choose if you want to set up your own *safe* and *blocked* lists for handling where your e-mail comes from or goes to. You can make a list of people whose messages should *always* be moved to the Junk E-Mail folder (or people whose messages should *never* be moved there). Check out the other tabs of the Junk E-Mail Options dialog box for descriptions of the types of senders you can enter:

✔ **Safe Senders:** When a message arrives with an e-mail address or domain on this list in the From field of the message, Outlook makes sure not to treat the message as junk e-mail — no matter what else the message says.

✔ **Safe Recipients:** If you receive messages from an online mailing list, the messages often appear to come from many different people, but they're always addressed to the list. (For example, if you belong to any of the groups on Yahoo! Groups, you'll see this.) In this case, you'd put the name of the list in your Safe Recipients list.

✔ **Blocked Senders:** This is the opposite of the two preceding choices: Messages from the addresses or domains on this list are always treated as junk e-mail.

✔ **International:** Quite a lot of spam comes from overseas. You might see a seemingly endless stream of spam from senders whose e-mail addresses end in strange letters, such as spamsender@spam.ru. Those odd letters at the end of the address are called *top-level domains*, and they indicate the country of origin of the sender. For instance, ru is the top-level domain for Russia — a common source of spam these days.

If you receive frequent spam from some of these top-level domains, you can have Outlook automatically send all incoming messages from them directly to the Junk E-Mail folder by selecting the respective top-level domains from the list that appears when you click the Blocked Top-Level Domain List button; see Figure 6-7. Similarly, if you get lots of spam that appear in foreign languages, you can have Outlook ban those messages as well, by selecting the respective languages from the list that appears when you click the Blocked Encoding List button.

If you regularly get legitimate mail from senders whose messages use a particular top-level domain, you don't want to block that domain — even if you get lots of spam from it. The same goes for messages that are encoded with foreign language sets — don't block languages that are used by legitimate senders.

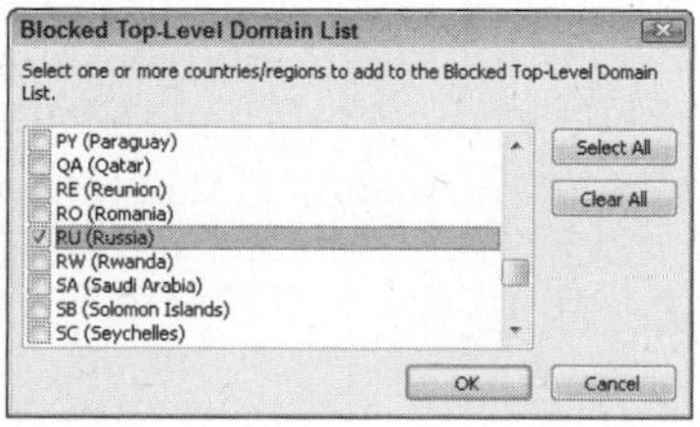

Figure 6-7:
Block messages from senders in specific countries with the Blocked Top-Level Domain list.

Blocked Top-Level Domain List

Select one or more countries/regions to add to the Blocked Top-Level Domain List.

- PY (Paraguay)
- QA (Qatar)
- RE (Reunion)
- RO (Romania)
- ✓ RU (Russia)
- RW (Rwanda)
- SA (Saudi Arabia)
- SB (Solomon Islands)
- SC (Seychelles)

Select All
Clear All

OK   Cancel

Adding an individual to your Blocked Senders list is pretty simple: When you receive a message from someone you don't want to hear from anymore, select the message and click the Junk button on the Home tab of the Ribbon and choose Block Sender. This same method works for adding people, domains, or groups to the Safe Senders and Safe Recipients lists. Just select the message, click the Junk button on the Home tab of the Ribbon, and choose the list to which you want the sender added.

Of course, if you want to be more precise, you can go directly to the appropriate tab in the Junk E-Mail Options dialog box and type in the addresses or domains you want to filter.

Some other junk e-mail options that could save you time are as follows:

- **Contacts:** A check box at the bottom of the Safe Senders tab is labeled Also Trust E-Mail from My Contacts. If that box is selected, messages from anyone in your Address Book automatically get treated as safe messages.

- **Recipients:** If you select the check box labeled Automatically Add People I E-Mail to the Safe Senders List, Outlook will automatically accept messages from the people to whom you've sent messages.

- **Import and Export:** If you have a particularly long list of people to add to your Safe Senders list or your Blocked Senders list, you can create a list in Notepad and then import that list to Outlook. Companies with lengthy client lists might make this feature available to all its employees.

Filtering domains

Outlook gives you one rather powerful option among your junk e-mail choices that you need to be careful about. That option involves filtering domains. If you do business with people at a certain company, you can enter that entire company in your Safe Senders list by selecting the message and then clicking the Junk button on the Home tab of the Ribbon and choosing Never Block Sender's Domain (`@example.com`).

However, if you accidentally add the domain of a friend who sends you e-mail via America Online to your Safe Senders list, you partly defeat the purpose of your junk e-mail filters (because so much junk e-mail comes from `Aol.com` — or at least pretends to come from `Aol.com`). So use the domain-filtering feature with care.

Archiving for Posterity

It doesn't take long to accumulate more messages than you can deal with. Some people just delete messages as they read them. Others hold on to old messages for reference purposes. I hold onto all the messages I've ever sent or received in Outlook because I never know when I'll need to check back to see what someone said to me (or, for that matter, what I said).

Also, some companies are required by law to retain all messages for a certain period of time. This is a serious issue if you work in a highly regulated industry such as banking, finance, or health care. Failure to save messages for the right amount of time can land you or your company in deep doo-doo, so it pays to be aware of your company's retention policy. On the other hand, many large companies automatically back up all messages and save the backups in a "secure, undisclosed location," which lets individual employees off the hook when it comes to document retention.

The problem with storing lots of messages is that Outlook slows down when you store too many of them. A huge collection of messages is not only cumbersome to manage, but system administrators at a large company may not let you store more than a certain amount of e-mail because it clogs up the system.

Archive is a feature that's built right into Outlook to help you store messages and other Outlook items that you don't need to look at right now, but that you still might want to refer to in the future. If you use Outlook on an Exchange network at work, archiving makes it easy for you to get along with your system administrators by slimming down the number of messages you're storing in the e-mail system.

Even if you don't want to use the Archive feature right now, you may want to understand how it works. Outlook sometimes archives items automatically using the AutoArchive feature — which may look to you as if your Outlook items are disappearing. In the following sections, I show you how to find the items that Outlook has archived for safekeeping.

If the Archive feature seems scary and complicated to you, try not to worry. I agree that Microsoft hasn't done a good job of making the Archive feature understandable. When you get the hang of it, however, archiving could become valuable to you.

Although e-mail messages are what people archive most often, nearly all Outlook items can be sent to the archive — Calendars, Tasks — everything, except for Contacts.

Setting up AutoArchive

Unless you change Outlook's AutoArchive settings after it is installed, Outlook does *not* archive your items automatically. Some businesses, however, might have it enabled for their users. Other companies might instead use an autodelete service to purge old messages — check your company's e-mail retention policy before you make any changes to the AutoArchive settings. If you want to turn on AutoArchive, see how Outlook is set up to archive your old items, or change the way Outlook does the job, follow these steps:

1. **Select the File tab in the Ribbon, and click the Options button.**

   The Outlook Options dialog box appears.

2. **Click the Advanced button in the Navigation pane on the left.**

   The Options for working with Outlook pages appears.

3. **In the AutoArchive section, click the AutoArchive Settings button.**

   The AutoArchive dialog box appears (as shown in Figure 6-8).

Figure 6-8:
The
AutoArchive
dialog box.

Don't go barging through the AutoArchive dialog box changing things willy-nilly — at least not until you look to see what's already set up. Four important tidbits that the AutoArchive dialog box normally tells you are as follows:

- ✔ Whether the AutoArchive feature is turned on
- ✔ How often Outlook archives items
- ✔ How old items have to be for Outlook to send them to the archive
- ✔ The name and location of the archive file

If you turn on AutoArchive without changing any of the other AutoArchive settings, Outlook automatically archives items every 14 days, sending items that are over six months old to the archive file listed in the AutoArchive dialog box. For most people, those settings are just fine. Some people prefer to turn off the AutoArchive feature and run the archive process manually, as I describe shortly. You can turn on or off the AutoArchive process by selecting or deselecting the Run AutoArchive Every check box at the top of the AutoArchive dialog box. You can also change how often AutoArchive runs by replacing the 14 in the text box with any number between 1 and 60.

If all you do is enable AutoArchive and make no other changes here, you might be surprised to find out that your Inbox, as well as some other folders, will *not* actually be autoarchived. Each folder has its own AutoArchive settings, which can be different from other folders' AutoArchive settings. If you want to autoarchive all your folders with identical settings, make sure to also click the Apply These Settings to All Folders Now button in the AutoArchive dialog box — that is, all folders except for the Contacts folder, which cannot be archived. Autoarchiving *all* your folders might not be a great idea if you never clean out your Deleted Items or Junk E-Mail folders — you'd wind up archiving lots of spam and deleted messages.

Setting AutoArchive for individual folders

It might be a better idea to set up the AutoArchive settings for each of your folders individually so that you can have more control of what gets autoarchived and what doesn't. For this example, I use the Inbox folder and set it to autoarchive every three months:

1. **Click the Mail button in the Navigation pane (or press Ctrl+Shift+I).**

   The Mail module appears.

2. **Select the word *Inbox* in the Folder list.**

   The word *Inbox* is highlighted.

3. **Select the Folder tab in the Ribbon, and click the AutoArchive Settings button.**

   The Inbox Properties dialog box opens, displaying the AutoArchive tab.

4. **Select Archive This Folder Using These Settings.**

5. **Click the box with the triangle and select Months.**

   If you would rather autoarchive messages from your Inbox that are much more recent, you can instead choose Weeks or Days.

6. **In the Clean Out Items Older Than text box, type the number 3.**

   The Inbox Properties dialog box should now indicate that items older than three months will be cleaned out; see Figure 6-9. You can put any number between 1 and 999 in the text box — which means that you can autoarchive messages from the Inbox that are anywhere from a day old to 999 months old.

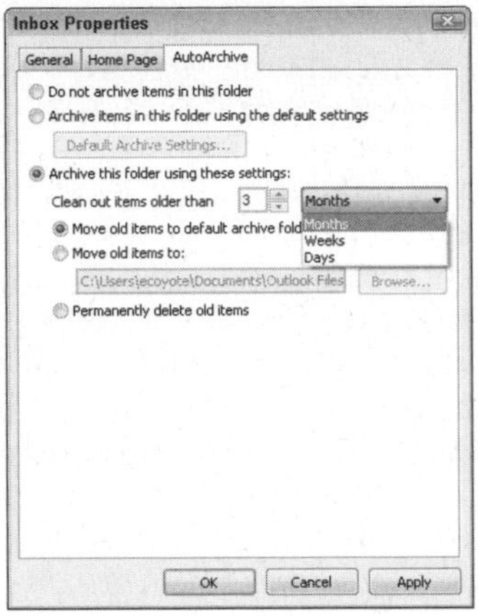

Figure 6-9:
Setting
the Inbox
folder to
autoarchive
messages
that are
older than
three
months.

Inbox Properties

General | Home Page | AutoArchive

○ Do not archive items in this folder
○ Archive items in this folder using the default settings
   [Default Archive Settings...]
● Archive this folder using these settings:
   Clean out items older than [3 ⏶⏷] [Months ▼]
   ● Move old items to default archive fold Months
   ○ Move old items to: Weeks
                                           Days
   C:\Users\jecoyote\Documents\Outlook Files   [Browse...]
○ Permanently delete old items

[OK] [Cancel] [Apply]

7. **Select Move Old Items to Default Archive Folder.**

   This setting will probably already be selected — but you should addi-
   tionally make sure that the Permanently Delete Old Items option is *not*
   selected. If you select this option, all old Inbox messages will be deleted
   instead of archived.

8. **Click the OK button.**

   Even though you are only setting the AutoArchive settings for a single
   folder, Outlook's AutoArchive setting still needs to be enabled. If
   AutoArchive is already turned on as I describe in the previous section,
   the Inbox Properties dialog box will close and you are all set.

   If, after you click OK, a window pops up stating `There are no global`
   `AutoArchive options set,` this means that Outlook's AutoArchive
   setting is not enabled. Luckily, this window gives you the option of
   turning it on just by clicking the OK button. Click OK to turn on autoarchiving for Outlook and for the Inbox.

Repeat these steps for each folder you want to set the AutoArchive settings
for. Even if you have a folder that you don't want to autoarchive, you should
still at least check what its current AutoArchive settings are. When you
enabled Outlook's AutoArchive feature, you also probably inadvertently activated AutoArchive for some other folders that you might not want to have
archived — there is no way to autoarchive a folder without also turning on
Outlook's AutoArchive setting. When Outlook is first installed, the Calendar,
Tasks, Journal, Sent Items, and Deleted Items folders are all set to autoarchive if Outlook's AutoArchive setting is turned on. I did say this was scary
and complicated, didn't I?

If this all seems confusing, this should help: If you followed the previous
examples exactly (and why wouldn't you?), every 14 days, Outlook will run
AutoArchive. When Outlook runs AutoArchive, it will move all messages from

the Inbox (as well as any subfolders in the Inbox folder) that are *older than* 3 months old into the archive. Any messages that are newer than three months will stay in the Inbox. Now it doesn't seem so scary or complicated, does it?

Whenever you create a new folder, it is automatically set *not* to autoarchive — even if you previously applied your autoarchiving settings for all folders. If you want your new folder to autoarchive, you'll need to go through the previous steps for that folder. Also, when you turn on AutoArchive for Outlook, the Deleted Items folder is set to autoarchive using the default settings. If you don't clean out your Deleted Items folder, all the e-mails that you thought you'd never see again will instead be archived for posterity. You should consider setting the Deleted Items folder to not autoarchive.

Activating the archive process manually

You can archive messages anytime you want by choosing the File tab from the Ribbon, selecting the Info button in the Navigation pane on the left, clicking the Cleanup Tools button, clicking the Archive button, and following the prompts; see Figure 6-10. The advantage of running the archive process manually is that you get slightly better control of the process; you can give Outlook a cutoff date for archiving items, say, the first of the year. You can also tell Outlook which folders to archive and where to send the archived items. You can even archive different Outlook folders to different archive files. The disadvantage to all this control is that it's possible to make an innocent mistake and send archived items to a place you can't find again easily. Try not to change the name or location of the files to which your archived items are sent, because it's surprisingly easy to lose track of what went where, and Outlook doesn't provide much help with keeping track of archived files.

Figure 6-10: Manually archiving the Inbox folder.

Finding and viewing archived items

Sometimes AutoArchive seems like magic. Older items are mysteriously filed away without any action on your part. Isn't that easy? Sure — until you suddenly need to *find* one of those items that moved magically to your archive. Then you have to figure out where it went and how to get at it again.

I usually like to talk up the good points of Outlook, but honestly, this is one place where the Outlook developers fell down on the job. Although it's easy to move items into your archive, it's pretty confusing to get them back. What's the point of archiving items if you can't find them again?

Anyway, when you want to take another look at the items you've archived, open the Archive folder, which Outlook also refers to as a *data file*.

To open a data file that contains your archive items, follow these steps:

1. **Select the File tab in the Ribbon, click the Open button in the Navigation pane on the left, and click the Open Outlook Data File button.**

   The Open Outlook Data File dialog box appears.

2. **Select the file that you want to open from the file list.**

   The file you selected appears in the File Name text box.

3. **Click the OK button.**

   The name of the data file you opened appears in the Navigation pane, below your normal set of folders.

Simple enough, right? Yes, but there's a virtual fly in the virtual ointment. You probably don't know the name of the archive file you want to open, and it might not show up in the list of files in the Open Outlook Data File dialog box.

To find out the name of the archive data file to open, choose the File tab in the Ribbon, click the Info button in the Navigation pane on the left, click the Cleanup Tools button, click the Archive button, and then look in the Archive File text box. Be careful not to change anything about the information; otherwise, Outlook may start sending your archived items someplace else. The information in the Archive File text box is usually complex gobbledygook with colons and slashes and all sorts of stuff that normal people can't remember.

My favorite trick for capturing a long name in a dialog box is to copy the information. Here's what it looks like in fast forward: Click the name once, press Tab, press Shift+Tab, press Ctrl+C, and then click the Cancel button. After you copy the filename, you can follow the steps given earlier in this section — pasting the name you want into the Open Outlook Data File dialog box's File

Name text box by pressing Ctrl+V and rejoicing that you don't have to remember that long, crazy filename.

Closing the archive data file

You can keep your archive data file open in the Outlook Folder list as long as you want, but most people prefer to close it after they find what they need. Outlook runs a little faster when you close any unnecessary data files.

To close an archive data file, follow these steps:

1. **In the Navigation pane, right-click the name of the archive data file.**

   A shortcut menu appears.

2. **Choose Close *Archive* from the shortcut menu.**

   The archive data file might be called something other than *archive* — if so, the name of your particular archive data file will appear instead of the term *archive*. Your archive folder disappears from the Navigation pane.

The way folders are named in Outlook is odd. You may find Inbox folders appearing several times in the Navigation pane. To make Outlook run as quickly as possible, close as many of the duplicate folders as you can. Your main set of folders — the set you use every day — won't close, so you don't have to worry about closing the folders you use every day.

Arranging Your Messages

Nobody gets a *little* bit of e-mail anymore. If you get one message, you get a ton of 'em, and they quickly clog your Inbox. In no time, you find yourself scrolling through an endless stream of new messages, trying find that one proverbial needle in the haystack that you needed a week from last Tuesday. Fortunately, Outlook offers you a whole bunch of different ways to arrange that mess of messages so that you have a fighting chance of figuring out what's important, what can wait, and what can be ignored.

When Outlook is set up to display the Reading pane on the right side of the screen, you'll see two buttons at the top of the list of messages. The leftmost button is labeled something like Arranged By: Date (Conversations). The Arranged By button describes the system Outlook is using to organize how your messages are displayed. To the right of the Arranged By button sits another button with a label that offers some detail about the arrangement Outlook is currently using. (For example, if your messages are currently arranged by date, the button on the right will say either Newest on Top or Oldest on Top.)

To change the way Outlook arranges your messages, simply click the Arranged By button to reveal a shortcut menu of all the arrangements you can use. These are the arrangements Outlook offers (see Figure 6-11):

✔ **Date (Conversations):** When you first set up Outlook, this is how your Inbox is arranged. This arrangement groups messages of the same subject together. If you've been exchanging a series of messages with others about a specific project or idea, this arrangement makes it much easier to follow the entire thread of the conversation — and it also cleans up a lot of the clutter in your Inbox, making it much easier to find what you are really looking for.

This is different from previous versions of Outlook — or even most other e-mail programs, for that matter — which usually sort e-mail just by date. After you get used to this arrangement, you'll wonder how you ever got along without it. I explain the Conversations arrangement in more detail in the next section of this chapter.

✔ **From:** As you might guess, this arrangement organizes your message collection according to the person from whom the message was sent. Choosing the From arrangement is a little bit faster than setting up a search folder, but sometimes a search folder is still the best way to track messages from *specific* important people.

✔ **To:** Most messages you receive are addressed to you, but not always. Sometimes you receive messages addressed to a list of people, so your name doesn't appear in the To field of the message. This arrangement separates your messages according to whether your name is in the To field of each message.

✔ **Categories:** You can assign categories to any message you send, and sometimes other people assign categories to the messages they send you. To see which messages fall into which category, use the Categories arrangement.

✔ **Flag: Start Date:** If you use flags with your messages to help you remember the tasks you need to do, using this arrangement can help — it organizes your messages based on when the start date for flags are set.

✔ **Flag: Due Date:** This is merely the opposite of the previous arrangement — messages are organized according to when the due date for flags are set.

✔ **Size:** Everyone knows that size doesn't matter; it's the sentiment that counts. Well, okay, not always. Size is important to certain system administrators — and it isn't *always* a personal problem. Some e-mail messages include photographs, music, and all sorts of heavyweight files that can really clog your company's e-mail servers. So when your system administrator asks you to thin out your Inbox, make some use of this feature: Identify and delete or archive the messages that are the most overweight. Outlook identifies messages as Tiny, Small, Medium, Huge, or Enormous — perhaps in the next version of Outlook, Microsoft will add Ginormous to the list.

✔ **Subject:** This arrangement is similar to the Conversation arrangement, except it doesn't follow the thread of a conversation; it just lumps together messages that have the same subject. Not every message with the same subject is necessarily part of the same conversation.

✔ **Type:** Not every item that arrives in your Inbox is a simple message; you may also receive Meeting Requests, Task Requests, and all sorts of other items. When you want to separate the messages from the Meeting Requests and so on, switch to the Type arrangement so that the most interesting messages rise to the top of the list.

✔ **Attachments:** When you go to your Inbox, you may not be looking for a message; you may be hunting for an attachment. Arranging your messages by attachment enables you to examine the likely suspects first.

✔ **Account:** You can set up Outlook to collect e-mail from several different e-mail addresses at the same time, and each of your e-mail addresses gets its own Inbox. But if you move messages from your different e-mail addresses into the same folder — as you might do when you periodically clean up your Inboxes — there may come a point down the road when you want to see which of those messages in the folder came from which of those addresses, or just to look at the messages sent to one of those addresses. If you want to see only the messages sent to a single address, choose the Account arrangement and then click the arrow next to the names of accounts you don't want to see. With this arrangement, Outlook shows you only the messages from the accounts that interest you. Unless you mush all your incoming mail from your different mailboxes into a single Inbox, the Account arrangement won't help you much when you are viewing the Inbox.

✔ **Importance:** First things first — you know the saying. When you need to see the messages marked with High Importance first, this is the arrangement you want to use.

When you click the Arranged By button to see the list of various arrangements, you'll notice an entry close to the bottom of the list that says Show in Groups. When the Show in Groups check box is selected, all the different arrangements group similar items together with a descriptive heading, and a thin line separates the different groups. If there is no check mark, Outlook still groups together similar items based on the arrangement you chose, but you don't have any visible clues as to where one group of message ends and the next group starts. Selecting Show in Groups makes it much easier to scan your messages when you are looking for similar items.

Figure 6-11:
Outlook
offers plenty
of ways to
arrange
your folders.

The Arrange By button appears at the top of your Message list only when the Reading pane is set to appear on the right side of the screen. You can turn the Mail module's Reading pane on by selecting the View tab in the Ribbon, clicking the Reading pane button, and choosing Right. You can use any of the arrangements to view the content of any message folder. If you want to arrange your messages when the Reading pane is off, select the View tab in the Ribbon and choose the arrangement you want to use from the Arrangement window in the middle of the Ribbon.

Viewing conversations

Whether you just trade a few e-mails back and forth with one other person or engage in large group discussions that continue for weeks, Outlook's Conversations arrangement groups together all related messages that have the same subject. With a single glance, you can see the latest entry in a conversation thread, as well as older messages from the conversation. A conversation starts as soon as someone replies to a message, clicking either the Reply or Reply All button. No matter who else responds or contributes additional messages to the back-and-forth discussion, all new messages become part of the conversation.

You can tell whether a message in your Inbox is part of a conversation in two different ways:

- The mail icon to the left of the message in the Message list looks like a pair of overlapping envelopes, instead of just the normal single envelope.

- A small triangle is positioned just to the left of this Mail icon, indicating that more messages are inside.

When you click a message that is part of a conversation, the most recent message received in the conversation is displayed in the Reading pane. Click the triangle to the left of the message's Mail icon to expand the complete list of messages you have sent or received that are part of the conversation; see Figure 6-12. Even if some of these messages are located in the Sent folder or were moved to another folder, they still appear in the conversation list. If a message is moved to the Deleted Items folder, however, it will not appear in the conversation list. Clicking any of the messages in the conversation list displays the message's text in the Reading pane.

The "Who stole the cookies from the cookie jar" conversation.

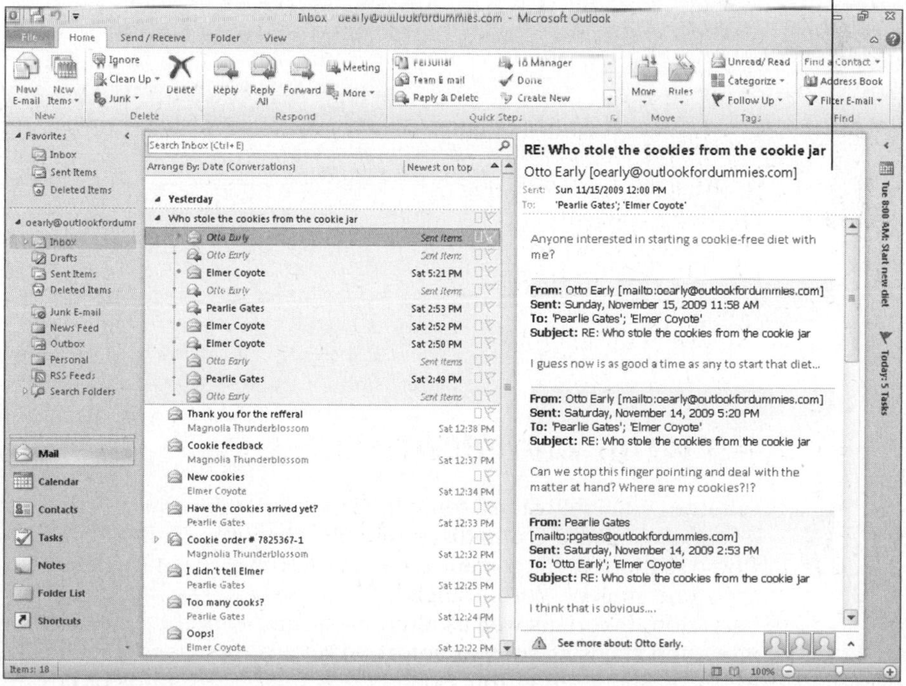

Figure 6-12: All the messages from a conversation are grouped together.

When you click a message in the conversation list, a set of lines appears to the left of the message list. These lines trace a map of the conversation by showing who replied to whom. You can reply to any message in the conversation list. If you reply to message that isn't the most recent, a warning appears at the top of the Message form telling you so and gives you the opportunity to open the latest message in the conversation.

When you reply to a message that is part of a conversation, don't change the subject of the message. If you do, Outlook does not consider it part of the conversation anymore — Outlook identifies a conversation partially by a message's Subject field. Don't worry if messages come in with the same Subject field that aren't part of a conversation — Outlook is smart enough to know the difference and doesn't inadvertently add them to the conversation.

Ignoring conversations

There often comes a point in a conversation where the discussion is no longer of interest or relevance to you. It's not uncommon for a conversation to completely spiral off topic — what started out as a conversation about when to have the next team meeting becomes a seemingly endless string of back-and-forth jokes about how hot the conference room gets in the winter.

At any point that you no longer want to follow a conversation, you have an easy way to ignore it. Select any message from the conversation and click the appropriately named Ignore button on the Home tab of the Ribbon. (You can also ignore a conversation by right-clicking on any of the messages in the conversation and selecting Ignore from the drop-down list — or with any message selected from the conversation you can press Ctrl+Delete). When you ignore a conversation, all messages from the conversation that are in the Inbox, and any other folder you moved messages from the conversation to, are dumped into the Deleted Items folder — messages from the conversation that are in your Sent folder are not moved. All traces of the conversation are gone from your Inbox and other folders. Even better, if any new messages from the conversation arrive, they too are automatically diverted to the Deleted Items folder.

If you accidentally ignore a conversation, you can unignore it. Simply move the messages from the conversation in the Deleted Items folder back into the Inbox.

Cleaning up conversations

When someone replies to a message, most e-mail programs, by default, include the text of the original message in the reply. When Outlook is first installed, it is set to do this. To see this setting, select the File tab in the

Ribbon, click the Options button in the Navigation pane on the left, click the Mail tab, and scroll down to the Replies and Forwards section in the Outlook Options dialog box. If everyone who sends a reply in a conversation includes the text of previous messages from the conversation, each subsequent message becomes a snapshot of the entire conversation thread up to that point. This creates a lot of redundancy, because a lot of the same information is repeated in each message. (Do I need to repeat that?)

Outlook can detect this redundancy and remove messages from a conversation that contain information that is already included elsewhere in the conversation — Outlook calls this *cleaning up.* The quick-and-dirty way to clean up a conversation is to simply select a message in the conversation that you want to clean up and press Alt+Delete. The longer way to do this is as follows:

1. **Select the conversation you want to clean up.**

   The most recent received message of the conversation is selected. You can do this in any folder that contains a message from the conversation.

2. **Select the Home tab in the Ribbon and click the Clean Up button.**

   A list drops down with three options; see Figure 6-13.

Figure 6-13:
The Clean
Up menu.

3. **Select Clean Up Conversation.**

   All messages from the conversation that Outlook detects as redundant are removed from all the folders they are in and moved to the Deleted Items folder. Messages in the Sent folder are not moved.

   From the drop-down list, you can also select Clean Up Folder to clean up *all* the conversations within the selected folder. Clean Up Folder & Subfolders goes one step further and cleans up *all* conversations that are in the selected subfolders and *all* subfolders. For instance, if you created a Personal folder that lives inside your Inbox folder, selecting the Inbox folder and then choosing Clean Up Folder & Subfolders automatically cleans up all conversations in both folders.

Don't be surprised if Outlook doesn't remove many messages. Outlook takes a rather conservative view on what it considers redundant, and it also doesn't move replies that have modified a previous message or messages that have Follow Up flags. If you want to give Outlook more latitude with what it can move when it cleans up a conversation, you need to change a few settings:

1. **Select the File tab and click the Options button.**

   The Outlook Options dialog box appears.

2. **Click the Mail button in the Navigation pane.**

   The Mail settings appear.

3. **Scroll down to the Conversation Clean Up section.**

   A number of options are listed that affect when Outlook will and won't move messages from a conversation; see Figure 6-14. Make adjustments to the settings that best fit your needs.

   Pay close attention to the Cleaned-Up Items Will Go to This Folder box. Outlook sends cleaned-up items to the Deleted Items folder by default. But if you want to send cleaned-up items someplace else, such as a folder in an archive file, this is where you make that change. Click the Browse button and select where your cleaned-up items should go.

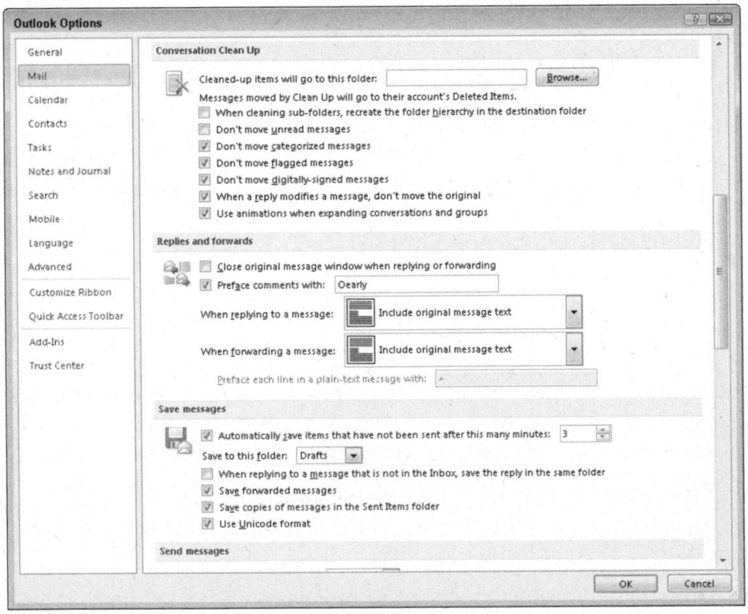

Figure 6-14:
Conver-
sation Clean
Up options.

If you find that Outlook doesn't move any messages when you click Clean Up, it is probably because someone made changes somewhere within the previous message text in their message reply before clicking the Send button. To get Outlook to clean up a conversation where this happens, make another change to the Conversation Clean Up settings: Deselect the When a Reply

Modifies a Message, Don't Move the Original check box. The danger in doing this is that the text from previous messages may have been changed for good reason — such as someone answering someone else's questions within the text of the original message.

Simplifying Tasks Using Quick Steps

By now, you've no doubt noticed that some Outlook actions take multiple clicks of the mouse to complete, such as the process of replying to a message and then deleting it. That's not a big deal if you only perform a particular action every once in while — but if it's something you do regularly in Outlook, it can quickly become a pain. If you do certain tasks on a regular basis, Outlook's Quick Steps feature can come to your rescue. Quick Steps lets you reduce multistep tasks to a single click of the mouse. You'll find Quick Steps in the Mail module, sitting in the middle of the Ribbon's Home tab. Even though the Quick Steps box is visible only when using the Mail module, you can use Quick Steps to speed up actions with most of Outlook's modules, such as Calendar or Tasks.

When you first install Outlook, the Quick Steps box already has six quick steps in it (see Figure 6-15):

- ✔ **Move To:** Use this quick step if you frequently move messages to a specific folder. If you've yet to move a message to a folder in Outlook, the quick step will display `Move to: ?`. If you have already moved messages to folders, this quick step will replace the ? with the name of the last folder you moved a message to, such as `Move to: Personal`.

- ✔ **Team E-Mail:** Use this quick step to open the New Message form and populate the To field with a particular set of recipients.

- ✔ **Reply & Delete:** The name pretty much says it all — when you select this quick step, Outlook automatically opens a Message form for replying to the sender of the selected message, and moves the selected message to the Deleted Items folder.

- ✔ **To Manager:** This quick step automatically opens a Message form for forwarding the selected message to a particular recipient, but it doesn't delete the selected message.

- ✔ **Done:** This marks the selected message with the Mark Complete flag, marks the message as read, and moves the message to a designated folder.

- ✔ **Create New:** Strictly speaking, this isn't really a quick step — it opens the Edit Quick Step Wizard, which allows you to create your own custom quick steps.

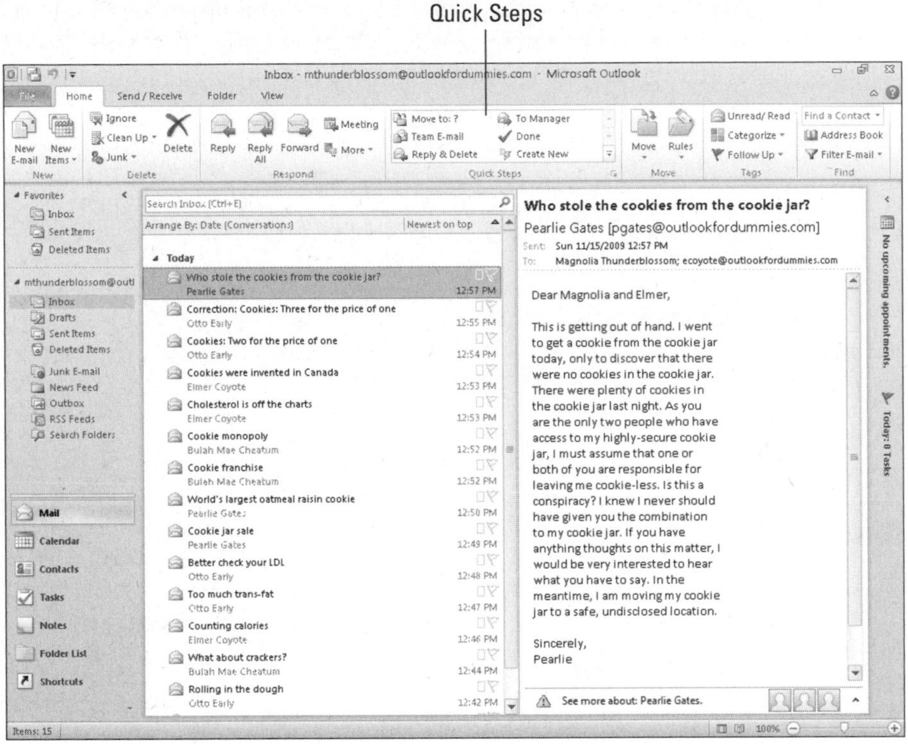

Quick Steps

Figure 6-15:
The Quick
Step box
is in the
middle of
the Ribbon's
Home tab.

Except for the Reply & Delete quick step, each of these quick steps requires you to make some decisions the first time you use them. This is because Outlook doesn't know yet where you want your messages moved to or who your manager is. If it did, that might be a little scary. So, you're going to have to tell Outlook what it needs to do when you select a particular quick step. After you do this, you never have to do it again — Outlook will remember what you want it to do whenever you select the quick step.

Each of the quick steps is a bit different — but I use the Move To quick step as an example here:

1. **Select the Inbox icon in the Mail module (or press Ctrl+Shift+I).**

   Your list of incoming mail messages appears.

2. **Select a message in the Inbox.**

   It can be any message. Don't worry about it actually being moved. As long as this is the first time you're using the Move To quick step, the message you select will not be moved — Outlook just needs to know which type of Outlook element you are creating the quick step for.

3. **Select the Home tab in the Ribbon, and click the icon in the upper-left corner of the Quick Steps box — this may or may not say** `Move to: ?`.

   The First Time Setup dialog box opens; see Figure 6-16. Your system may not say `Move to: ?`, but might instead have just a folder name, such as Personal. If the dialog box already has a folder name in it, Outlook is just trying to be helpful by suggesting the last folder to which you moved a message — the First Time Setup dialog box will still open.

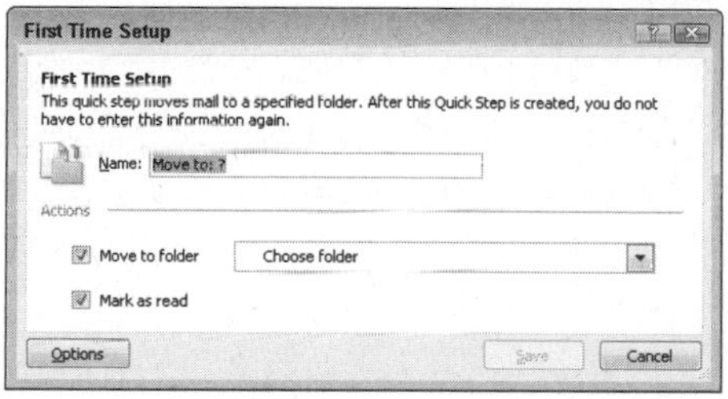

Figure 6-16:
The Quick
Step First
Time Setup
dialog box.

4. **Select the folder where the quick step will move messages.**

   Select a folder in the Move to Folder box by clicking the arrow at the end of the box. If the folder you want isn't shown, choose the Other Folder selection, which opens the Select Folder window so that you can see a detailed list of all available folders. You can even create a new folder using the Select Folder window.

   Make sure that the Move to Folder check box is selected. If you want each message marked as read when the quick step moves it, make sure that the Mark as Read check box is also selected.

   If you want to change the quick step's icon, add additional actions to it, or create a keyboard shortcut that will activate the quick step, click the Options button to access those settings.

5. **Type a name for the quick step in the Name text box.**

   In the previous step, you probably noticed that as soon as you selected a folder in the Move to Folder box, Outlook also placed that folder name in the Name text box. If you are happy with the Name that Outlook chose for the quick step, skip ahead to the next step. If you want to give the quick step a different name, just type it into the Name text box. You should give the quick step a name that will help you remember what the quick step does — "Move to Personal folder" would be a pretty good name for a quick step that moves a message to a folder called Personal, don't you think? For those who prefer brevity, "Personal" works just as well.

6. **Click the Save button.**

   The First Time Setup dialog box closes.

Now, whenever you want to move a message to the specific folder, just select the message and click the quick step you created, and the message will automatically move to the folder and be marked as read.

Once you get the hang of using Quick Steps, you should be able to create quick steps that perform many functions with a single click of the mouse — creating a quick step that does your job for you might be beyond the reach of Outlook.

Creating and managing quick steps

In addition to the six quick steps that appear in the Quick Step box when Outlook is first installed, you have even more Quick Step templates that you can choose from. To use these additional Quick Step templates, follow these instructions:

1. **Click the Inbox icon in the Mail module (or press Ctrl+Shift+I).**

    Your list of incoming mail messages appears.

2. **Select the Home tab in the Ribbon and locate the Quick Step box's scroll bar — it's on the right side of the Quick Step box and has one up and two down arrows. Click the arrow on the bottom — it's the arrow with a line above it.**

    A list drops down with two options: New Quick Step and Manage Quick Steps.

3. **Select New Quick Step.**

    A list of additional Quick Step templates appears; see Figure 6-17. Selecting any of these Quick Step templates opens the First Time Setup dialog box with choices that are relevant to the particular type of task you selected — for instance, if you select Move to Folder, the First Time Setup asks you to pick which folder it will move the messages to, and it additionally gives you the option of marking the messages as read. These additional Quick Step templates are as follows:

    • *Move to Folder:* This is essentially the same as Move To.

    • *Categorize & Move:* This moves the selected message to a specific folder, marks the message as read, and assigns a category to the message.

    • *Flag & Move:* This moves the selected message to a specific folder, marks the message as read, and assigns a flag to the message.

    • *New E-Mail To:* This opens a New Message form with the To field already filled out with a particular recipient.

    • *Forward To:* This is essentially the same as To Manager.

- *New Meeting:* If you often send meeting invites to the same group of people, use this quick step to open a New Meeting form with the To field already filled in with the invitees.

- *Custom:* This opens the Edit Quick Step dialog box so that you can create you own custom quick step.

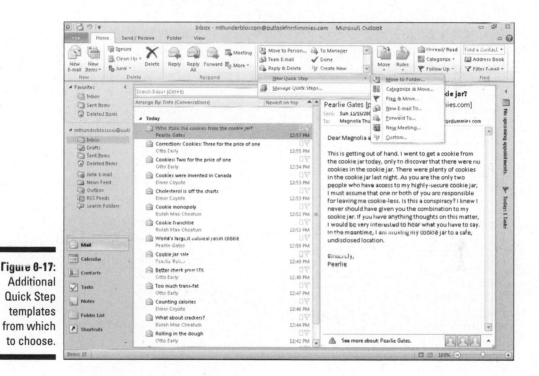

Figure 6-17: Additional Quick Step templates from which to choose.

4. **Select a Quick Step template.**

   As you saw with the Move To quick step, a First Time Setup dialog box appears. Depending on the task, you'll need to tell Outlook where to move a message, how to categorize a message, what flag to set, to whom to send or forward a message, or to whom to send a meeting invitation. After you input this information into the First Time Setup dialog box, be sure to also give this quick step a name that will help you remember what it does.

5. **Click the Finish button.**

   The First Time Setup dialog box closes.

Instead of selecting New Quick Step from the drop-down list, you could choose Manage Quick Steps, which opens the Manage Quick Steps dialog box, as shown in Figure 6-18. Here you can do a bunch of different things to your quick steps, such as change the order in which they are displayed in the Quick

Step box in the Ribbon, change what they do, duplicate them, delete them, and create new ones. If your quick steps are becoming an unruly mess and you want start over from square one, click the Reset to Defaults button and all the quick steps will revert to what they looked like when Outlook was first installed.

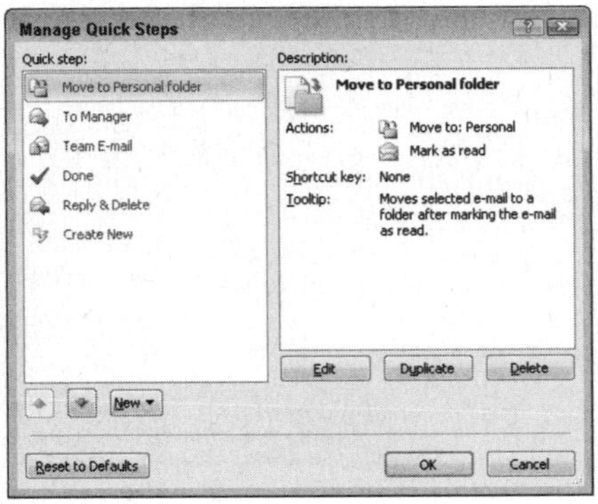

Figure 6-18:
The Manage
Quick Steps
dialog box.

Part III
Managing Contacts, Dates, Tasks, and More

The 5th Wave   By Rich Tennant

"Hold on, Barbara. Let me launch Outlook and
see if I can find an RSS feed on this."

In this part . . .

Research shows that most people only use a tiny fraction of Outlook's power. In this part, I show you how Outlook's organizing features can help you make quick work of your daily tasks, appointments, and other obligations. There's nothing difficult in these chapters — in fact you'll be surprised to discover how easy it is to get vastly more productive when you take full advantage of the power of Outlook.

Chapter 7

Your Little Black Book: Creating Contacts Lists

*Y*ou've heard people say "It's not what you know; it's who you know." Well, how do you keep track of what you know about who you know? You either need a terrific memory or a convenient tool for keeping track of all those whatshisnames and whoziwhatzits out there.

Years ago I had a habit of keeping track of all the people I needed to know by memory. Then something happened that changed that habit. What was it? I forget. But take my word for it: I don't go around memorizing names and numbers anymore. I put them all into Outlook and make my computer do the memorizing. Now, instead of wasting hours memorizing, I can spend quality time with my dear friends whatshisname and whoziwhatzit.

All kidding aside, I work as a consultant and speaker and writer for computer magazines and tech companies. The information I need to keep about consulting clients (hours, locations, and whatnot) differs from the information I need for dealing with people in the publishing business (editors, deadlines, topics, and so on). I'm also active as a musician and filmmaker, and my contacts in those businesses are two entirely different kettles of fish. But when someone calls on the phone, or when I want to do a mailing to a group from one world or another, I need to be able to look up the person right away, regardless of which category the person fits in.

Outlook is flexible enough to let you keep your entire collection of name and address information in a single place — but you can also sort, view, find, and print it differently, depending on what kind of work you're doing. You can also keep lists of family and friends stored in Outlook right alongside your business contacts, and still distinguish them from one another quickly when the need arises.

Storing Names, Numbers, and Other Stuff

Storing lots of names, addresses, and phone numbers is no big trick, but finding them again can take magic unless you have a tool like Outlook. Other programs can store names and related numbers, but Outlook, by far, is the most popular program for doing work that uses names, addresses, and phone numbers.

If you've ever used a little pocket address book, you pretty much know how to use the Outlook Contacts feature. Simply enter the name, address, phone number, and a few juicy tidbits, and there you are!

The quick-and-dirty way to enter contacts

Entering a new name in your Contacts list is utterly simple. With the Contacts list open, click the New Contact button in the Ribbon to open the New Contact entry form, fill in the blanks on the form, and then click the Save & Close button. That's really all there is to it. If you don't enter every detail about a contact right away, it's okay — you can always add more information later.

The slow, complete way to enter contacts

If you want, you can enter scads of details about every person you enter in your Contacts list and choose from literally dozens of options, but if all you do is enter the essentials and move on, that's fine. If you're more detail-minded, here's the way to enter every jot and tittle for each contact record:

1. **Click the Contacts button in the Navigation pane (or press Ctrl+3).**

   The Contacts list appears; see Figure 7-1.

2. **Click the New Contact button.**

   The New Contact form appears.

   To be really quick, press Ctrl+Shift+C to see the New Contact form shown in Figure 7-2.

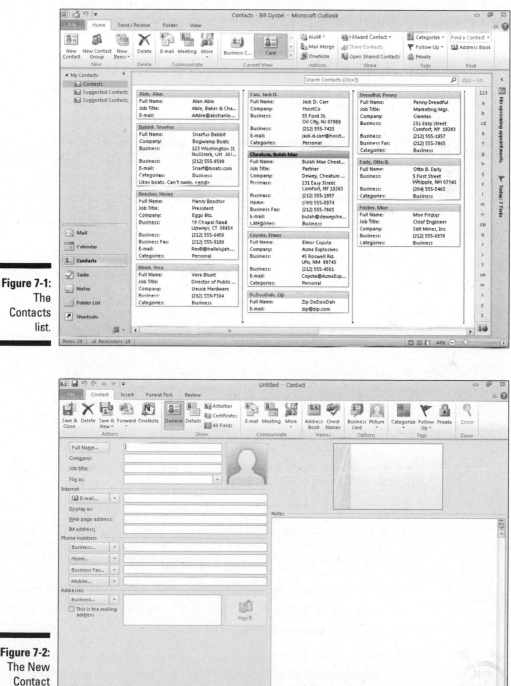

Figure 7-1:
The
Contacts
list.

Figure 7-2:
The New
Contact
form.

3. **Click the Full Name button.**

   The Check Full Name dialog box appears (as shown in Figure 7-3). You can do any of the following:

   - Click the triangle (called the *scroll-down button*) on the right edge of the Title text box and choose a title (such as Mr., Ms., or Dr.) from the list that drops down, or type one — such as *Reverend, Guru,* or *Swami.*

   - Click in the First text box and type the contact's first name.

   - Click in the Middle text box and type the contact's middle initial (if any). If there's no middle initial, you can leave this box blank.

   - Click in the Last text box and type the contact's last name.

   - Click in the Suffix drop-down list and choose a suffix, such as Jr. or III, or type one in the box, such as *Ph.D., D.D.S.,* or *B.P.O.E.*

   - Click the OK button. The Check Full Name dialog box closes, and you're back in the New Contact form, where the name you entered is now shown in both the Full Name and File As text boxes.

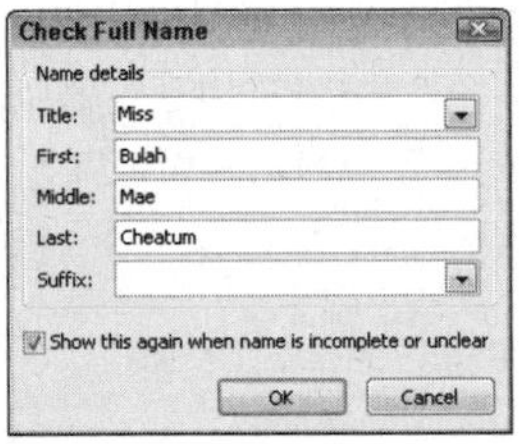

Figure 7-3:
The Check
Full Name
dialog box.

4. **Click in the appropriate box and enter the information requested on the New Contact form.**

   If the information isn't available — for example, if the contact has no job title — leave the box blank. A triangle after the box indicates a drop-down list with choices. If your choice isn't listed, type it in the box.

   - If you've entered a name in the Full Name box, the File As box will already contain that name.

   - If you want this person filed under something other than his or her name, click in the File As box and type in your preferred designation.

     For example, you may want to file your dentist's name under the term *Dentist* rather than by name. If you put Dentist in the File As box, the name turns up under Dentist in the alphabetical listing rather than under the name itself. Both the Full Name and the File As designation exist in your Contacts list. That way (for example), you can search for your dentist either by name or by the word *Dentist.*

5. **Click in the E-Mail text box and enter your contact's e-mail address.**

   If your contact has more than one e-mail address, click the triangle at the left edge of the E-Mail box (shown in Figure 7-4), select E-Mail 2, click in the text box, and then enter the second address.

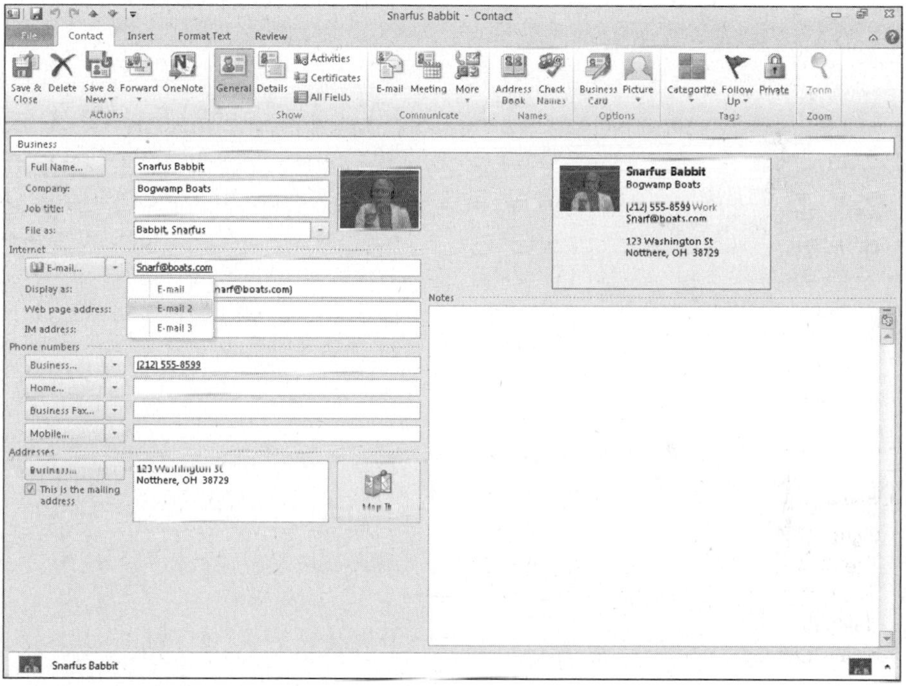

Figure 7-4:
You can enter more than one e-mail address for each person in your Contacts list.

6. **Click in the text box to the right of the Business Phone box and type in the contact's business phone number.**

7. **Click in the text box to the right of the Home Phone box and type in the contact's home phone number.**

   For numbers other than Business and Home phones, click the triangle to the right of the phone-number type block, choose the kind of number you're entering, and then enter the number.

   The New Contact form has four phone-number blocks. You can use any of them for any of the 19 phone-number types available in the drop-down list. You can also add custom fields so that you can include more than four phone numbers for a single contact. For the person who has everything, you can create custom fields for that person's Ski Phone, Submarine Phone, Gym Phone — as many as you want.

   You can choose any of 19 phone-number types to enter, depending on what types of phone numbers your contacts have; see Figure 7-5.

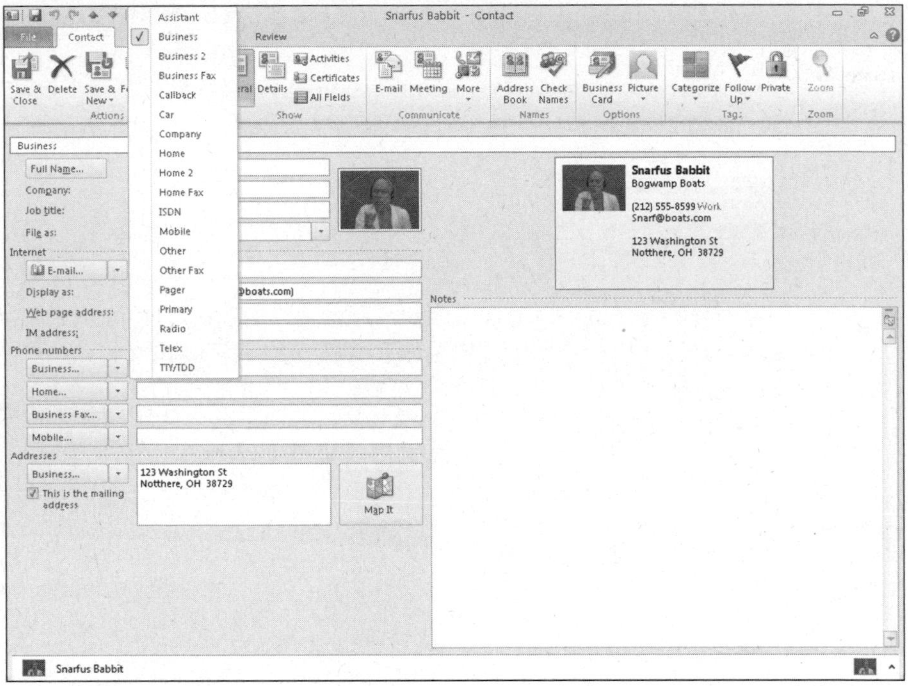

Figure 7-5:
You can
always
reach your
contact at
one of these
phone
numbers.

8. **Click the triangle in the Addresses section to choose the type of address you want to enter.**

    You can choose to enter a Business address, Home address, or Other type of address.

9. **Click the button in the Addresses section to open the Check Address dialog box, and then enter the following information in the appropriate boxes:**

    - Street
    - City
    - State/Province
    - ZIP/Postal Code
    - Country

    See Figure 7-6 for a look at a completed Check Address dialog box.

10. **Click the OK button.**

    The Check Address dialog box closes.

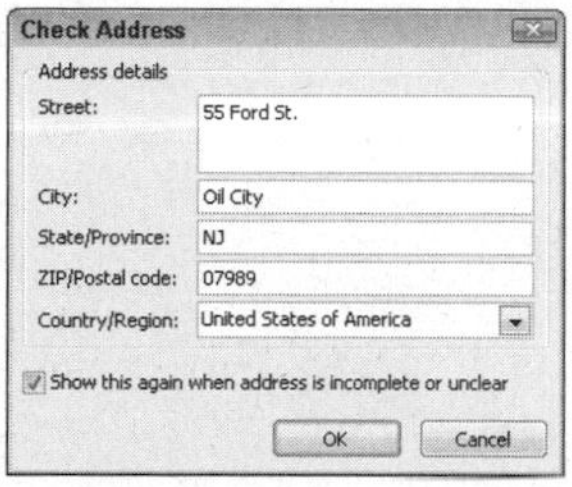

Figure 7-6:
The Check
Address
dialog box.

11. **On the New Contact form, select the This Is the Mailing Address check box if the address you just entered is the one you'll use for sending mail to the contact.**

12. **Click in the Web Page Address text box and type the page's address if you want to link to that page directly from the Address Card.**

URL is a fancy name for the address of a page on the World Wide Web. When you see ads on TV that refer to www.discovery.com or www.dummies.com, what you're seeing is a *Uniform Resource Locator* (the even fancier term that URL stands for — essentially an Internet address).

You can view a Web page by entering the URL for the page in the Address box of your Web browser. If a person or company in your Outlook Contacts list has a Web page, you can enter the URL for that page in the Web Page Address box. To view the Web page for a contact, open the contact record, click the More button, and choose Web Page (or press Ctrl+Shift+X); your Web browser opens and loads the contact's Web page.

13. **Click in the large text box at the bottom right of the form and type in anything you want.**

You can enter directions, details about meetings, the Declaration of Independence — anything you want (preferably something that can help you in your dealings with the contact).

Format the text in the big text box (see Figure 7-7) by clicking the Format Text tab and using the buttons in the Formatting Ribbon, if you want. The tools on the Formatting Ribbon are just like the ones that all other word processing programs use: font, point size, bold, italic, justification, and color. Select the text you want to format. You can change the formatting of a single letter or the whole text box. You can't format the text in the smaller data text boxes in the other parts of the Contact form — only the text in the big text box at the bottom right of the form.

14. **When you're done, click the Save & Close button.**

After you enter anything you want or need (or may need) to know about people you deal with at work, you're ready to start dealing.

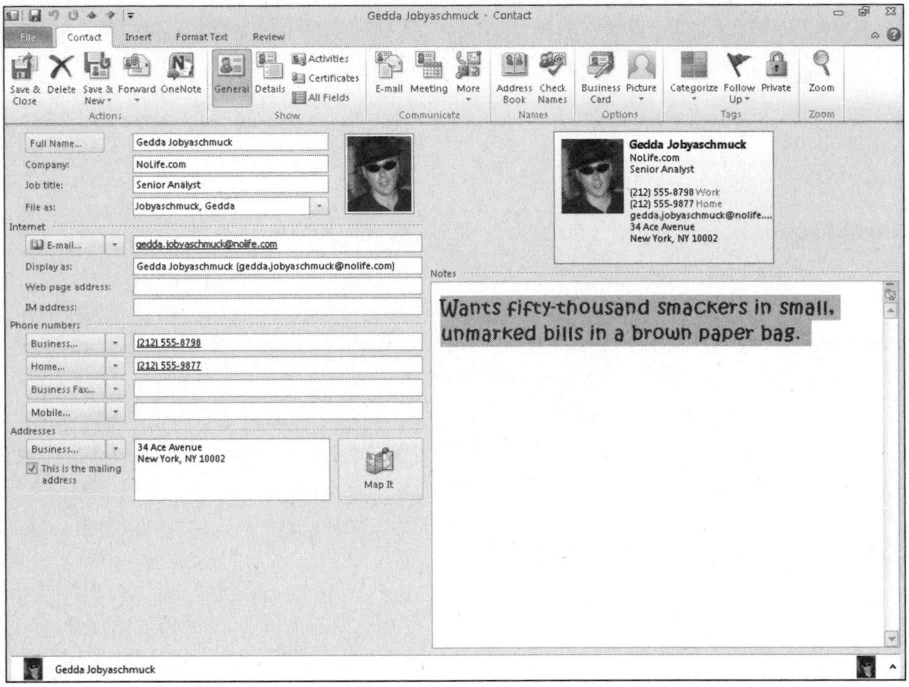

Figure 7-7:
Have fun
with format-
ting in the
Contact
text box.

Viewing Contacts

After you enter your contact information, Outlook lets you see the information arranged in many different and useful ways, called *views*. Viewing your
contact information and sorting the views are quick ways to get the big picture of the data you've entered. Outlook comes with from 5 to 12 predefined
views in each module. You can easily alter any predefined view. Then you
can name and save your altered view and use it just as you would the predefined views that come with Outlook.

To change the view of your Contacts list, follow these steps:

1. **Click the Contacts button in the Navigation pane (or press Ctrl+3).**

   The Contacts list appears in the main part of the Outlook screen; a list of
   views appears in the top part of the Navigation pane.

2. **Pick the view you want from the Current View category of the Ribbon.**

   The view you picked appears. If you chose the Business Cards view,
   you'd get something like what's shown in Figure 7-8. You can also
   choose Card view, Phone view, List view, or whatever other views are
   listed.

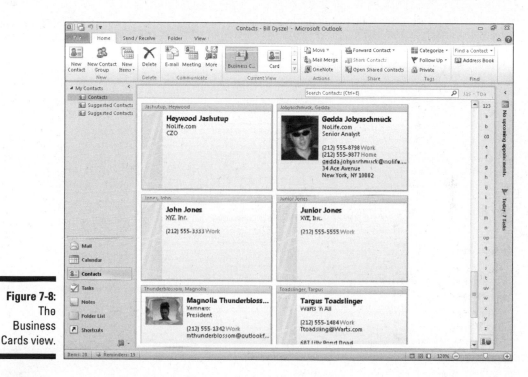

Figure 7-8:
The
Business
Cards view.

You can shift among views as you can switch television stations, so don't worry about changing back and forth. When you change views, you're just seeing different ways to organize the same information.

Sorting a view

Some views are organized as simple lists, such as the Phone List view of the Contacts module. Figure 7-9 shows the Phone view: a column of names on the left, followed by a column of company names, and so on.

If you're unable to find a certain contact in a view that is arranged in columns, all you have to do to sort that column is click once on the title of the column. For example, suppose that you want to see the names of the people who work for IBM who are entered in your Contacts list. One easy way to see all their names simultaneously is to run a sort on the Company column, like this:

1. **Click the Contacts button in the Navigation pane (or press Ctrl+3).**

   The Contacts list appears in the main part of the Outlook screen, and a list of views appears in the top part of the Navigation pane.

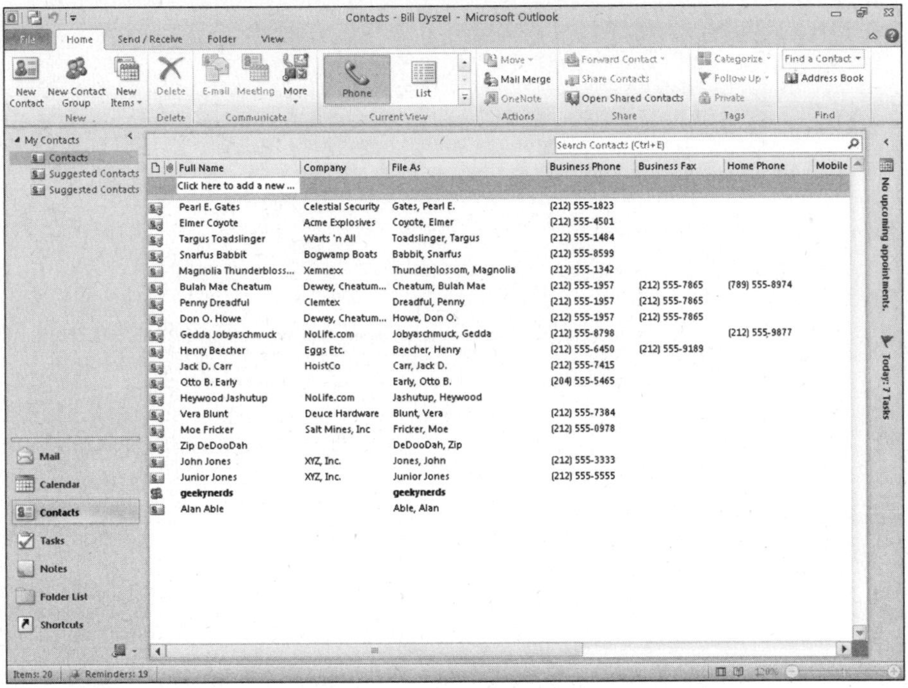

Figure 7-9:
The Phone
view.

2. **Choose the Phone view.**

   Your list of contacts appears in the Phone view.

3. **Click the heading at the top of the Company column.**

   Your contacts appear in alphabetical order according to the name in the Company column. If you click the heading a second time, your contacts appear in reverse alphabetical order.

After you sort your list, it's easier to find someone's name by scrolling down to that part of the alphabet. If you sort by company, all the contacts line up in order of company name, so you can scroll down to the section of your list where all the people from a certain company are listed.

Rearranging views

You can rearrange views simply by dragging the column title and dropping the title where you want it. For example, to move the Business Phone column in the Phone view, follow these steps:

1. **Choose the Phone view from the list in the Navigation pane.**

   The Phone List view of your contacts appears.

2. **Click the Business Phone heading and drag it on top of the column to its left.**

   You see a pair of red arrows pointing to the border between the two columns to the left of the Business Phone column. The red arrows tell you where Outlook will drop the column when you release the mouse button (as shown in Figure 7-10).

3. **Release the mouse button.**

   The Business Phone column is now to the left of the File As column (instead of to the right). If it makes more sense to you to have File As to the right of Business Phone, you can set up your view in Outlook to put it there.

Drag the column head.

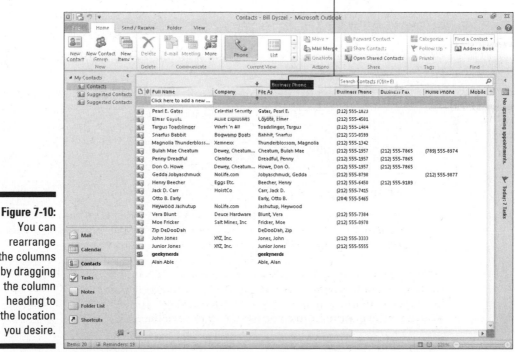

Figure 7-10: You can rearrange the columns by dragging the column heading to the location you desire.

You can use the same process to move any column in any Outlook view. Because the screen is not as wide as the list, you may need to move columns around at times to see what you really want to see. For example, the List view in Figure 7-11 shows 6 columns, but the list in that view really has 12 columns. You must use the scroll bar at the bottom of the list to scroll to the right to see the last column, Categories. If you want to see the Categories column at the same time as the Full Name column, you have to move the Categories column to the left.

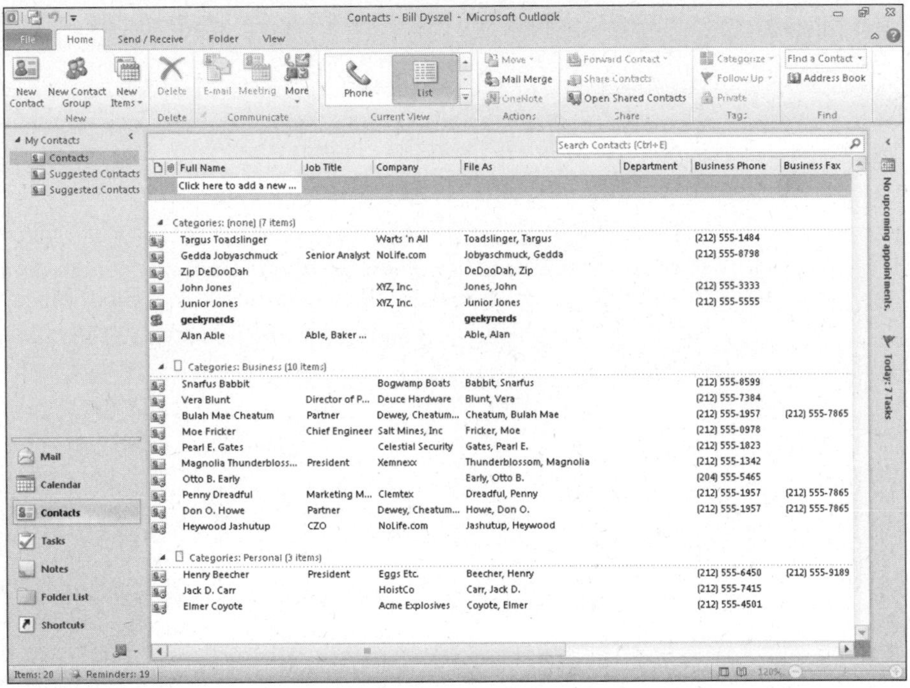

Figure 7-11:
The List
view.

Using grouped views

Sometimes sorting just isn't enough. Contacts lists can get pretty long after a while; you can easily collect a few thousand contacts in a few years. Sorting a list that long means that if you're looking for something starting with the letter *M,* for example, the item you want to find will be about three feet below the bottom of your monitor, no matter what you do.

Groups are the answer, and I don't mean Outlook Anonymous. Outlook already offers you several predefined lists that use grouping.

You can view several types of lists in Outlook: A sorted list is like a deck of playing cards laid out in numerical order, starting with the deuces, then the threes, then the fours, and so on up through the picture cards. A grouped view is like seeing the cards arranged with all the hearts in one row, then all the spades, then the diamonds, and then the clubs.

Gathering items of similar types into groups is handy for tasks such as finding all the people on your list who work for a certain company when you want to send congratulations on a new piece of business. Because grouping by company is so frequently useful, the List view sorts your contacts by company, and it's set up as a predefined view in Outlook.

To use the List view, follow these steps:

1. **Click the Contacts button in the Navigation pane.**

   The Contacts module opens with its current view displayed.

2. **Choose the List view from the list in the Navigation pane.**

   Each heading labeled Company: *name of company* tells you how many items are included under that heading, and it also has a little triangle at the left. Click a triangle to see additional names under the company's heading.

3. **Click the triangle to see entries for the company listed on the gray bar.**

If the predefined group views don't meet your needs, you can group items according to just about anything you want, assuming that you've entered the data.

Grouping is a good way to manage all Outlook items, especially contacts. After you get a handle on using groups, you'll save a lot of time when you're trying to find things.

Flagging Your Friends

Contacts aren't the only items you can flag. You can add reminders to tasks, e-mail messages, and appointments to achieve the same effect.

To attach a flag to a contact, follow these steps:

1. **With the Contacts screen open, right-click the contact you want to flag.**

   A shortcut menu appears (as shown in Figure 7-12).

2. **Choose Follow Up.**

   The Follow Up menu appears.

3. **Choose the date you plan to follow up with the contact you chose.**

   Your choices include Today, Tomorrow, This Week, and Next Week. Sadly, When Heck Freezes Over is not included.

Flagging a contact for a specific day makes that contact's name appear on your Outlook calendar on the day you chose. If you prefer, you can add a reminder to your flag by choosing Add Reminder. That makes a reminder window pop up and play a sound at the time you choose, just in case you have big reasons to avoid talking to that person. A reminder is Outlook's way of telling you to get it over with.

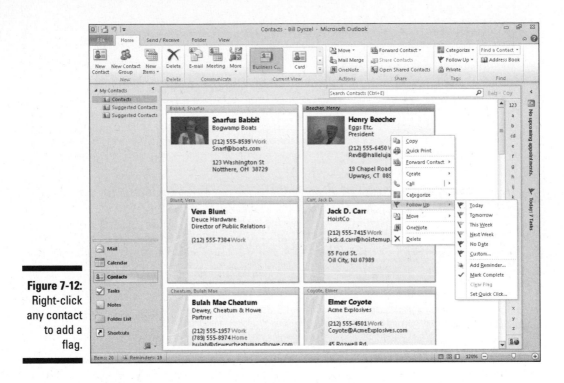

Figure 7-12:
Right-click
any contact
to add a
flag.

Using Contact Information

Call me crazy, but I bet you actually plan to use all that contact information you enter. I'm sure you'll indulge me while I show you a few ways to dig up and exploit the valuable nuggets you've stashed in your Contacts list.

Searching contacts in the Contacts module

The whole reason for entering names in a Contacts list is so that you can find them again. Otherwise what's the point of all this rigmarole?

Finding names in the Outlook Contacts module is child's play. The easiest way is to look in the Address Cards view under the last name.

To find a contact by last name, follow these steps:

1. **Click the Contacts button in the Navigation pane.**

   Your list of contacts appears.

2. **Choose the Card view in the Ribbon.**

   The Card view appears (as shown in Figure 7-13).

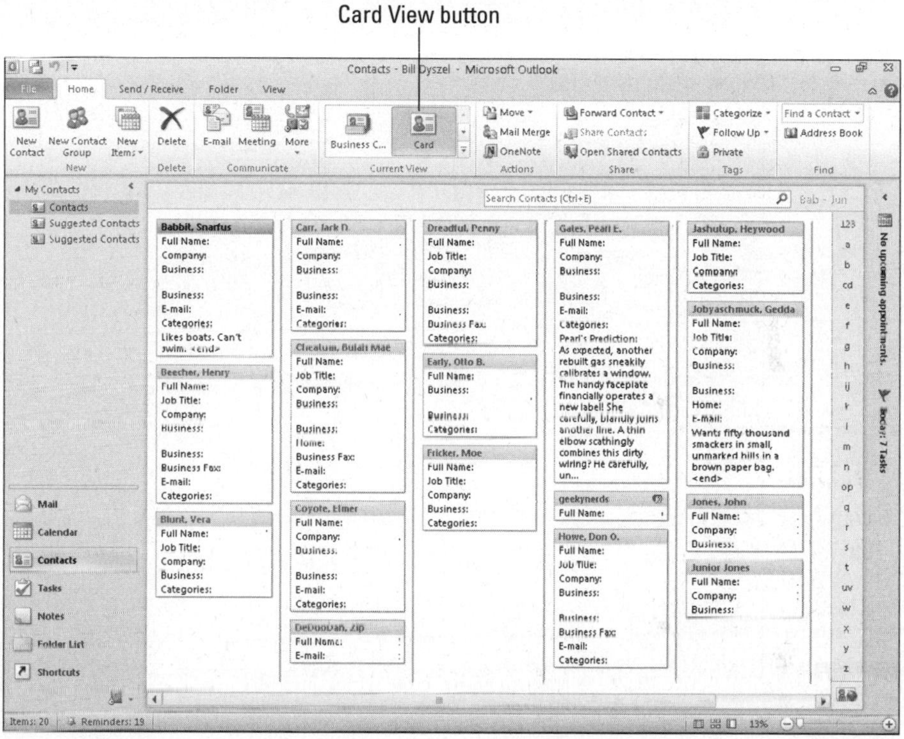

Card View button

Figure 7-13:
The Card
view.

The Card view has a set of lettered tabs along the right edge. You can click a tab to go to that lettered section, but you can use an easier method: Simply click any card, then type the first letter of the name you're looking for. For example, if you're looking for Magnolia Thunderblossom (and you've had Outlook make her File As name *Thunderblossom, Magnolia*), type the letter *T*. You see the names that start with *T*.

Of course, you may need to base a search for a contact name on something like the company the contact works for. Or, you may want to find all the people on your list who live in a certain state — or people who put you in a certain state of mind (now, *there's* a useful tidbit to include in their contact records). In such a case, the Search tool takes you to your contact.

To use the Search tool to search for a contact, follow these steps:

1. **With the Contacts screen open, type the text you want to find in the Search Contacts box and press Enter.**

   The search box is found at the top of your list of contacts, right below the Ribbon. The list of contacts shrinks to those that contain the information you typed (as shown in Figure 7-14).

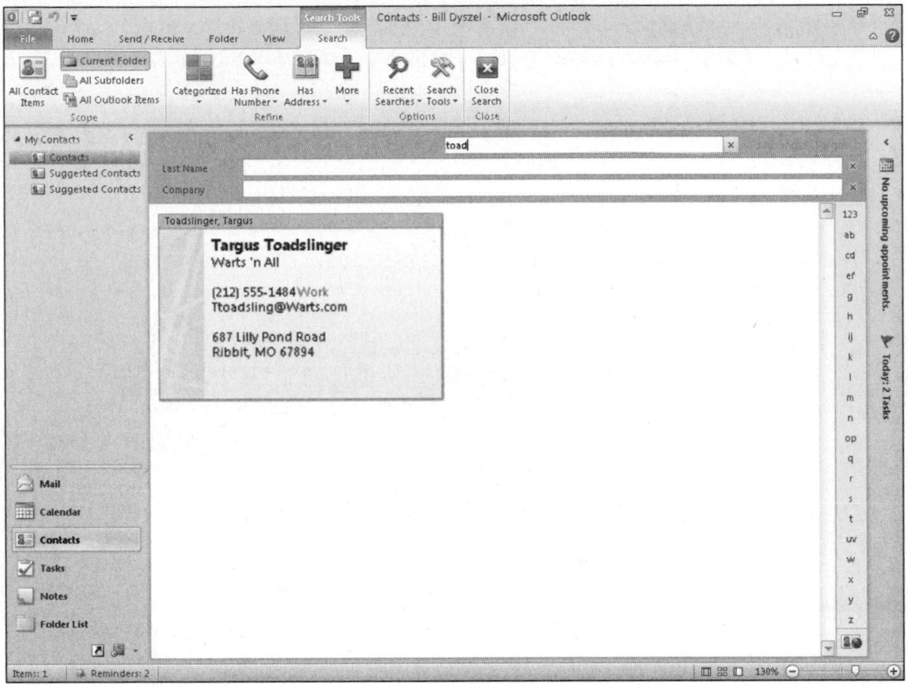

Figure 7-14:
Choose
what kind of
item you're
looking for
with the
Search tool.

2. **Double-click the name of the contact in the list at the bottom of the screen to see the Contact record.**

   If you get no contacts that match your search, check to see whether you correctly spelled the search text you entered.

It's hard to be as stupidly literal as computers — close doesn't count with them. If you see *Grg Wshngtn,* you know to look for *George Washington,* but a computer doesn't. George would have to have his vowels removed before a computer would see those two names the same way.

On the other hand, if you have only a scrap of the name you're looking for, Outlook can find that scrap wherever it is. A search for *Geo* would turn up George Washington, as well as any other Georges in your Contacts list, including Boy George and George of the Jungle (provided they're all such close, personal friends of yours that they're featured in your Contacts list).

Finding a contact from any Outlook module

The Find a Contact box in the Ribbon can help you dig up a contact record in a jiffy from any Outlook module. Follow these steps:

1. **Click the Find a Contact box.**

2. **Type the contact name.**

3. **Press Enter to make Outlook open the record for that contact.**

    If you just type in a fragment of a name, Outlook lists names that contain that fragment and enables you to choose which contact you had in mind. For example, if you type *Wash,* you get George Washington, Sam Washburn, and anyone else in your list whose name includes *Wash.* Double-click the name of the contact record you want to see.

The Find a Contact box has a scroll-down button (triangle) at the right side.

If you click the button, you see a list of the last dozen people you looked up, which is handy when you look for the same people repeatedly. When the list appears, just click the name of the contact you want to see.

Using the Activities page

When you open a contact record, you see a button labeled Activities in the Ribbon. That's the place to look for a summary of every Outlook item you've associated with that person. When you click the Activities icon, Outlook opens a page that displays all items linked with your contact. If you're sure that you want to find something specific, such as an e-mail message, click the scroll-down button (triangle) next to the word *Show* and choose the type of item you want. That way, Outlook looks only at the kind of items you've specified.

A new feature called the Outlook Social Connector displays some of the same information you'll see on the Activities page, along with recent postings from popular social media services. See Chapter 11 for more details about the Social Media Connector.

Forwarding a business card

Outlook can also forward an electronic "business card" to any other person who uses Outlook (or any other program that understands how to use digital business cards). It's a handy way to e-mail any contact record in your list to anybody else.

The most obvious thing you may want to send this way is your own contact information. Just create a contact record for yourself that contains all the information you want to send someone. Then follow these steps:

1. **Click the Contacts button in the Navigation pane.**

    Your list of contacts appears.

2. **Double-click the contact record that contains the information you want to send.**

   The contact record you double-clicked opens.

3. **Click the Forward button.**

   A menu offers three choices: Send as Business Card (both Internet Format and Outlook Format), In Internet Format, and In Outlook Format. If you've set up a text messaging service to work with Outlook, you'll see another choice labeled Forward as Text Message. See Chapter 18 for more about text messaging services.

4. **Choose the format you prefer.**

   If you're not sure, choose Send as Business Card. That sends both kinds of card, as seen in Figure 7-15.

5. **Type the address of the person to whom you want to send the message in the To text box.**

   You can also click the To button and pick a name from the Address Book.

6. **Click the Send button (or press Alt+S).**

   Your message and the attached vCard are sent to your recipient.

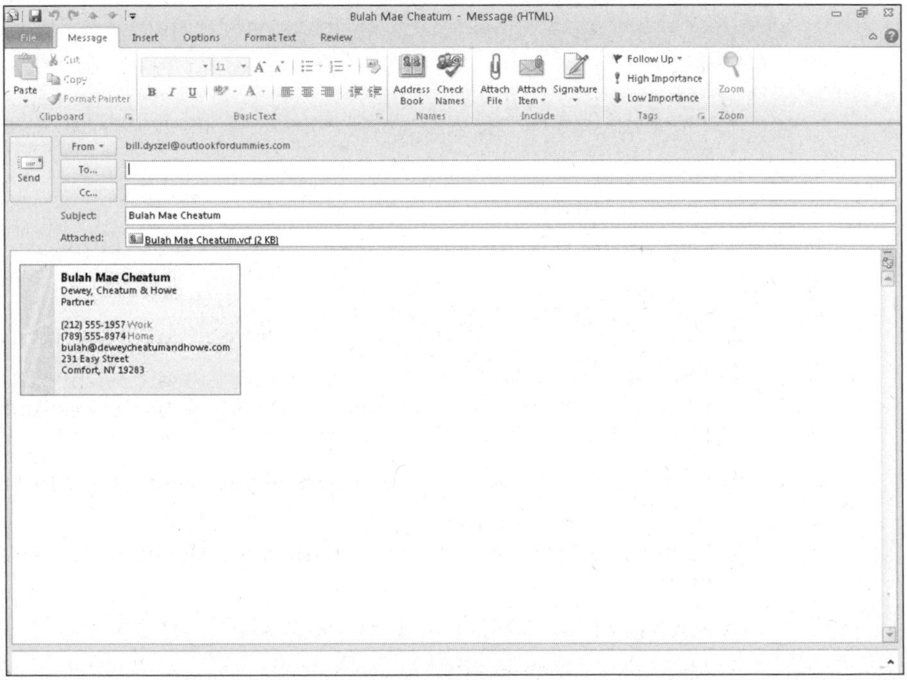

Figure 7-15:
Sending a
business
card.

When you receive a business card in an e-mail message, you can add the card to your Contacts list by double-clicking the icon in the message that represents the business card. Doing so opens a new contact record. Simply click the Save & Close button to add the new name — along with all the info on the business card — to your Contacts list.

Contact Groups

You can create a Contact group in your Contacts module that includes the name of more than one person for those times when you send a message to several people simultaneously. You can also assign categories to your Contact groups (just as you can with individual contacts), and you can send a Contact group to other people as an attachment to an e-mail message so that they can use the same list you do if they're also using Outlook.

Creating a Contact group

Creating a Contact group is a simple matter of making up a name for your list and choosing from the collection of names you've stored on your system. A Contact group doesn't keep track of phone numbers and mailing addresses, just e-mail addresses.

To create a Contact group in your Contacts module, follow these steps:

1. **Click the New Contact Group button in the Ribbon (or press Ctrl+Shift+L).**

   The Contact Group dialog box appears.

2. **Type the name you want to assign to your Contact group.**

   The name you type appears in the Name text box.

3. **Click the Add Members button and choose From Outlook Contacts.**

   The Select Members: Contacts dialog box appears, displaying a list of available names on the left side and a blank box at the bottom; see Figure 7-16.

4. **Double-click the name of each person you want to add to your Contact group.**

   Each name you double-click appears in the Members box at the bottom of the dialog box.

5. **When you're done picking names, click the OK button.**

   The Select Members dialog box closes.

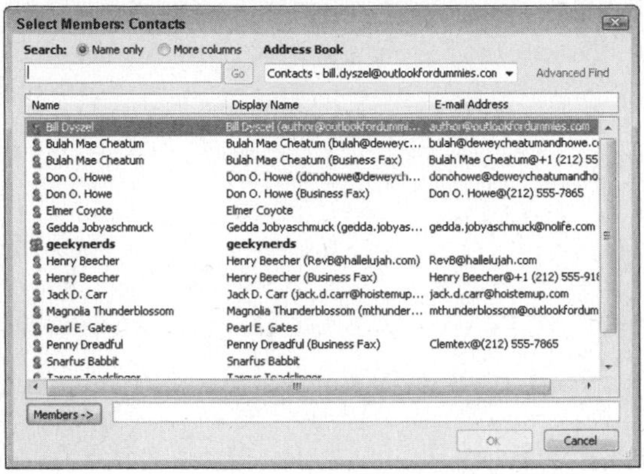

Figure 7-16:
Picking
members
for your
Contact
group.

6. **Click the Save & Close button (or press Alt+S).**

   The Contact Group dialog box closes and your Contact group appears in boldface in your list of contacts.

When you're creating a Contact group, you may also want to include the e-mail addresses of people who aren't included in your Contacts list or any of your other Outlook Address Books. To do so, click Add Members then choose New Email Contact (instead of From Outlook Contacts) in Step 3. Enter the name and e-mail address of the person you want to add in the Add Members dialog box, click the OK button, and follow the rest of the steps exactly the same way.

Editing a Contact group

People come and people go in Contact groups, just as they do everywhere else. It's a good thing you can edit the lists. Just click the Contacts icon in the Navigation pane and double-click the name of one of your Contact groups (the entries that show a little two-headed icon to the right of their names). When you open a Contact group entry, you see the same screen you saw when you first created the list. Here you have some useful options:

- ✔ To remove a member of the list, click that name and click the Remove Member button. (I hope Microsoft finds a better name for that button in the future. Ouch!)

- ✔ To select a new member from the names already in your Contacts list or Global Address list, click the Add Members button and follow the same routine you used when you created the list.

- ✔ To add a person whose e-mail address isn't listed in any of your Address Books, click the New Email Contact button, fill in the person's name and e-mail address, and click the OK button.

Using a Contact group

Contact groups show up as items in your Contacts list along with people's names — so (as you'd guess) you can use a Contact group to address an e-mail message just as you would with any contact. You can drag the card for a Contact group to your Inbox to create a new e-mail message to that list. You can also type the name of the Contact group in the To field of an e-mail message and click the Check Names button on the toolbar. When Outlook adds an underline to the name in the To box, you know that your message will go to the people in your Contact group.

Adding pictures to contacts

You can include a picture with the contact information you collect, and not just for decoration. Now that many cell phones and other mobile devices synchronize with the Outlook Contacts list, you can make someone's picture appear on your cell phone screen every time he or she calls or sends you a text message. Those pictures will also appear when you pick the Business Card view of your Outlook contacts. If you're the type who forgets names but never forgets a face, you can collect both names and faces.

Add a picture to a contact record by following these steps:

1. **With the Contacts screen open, double-click a contact to which you want to add a picture.**

   The contact record you chose opens.

2. **Double-click the picture icon at the top center of the contact record.**

   The Change Contact Picture dialog box opens; see Figure 7-17.

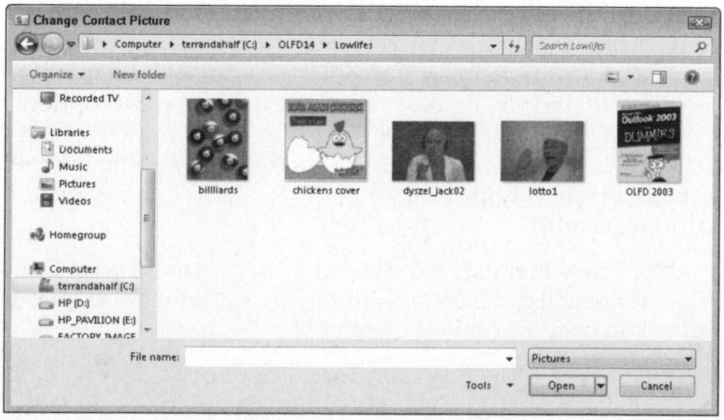

Figure 7-17: The Add Picture dialog box.

  3. **Double-click the picture you want to add.**

     The picture you chose appears in the contact record.

  4. **Click the Save & Close button.**

     Another smiling face now adorns your world, as shown in Figure 7-18. Isn't it wonderful? If you're likely to be sending out your own business card, it's probably worthwhile to add a nice-looking picture to help make a good impression.

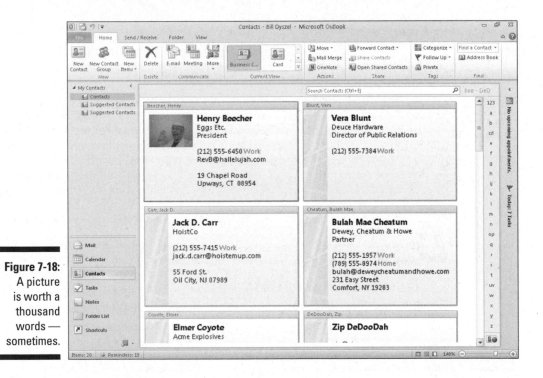

Figure 7-18: A picture is worth a thousand words — sometimes.

Also, if you have one of those fun picture-editing programs, you can add mustaches and blacked-out teeth to the people you find unappealing just for a laugh. But if your boss is likely to see his picture on your screen with some (ahem!) unflattering adjustments, you might think twice before "improving" his contact photo.

Chapter 8

The Calendar: How to Unleash Its Power

In This Chapter

▶ Using the Date Navigator

▶ Finding a date (the number kind)

▶ Making and breaking dates

▶ Viewing the calendar

▶ Printing your appointments

▶ Reminding yourself to celebrate

D o working people work all day? No. Most working people spend the day going to meetings. It's enough to send anyone to Over Meeters Anonymous. The Outlook Calendar can't halt the relentless tedium of meetings, but it can speed up the scheduling process and help you budget your time for more meetings!

Getting around the Outlook Calendar

No doubt you've been looking at calendars your whole life, so the Outlook Calendar will be pretty simple for you to understand. It looks like a calendar: plain old rows of dates, Monday through Friday plus weekends, and so on. You don't have to learn to think like a computer to understand your schedule.

If you want to see more information about something in your calendar, most of the time, you just click the calendar with your mouse. If that doesn't give you enough information, click twice. If that doesn't give you everything you're looking for, read on; I fill you in on the fine points.

The Date Navigator is actually the name of this feature, but don't confuse it with Casanova's chauffeur. The Date Navigator (shown at the upper-left of Figure 8-1) is a trick that you can use in Outlook to change the part of the calendar you're seeing or the time period you want to look at.

Date Navigator

Today button

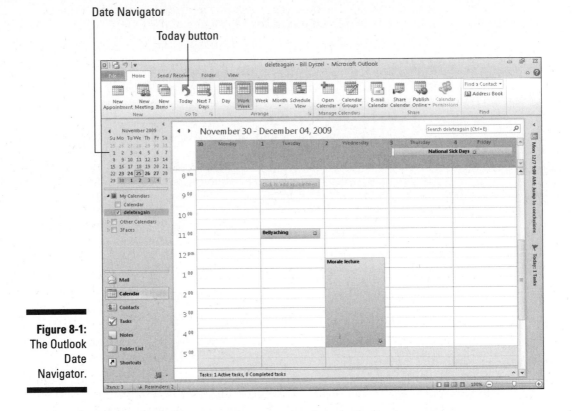

Believe it or not, that unassuming calendar scrap is probably the quickest way to change how you look at the calendar and make your way around in it. Just click the date you want to see, and it opens in all its glory. It couldn't be simpler.

To navigate your calendar, follow these steps:

1. **Click the Calendar button in the Navigation pane (or press Ctrl+2).**

   The calendar appears in the Information Viewer, while the top part of the Navigation pane displays the Date Navigator. If you have the To-Do Bar open, the Date Navigator appears there, instead.

2. **Click the Day, Week, Work Week, or Month button in the Ribbon.**

   The button you click appears highlighted to indicate which one you've selected:

   • To see the details of a single date, click that day wherever it's visible. You see the appointments and events scheduled for the day you clicked.

- To advance the Date Navigator one month at a time, click one of the triangles on either side of the name of the month.

- As time goes by (so to speak), you'll gravitate to the Calendar view that suits you best. I like the Week view because it includes both calendar and task information in a screen that's pretty easy to read. You can leave Outlook running most of the time to keep the information you need handy.

Time travel isn't just science fiction. You can zip around the Outlook Calendar faster than you can say "Star Trek." Talk about futuristic: The Outlook Calendar can schedule appointments for you well into the year 4500! Think about it: Between now and then, there are more than 130,000 Saturday nights! That's the good news. There are also more than 130,000 Monday mornings. Of course, in our lifetimes, you and I have to deal with only about 5,000 Saturday nights at most, so we have to make good use of them. Better start planning.

When you need to find an open date fast, follow these steps:

1. **Press Ctrl+G.**

   A dialog box appears (as shown in Figure 8-2) with a date highlighted.

2. **To go to another date, type the date you want in the Date box as you normally would, such as** January 15, 2011 **or** 1/15/11.

   A really neat way to change dates is to type something like **45 days ago** or **93 days from now**. Try it. Outlook understands simple English when it comes to dates. Don't get fancy, though — Outlook doesn't understand **Four score and seven years ago**. (But who does?)

Figure 8-2:
The Go to
Date dialog
box.

If you want to go to today's date, just click the Today button in the Ribbon at the top of the screen. No matter which date you land on, you can plunge right in and start scheduling. You can double-click the time and date of when you want an appointment to occur and then enter the particulars, or you can double-check the details of an appointment on that date by double-clicking the date and making changes to the appointment if necessary. You can also do something silly like find out what day of the week your birthday falls on 1,000 years from now. (Mine's on Saturday. Don't forget.)

Meetings Galore: Scheduling Appointments

Many people live and die by their datebooks. The paper type of datebook still exists. (How quaint.) I'll admit, I find them the easiest kind of datebook to put stuff in, although after it's in, the stuff can be a pain to find. Electronic gizmos like iPhones and BlackBerrys can also serve as datebooks, but sometimes it's hard to put appointments into them because they're small and usually have no mouse that you can use to select dates. Fortunately, many digital gadgets synchronize to Outlook, so you can have the best of both worlds!

Outlook makes it surprisingly easy to add appointments — and even easier to find items that you've entered. It also warns you when you've scheduled two dates simultaneously. (Very embarrassing!)

The quick-and-dirty way to enter an appointment

Some appointments don't need much explanation. If you're having lunch with Mom on Friday, there's no reason to make a big production out of entering the appointment. When you're looking at a view of your calendar that shows the hours of the day in a column, such as the Work Week view, just click the starting time of your appointment, type a description, such as **Lunch with Mom**, and press Enter. Your appointment is now part of your official schedule, faster than you can say "Waiter!"

The complete way to enter an appointment

Appointments you set up at work often require you to include a little more information than you'd need for your lunch date with Mom. You might want to add details about the location of a meeting and some notes about the meeting agenda. You might also want to assign a category to a meeting so that you can show the boss how much time you spend with your clients. When you want to give an appointment the full treatment, use the complete method.

Follow these steps to schedule an appointment the complete way:

1. **Click the Calendar button in the Date Navigator.**

   Your calendar appears.

2. **Click the New Appointment button.**

   The Appointment form opens (as shown in Figure 8-3).

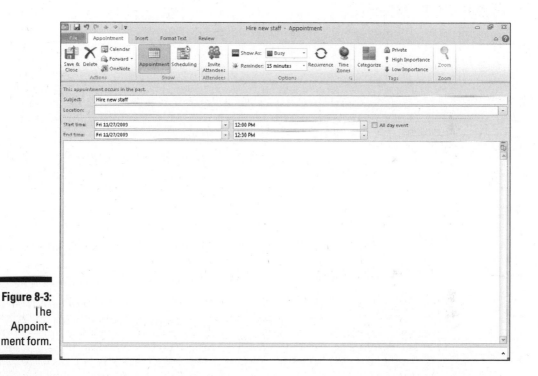

Figure 8-3:
The
Appoint-
ment form.

You can also press Ctrl+N to open the screen that lets you create a new item in your calendar. You can even press Ctrl+Shift+A from any other section of Outlook to create an appointment. The catch is that you won't see the appointment on the calendar until you switch to the Calendar view.

3. **Click in the Subject box and type something there to help you remember what the appointment's about.**

   For example, type **Dentist appointment** or **Deposit Lottery Winnings** or whatever. This text shows up on your calendar.

4. **(Optional) Click in the Location box and enter the location.**

   Notice the little triangle (scroll-bar button) at the right side of the box. If you click the triangle, you see a list of the last few locations where you scheduled appointments so that you can use the same places repeatedly without having to retype them. Another advantage to having this recallable list of locations is that it makes entering locations easy — you can (for example) sort your list of appointments by location to see whether any conference rooms are free.

5. **Add any other information you need to remember about your appointment.**

   The large, empty box in the Appointment form is a great place to save driving directions, meeting agendas, or anything else that might be helpful to remember when the appointment time arrives.

6. **Click the Save & Close button.**

   The appointment you created appears in your calendar (as shown in Figure 8-4). You may have to change your Calendar view by clicking the Date Navigator on the date the appointment occurs so that you can see your new appointment.

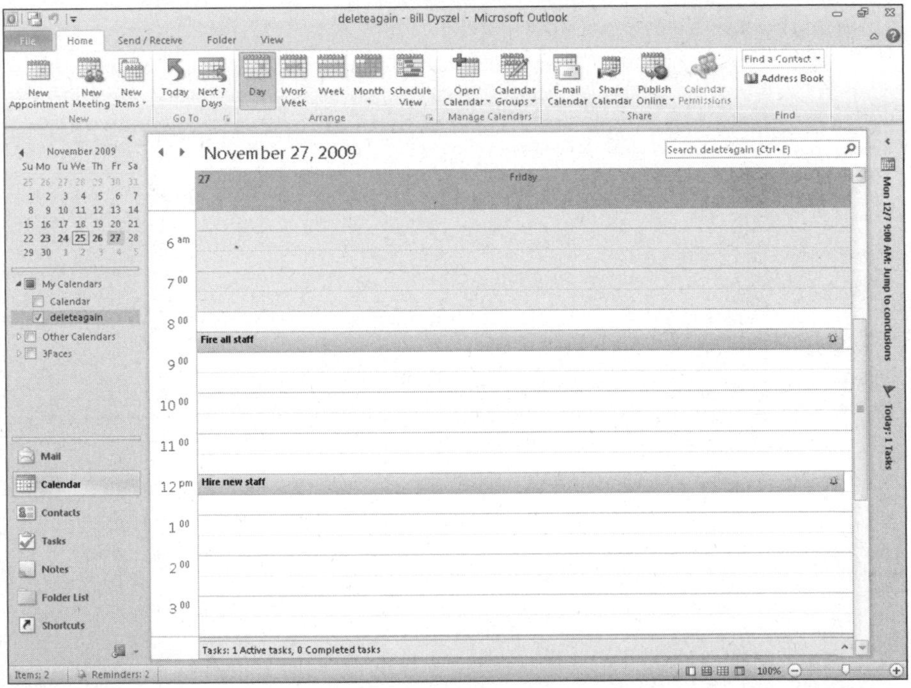

Figure 8-4:
When you finish creating an appointment, you'll find it in your calendar.

If you want to see reminders for all your important appointments, you must keep Outlook running so that the reminders pop up. You can keep Outlook running in the background if you start up a second program, such as Microsoft Word. When the reminder time arrives, you see a dialog box, similar to the one shown in Figure 8-5.

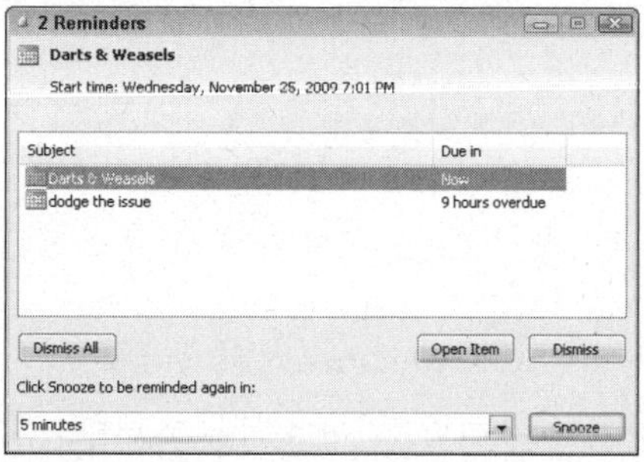

Figure 8-5:
A dialog
box pops up
to remind
you of your
appoint-
ment.

Not this time: Changing dates

You can be as fickle as you want with Outlook. In fact, to change the time of
a scheduled item, just drag the appointment from where it is to where you
want it to be (as shown in Figure 8-6). Or back again . . . maybe . . . if you feel
like it. . . .

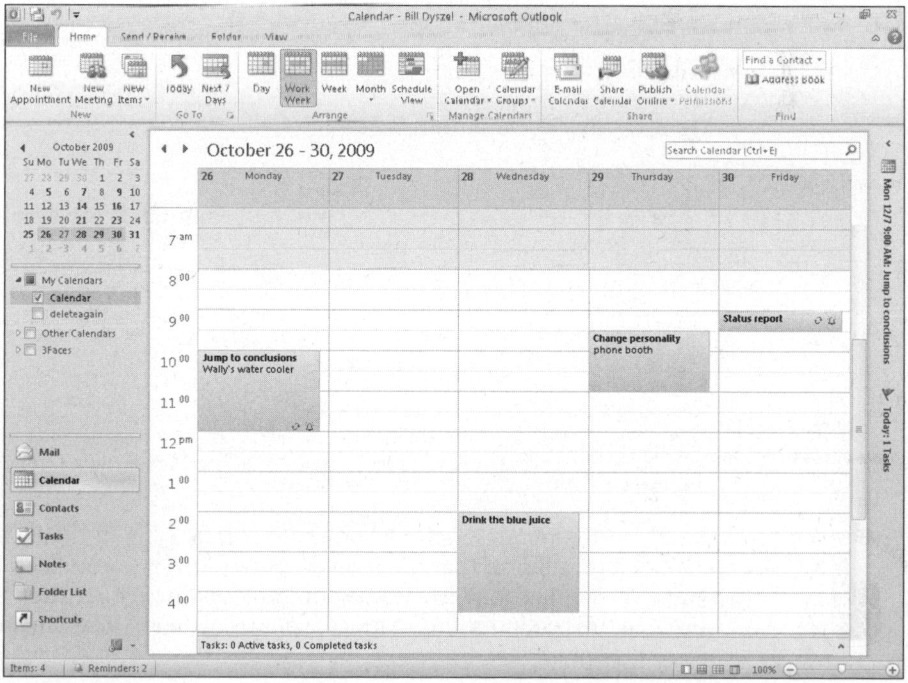

Figure 8-6:
If your
appointment
is a drag,
drop it in a
new time
slot.

To change an appointment, follow these steps:

1. **Click the appointment in the Calendar view.**

   A dark border appears around the edge of the appointment.

2. **Drag the appointment to the time or date you want it to be.**

   If you're in the One-Day view, switch to the Week view or Month view before you drag the appointment to a different date.

   If you want to create a copy of an appointment for another time, hold down Ctrl while you use the mouse to drag the appointment to another time or date. For example, if you're scheduling a summer intern orientation from 9:00 a.m. to 11:00 a.m. and again from 1:00 p.m. to 3:00 p.m., you can create the 9:00 a.m. appointment and then copy it to 1:00 p.m. by holding Ctrl and dragging the appointment. Then you have two appointments with the same subject, location, and date, but with different start times.

   If you copy an appointment to a different date by dragging the appointment to a date on the Date Navigator, you retain the hour of the appointment but change the date.

You can change an appointment to a date you can't see on the calendar by following these steps:

1. **Double-click the appointment.**

   The Appointment dialog box opens.

2. **Click in the leftmost Start Time box and then click the scroll-down button to the right of the date.**

   A drop-down calendar (shown in Figure 8-7) appears.

3. **Pick the month by clicking one of the triangles beside the month's name.**

   Clicking the left triangle moves you one month earlier; clicking the right triangle moves you one month later.

4. **Click the day of the month you want.**

5. **Click in the rightmost Start Time text box and enter the appointment's new time, if needed.**

6. **Make any other changes you need in the appointment by clicking the information you want to change and typing the revised information over it.**

7. **Click the Save & Close button.**

Save and Close button   Start time

Click these triangles to change the month.

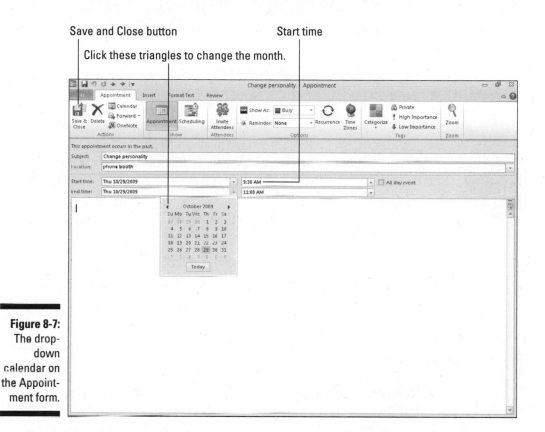

Figure 8-7:
The drop-
down
calendar on
the Appoint-
ment form.

Imagine that your dentist calls to tell you that you *won't* need a root canal after all, but you'll still need a routine checkup. To change the length of an appointment, follow these steps:

1. **Click the appointment.**

2. **Move the mouse pointer over the "handles" at the top or bottom of the appointment.**

   When the pointer is in the right place, it turns into a two-headed arrow that you can use to drag the lines of the appointment box.

3. **Drag the bottom line down to make the appointment time longer; drag the bottom line up to make the appointment shorter.**

   You can change an appointment's length by dragging.

You also can shorten an appointment to fewer than 30 minutes. Follow these steps:

1. **Double-click the appointment and click the End Time box.**

2. **Type the ending time.**

3. **Click the Save & Close button.**

You can enter times in Outlook without adding colons and often without using a.m. or p.m. Outlook translates 443 as 4:43 p.m. If you plan lots of appointments at 4:43 a.m., just type **443A**. (Just don't call *me* at that hour, okay?)

Not ever: Breaking dates

Well, sometimes things just don't work out. Sorry about that. Even if it's hard for you to forget, with the click of a mouse, Outlook deletes dates that you otherwise fondly remember — okay, *two* clicks of a mouse. *C'est la vie, c'est l'amour, c'est la guerre.* (Look for my next book, *Tawdry French Clichés For Dummies.*)

To delete an appointment (after you've called to break it, of course), follow these steps:

1. **Right-click the appointment (that is, click with the right mouse button).**

2. **Choose Delete.**

   As far as Outlook is concerned, your appointment is canceled.

By pressing Ctrl+D, you can delete an appointment in just one, brusque key-stroke. How cold.

We've got to keep seeing each other: Recurring dates

Some appointments are like a meal at a Chinese restaurant: As soon as you're done with one, you're ready for another. With Outlook, you can easily create an appointment that comes back like last night's spicy Szechwan noodles.

To create a *recurring* (that is, regularly scheduled) appointment, follow these steps:

1. **Click the appointment that you want to turn into a recurring appointment.**

    The appointment is highlighted to show that you've selected it.

2. **Click the Recurrence button in the Ribbon (as shown in Figure 8-8).**

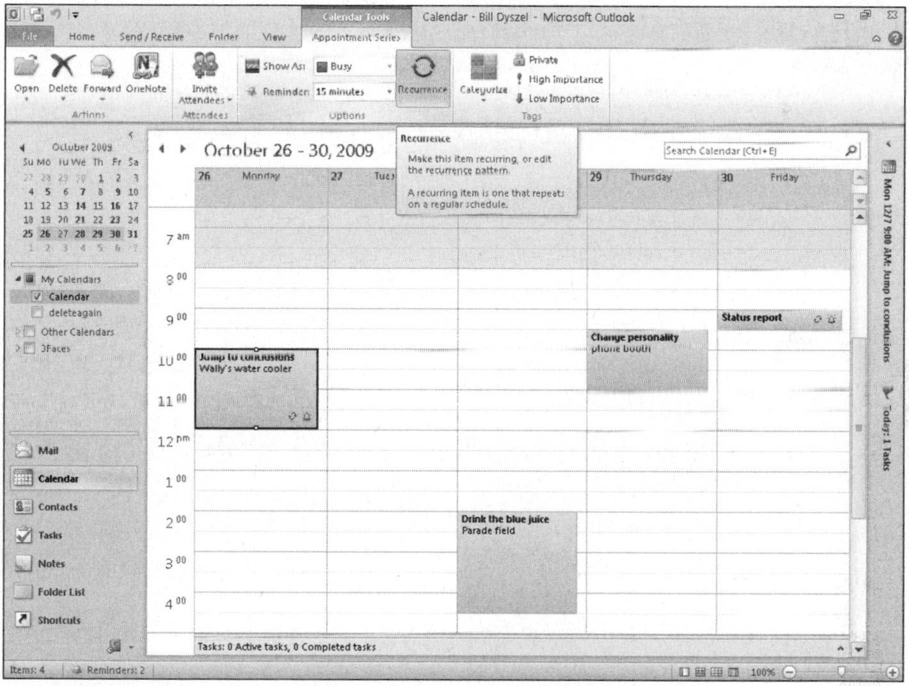

Figure 8-8:
Create recurring appointments from the Actions menu.

The Appointment Recurrence dialog box appears (as shown in Figure 8-9). If you simply click the OK button to accept the preset choices in the Appointment Recurrence dialog box, your appointment will repeat at the same time each week forever. However, you might not be prepared to schedule meetings from now until doomsday. Doomsday is not a federal holiday, by the way; you'll still have to work (unless you take a personal doomsday). So you might want to fill in the rest of the Appointment Recurrence dialog box just to be sure.

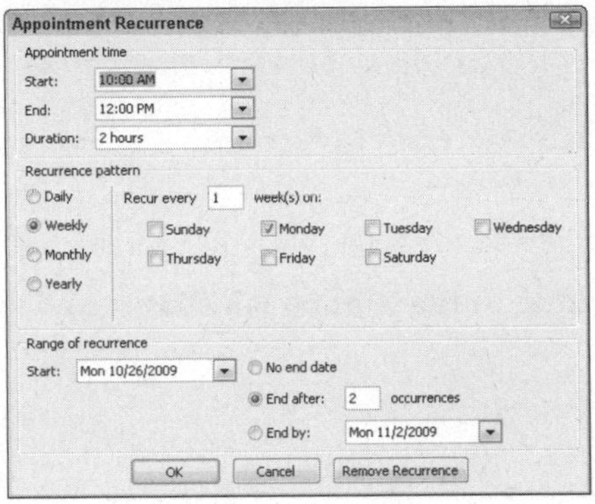

Figure 8-9:
The
Appoint-
ment
Recurrence
dialog box.

3. Click the Start text box and enter the starting time.

Outlook assumes that your appointment is 30 minutes long unless you tell it otherwise by entering an ending time as well. Click the End box and enter an ending time if you feel the need.

4. In the Recurrence Pattern section, click the Daily, Weekly, Monthly, or Yearly option button to select how often the appointment recurs.

5. In the next part of the Recurrence Pattern section, choose how often the appointment occurs.

6. In the Range of Recurrence section, enter the first occurrence in the Start box.

7. Choose when the appointments will stop.

You can select No End Date, End After (a certain number of occurrences), or End By (a certain date).

8. Click the OK button.

The Appointment Recurrence dialog box closes and the Appointment form appears; refer to Figure 8-3.

9. Click the Subject box and enter the subject.

10. Click the Location box and enter the location.

11. Click the Save & Close button.

Your appointment appears in your Outlook calendar with a symbol in the lower-right corner to show that it's a recurring appointment; see Figure 8-10.

The symbol looks like two little arrows chasing each other's tails, a little bit like people who go to too many recurring meetings. Coincidence? I don't think so.

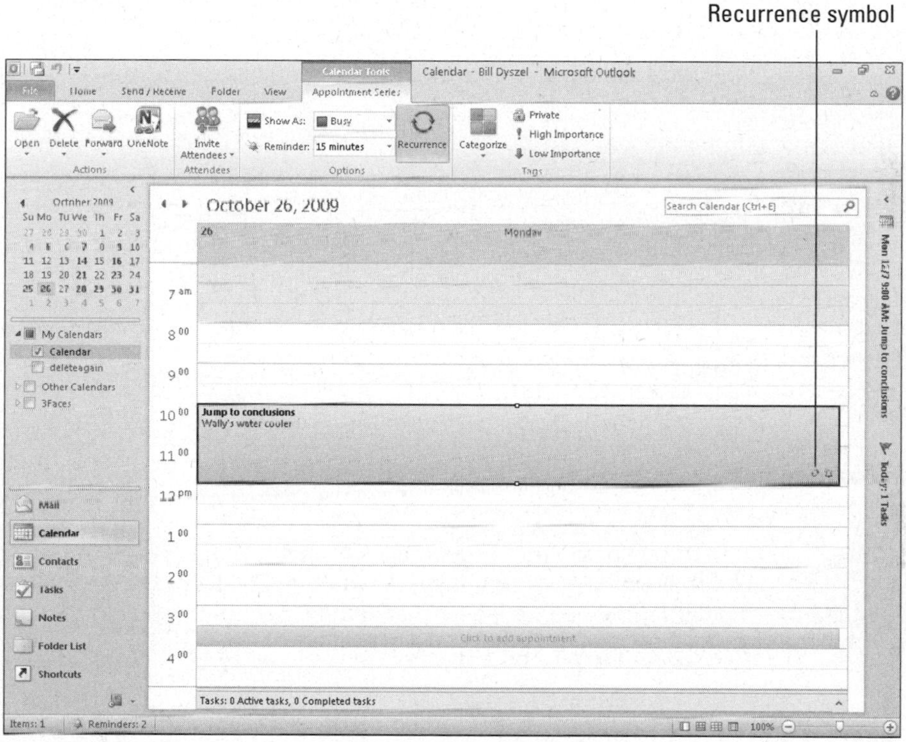

Recurrence symbol

Figure 8-10:
Repeating appoint-
ments display the Recurrence symbol in the lower-right corner.

Even a recurring appointment gets changed once in a while. Edit a recurring appointment this way:

1. **Double-click the appointment that you want to edit.**

   The Open Recurring Item dialog box appears, displaying the recurrence pattern above the subject (as shown in Figure 8-11).

2. **Choose whether you want to change just the occurrence you clicked or the whole series.**

3. **Click the OK button.**

   The Recurring Appointment dialog box appears.

4. **Edit the details of the appointment.**

   To change the pattern, click the Recurrence button, change the recurrence, and click the OK button.

5. **Click the Save & Close button.**

Figure 8-11:
A recurring appointment includes a description of how and when the appointment recurs.

 I find it helpful to enter regular appointments, such as classes or regular recreational events, even if I'm sure I won't forget them. Entering all my activities into Outlook prevents me from scheduling conflicting appointments.

Getting a Good View of Your Calendar

Outlook enables you to slice and dice the information in every section nearly any way you can imagine, using different views. You could easily fill a cookbook with the different views you can create, but I'm going to stick to the standard ways of looking at a calendar that most people are used to. If you want to cook up a calendar arrangement that nobody's ever thought of before, Outlook will probably let you. If you accidentally create a Calendar view you don't like — "Only Mondays? Yikes. What was I thinking?" — that's okay; you can delete it.

The basic Calendar views are Daily view (shown in Figure 8-12), Work Week view (shown in Figure 8-13), Week view (shown in Figure 8-14), and Month view (shown in Figure 8-15). Other views (such as the Schedule view) are helpful when you're trying to figure out when you did something or when you will do something.

Figure 8-12:
The Daily
view.

Figure 8-13:
The Work
Week view.

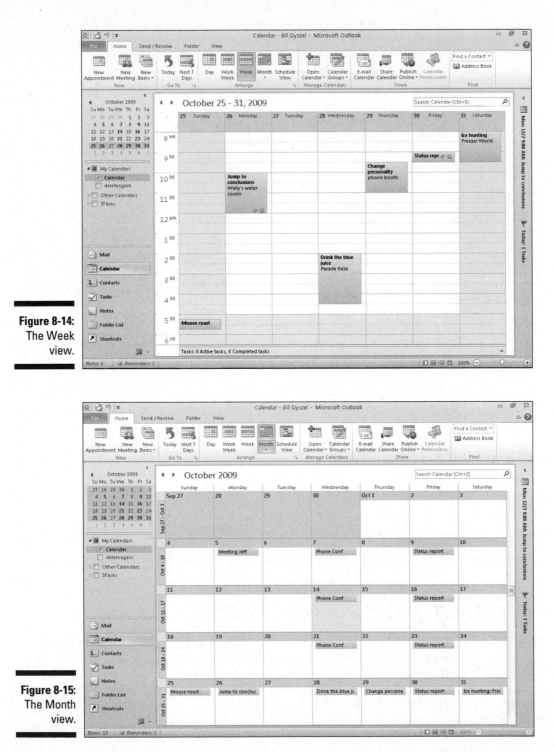

Figure 8-14:
The Week
view.

Figure 8-15:
The Month
view.

Outlook displays buttons for all of its Calendar views in the Ribbon. You can change Calendar views by clicking the name of the view you want to see. If the view you select doesn't suit you, don't worry — just click a different view. In the Schedule view (shown in Figure 8-16), you can view an arrangement of your calendar set on its side, which is useful if you nod off and fall over sideways during one of those interminable meetings you've scheduled. It's also a useful way to view your calendar in a more linear sequence for planning purposes.

Appointment date

Description of appointment | Time of Day

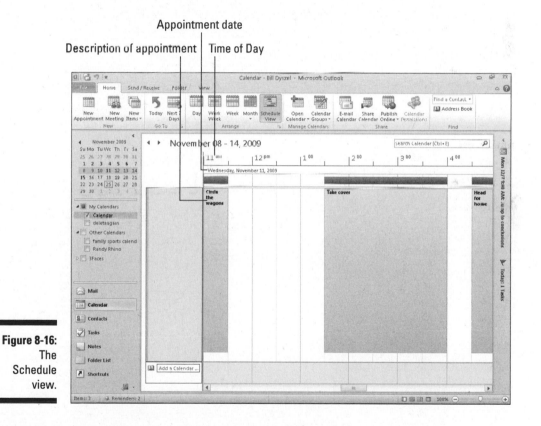

Figure 8-16: The Schedule view.

Printing Your Appointments

Plain old paper is still everybody's favorite medium for reading. No matter how slick your computer organizer is, you may still need old-fashioned ink on paper to make it really useful. To be brutally honest, Outlook's calendar-printing feature stinks. If you can't figure out how to print your calendar the way you want, it's probably not your fault.

You use the same basic steps to print from any module in Outlook. Here's how to print your appointments:

1. **Click a date within the range of dates you want to print.**

   If you want to print a single day, click just one day. If you want to print a range of dates, click the first date and then hold down Shift and click the last date in the range. The whole range is highlighted to show which dates you've selected.

2. **Click the File tab and choose Print (or press Ctrl+P).**

   The Print dialog box appears (as shown in Figure 8-17).

3. **In the Print What section, make a style choice.**

   Daily, Weekly, Monthly, Trifold, and Calendar Details are the basic choices. You can also define your own print styles in Outlook, so you may eventually have quite a collection of choices showing up in this box. Outlook also shows you a preview of the page you're about to print, which eliminates surprises.

4. **Click the Print button.**

   Your dates are sent to the printer.

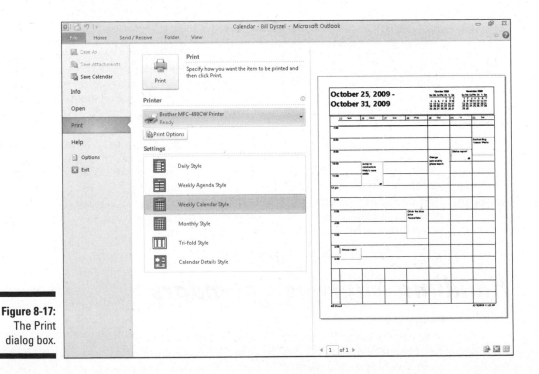

Figure 8-17:
The Print
dialog box.

TIP

Scheduling your main events

You can enter more than just appointments in your calendar. You can also add events by selecting the All Day Event check box in the Appointment form, or you can begin by clicking the New Items button and choosing All Day Event. Then follow the same steps you use to create an appointment. (Refer to the section "Meetings Galore: Scheduling Appointments," earlier in this chapter.)

Events correspond to occurrences that land on your calendar (such as business trips or conferences) that last longer than an appointment — and you can still enter routine appointments that may take place at the event. For example, you can create an event called "2011 Auto Show" and then add appointments to see General Motors at 9:00 a.m., Chrysler at noon, Ford at 3:00 p.m., and the Ghost of Christmas Past at 5:00 p.m.

Adding Holidays to Your Outlook Calendar

What days are most important to working people? The days when they don't have to work! Outlook can automatically add calendar entries for every major holiday so that you don't forget to take the day off (as if you'd forget!). In fact, Outlook can automatically add holidays from over 70 different countries and several major religions. So if you have a yen (so to speak) to celebrate Japanese Greenery Day, an urge to observe Estonian Independence Day, or suddenly want to send a gift for Ataturk's birthday, your Outlook calendar can remind you to observe those monumental events.

To add holidays to your calendar, click the File tab, choose Options and click the Calendar button, and then click the Add Holidays button. You then see a list of nations and religions whose holidays you can add to your calendar; just click the ones you want to add. Think about it: If you made a promise that you'd only eat chocolate on holidays, you can now make just about every day of the year a holiday by adding enough international celebrations to your calendar. It's just a thought (yum).

Handling Multiple Calendars

People who led double lives were once considered thrilling and dangerous. Now they're underachievers. You only have two lives? Well, get busy, pal — get three more. Outlook can manage as many calendars as you have lives. Even if you're a mild-mannered person who just likes peace and quiet, you might want to keep your personal calendar and your business calendar separate by creating two calendars in Outlook.

Creating multiple calendars

To create an additional Outlook calendar, click the Open Calendar button and choose Create New Blank Calendar. Give your new calendar a name and click the OK button. After you've done that, the name you've assigned to your new calendar appears in the Navigation pane, to the right of a blank check box. If you select the check box, your new calendar will appear in the Information Viewer screen side by side with your original calendar, using the same Day, Week, or Month view (see Figure 8-18). If you deselect the check box to remove the check mark, the calendar you deselected disappears, and you only see the calendar that remains selected.

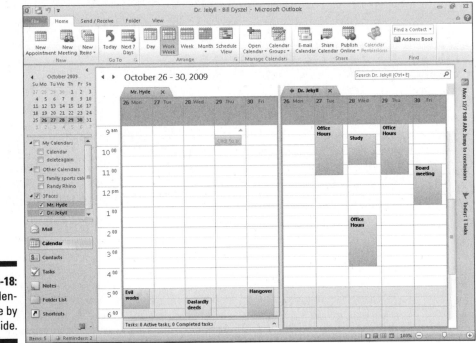

Figure 8-18:
Two calen-
dars side by
side.

Managing multiple calendars

You can't be in two places at once. Even if you could, you wouldn't want your boss to know that; otherwise, you'd end up having to be everywhere at once for the same pay. That's why you'll like the fact that you can superimpose Outlook calendars to avoid schedule conflicts. When you open two calendars side by side, one of the two calendars displays an arrow on the tab at the top of the screen. By clicking that arrow, you can superimpose the two calendars to see whether any appointments conflict (see Figure 8-19).

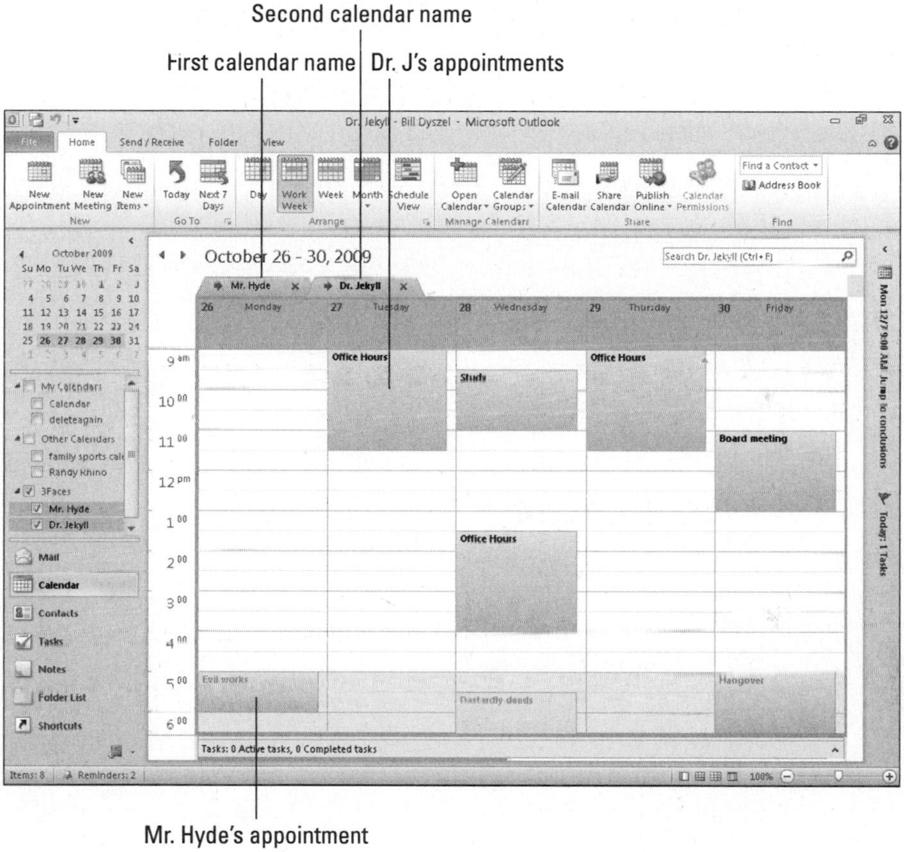

Second calendar name

First calendar name | Dr. J's appointments

Figure 8-19:
Super-
impose two
calendars
to prevent
shatter-
ing the
space-time
continuum
as well as
to keep your
appoint
ments
straight.

Mr. Hyde's appointment

Chapter 9

Task Mastery: Discovering All the Bells and Whistles

*Y*ou can store and manage more information about your daily tasks in Outlook than you may have wanted to know, but you'll certainly find that Outlook makes it easy to remember and monitor your daily work. Organizing your tasks doesn't have to be a task in itself.

Some people say that work expands to fill the available time — and chances are that your boss is one of those people. (Who else would keep expanding your work to fill your available time?) One way of saving time is to keep a list of the tasks that fill your time. That way, you can avoid getting too many more tasks to do.

I used to scrawl a to-do list on paper and hope I'd find the list in time to do everything I had written down. Now Outlook pops up and reminds me of the things I'm trying to forget to do just before I forget to do them. It also keeps track of when I'm supposed to have done my daily tasks and when I actually did them. That way, I can use all the work I was supposed to do yesterday as an excuse not to do the drudgery I'm supposed to do today. Sort of. (Outlook still won't *do* the stuff for me — it just tells me how far I'm falling behind. Be forewarned.)

The To-Do Bar

Outlook 2010 has a feature called the To-Do bar that pulls together all the things you need to do and displays them in a single part of the Outlook screen (see Figure 9-1). The goal of the To-Do bar is to let you know what you need to do at a glance rather than making you check your calendar, then check your e-mail Inbox, and then check your Task list. The items you'll see most often in the To-Do bar include

✔ Tasks you've entered

✔ Your next few appointments

✔ E-mail messages you've flagged for action

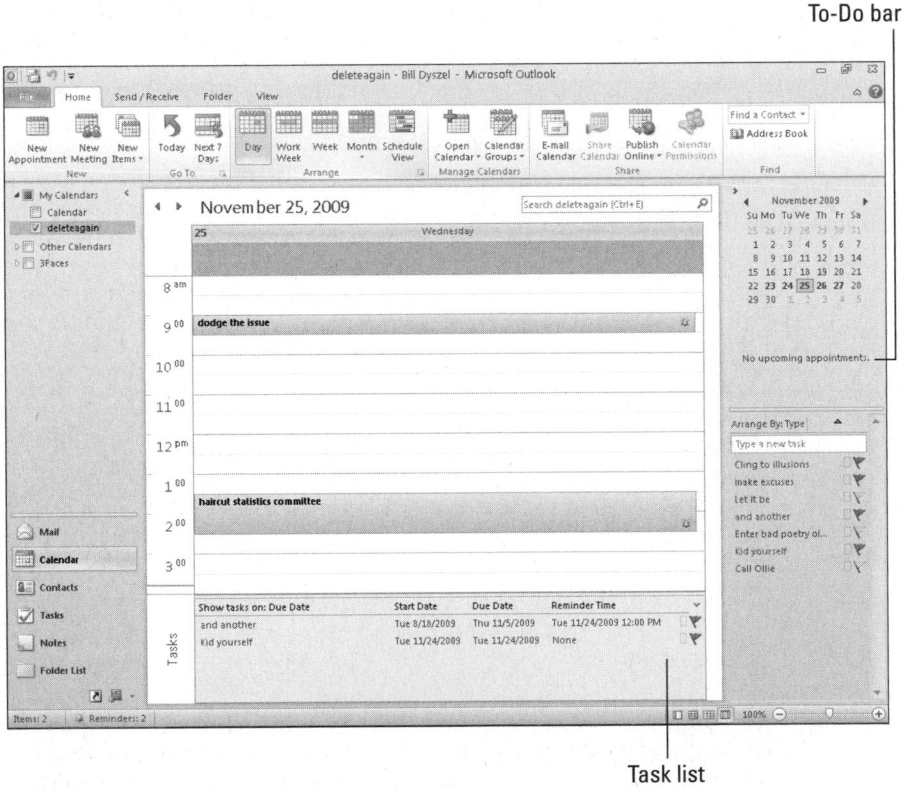

To-Do bar

Figure 9-1:
The To-Do
bar — more
than you'll
ever want
to do.

Task list

At first, the To-Do bar can seem a little confusing because things turn up there that you may not have put there directly. For example, if you receive an e-mail message on a Monday and apply the flag labeled This Week, it'll turn up for action two Fridays later, when you might have forgotten about it. That's what the To-Do bar is for — to prevent you from forgetting.

Adding a new item to the To-Do bar

I don't mean to add work to your busy schedule; you already have plenty of that. But adding an item to the To-Do bar in Outlook isn't such a big to-do. Even though you can store gobs of information about your tasks in Outlook, you have both a quick way and a really quick way to enter a new task.

There's a little box in the To Do bar on the right side of the screen that says Type a new task. Do what the box says. (If you can't see the box, go on to the following section to discover the regular, slightly slower way to enter the task.)

To enter a task by using the quick-and-dirty method, follow these steps:

1. **Click the box that says** Type a new task.

   The words disappear and you see the insertion point (a blinking line).

2. **Type the name of your task.**

   Your task appears in the To-Do bar Task list, as shown in Figure 9-2.

3. **Press Enter.**

   Your new task moves down to the To-Do bar Task list with your other tasks.

Isn't that easy? If only the tasks themselves were that easy to do. Maybe in the next version of Outlook, the tasks will get easier, too (in my dreams).

Of course, all you have is the name of the task — no due dates, reminders, or any of the cool stuff that really helps you get things done. I'll get to that later in this chapter.

Minimizing the To-Do bar

Although the To-Do bar is handy, it takes up quite a bit of space on the screen, which is a nuisance when you're reading e-mail or checking your calendar. You can clear the To-Do bar out of the way by clicking the To-Do Bar icon on the View tab of the Ribbon and choosing Minimized or Off from the drop-down list. You can also click the little arrow symbol at the top of the To-Do bar itself. That doesn't close the To-Do bar; it just shrinks it into a tiny ribbon along the right side of the screen (see Figure 9-3).

When you minimize the To-Do bar you can't add items to it or change anything in it. But it still nags you in a subtle way: it shows how many appointments you have coming up later in the day, and how many items are hidden behind that little ribbon.

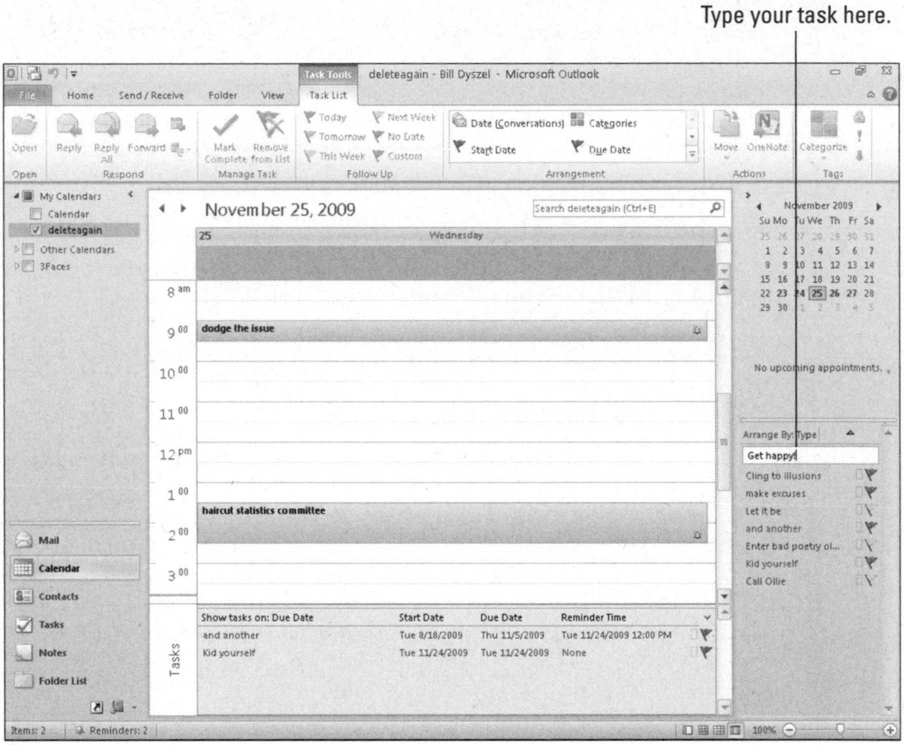

Type your task here.

Figure 9-2:
Entering
your task
in the
To-Do bar.

TIP

You can click the ribbon along the right side of the screen to get a quick glance at the To-Do bar; clicking anywhere else on the screen makes the To-Do bar shrink again.

Entering New Tasks in the Tasks Module

The official way to enter a task is through the Task form, which requires a tiny bit more effort but lets you enter much more detailed information. But you don't need to work your fingers to the bone — as long as you enter a name for the task, you've done all you really must do. If you want to go hog-wild and enter all sorts of due dates or have Outlook remind you to actually *complete* the tasks you've entered (heaven forbid!), you just need to put information in a few more boxes.

To add a task to your Task list, follow these steps:

1. **Click the Tasks button in the Navigation pane (or press Ctrl+4).**

   Your Task list appears.

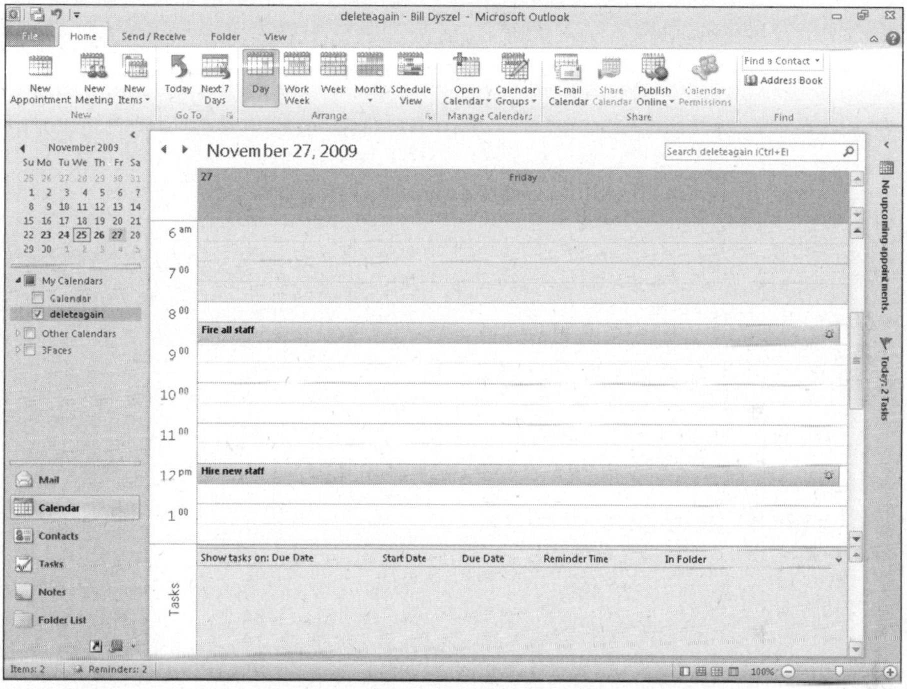

Figure 9-3:
The To-Do bar shrinks to a ribbon on the right side of the screen when you minimize it.

2. **Click the New Task button (or press Ctrl+N).**

   The Task form appears (see Figure 9-4).

3. **Type the name of the task in the Subject box.**

   Use a subject that will help you remember what the task is. The main reason to create a task is to help you remember to do the task.

   You can finish at this point by jumping to Step 13 (click the Save & Close button or press Alt+S) if you want to add only the name of the task to your list. If you want to note a due date, start date, reminders, and so on, you have more to do. All the rest of the steps are optional; you can skip the ones that don't interest you.

4. **(Optional) To assign a due date to the task, click the Due Date box.**

5. **(Optional) Enter the due date in the Due Date box.**

   You can enter a date in Outlook in several ways. You can type **7/4/10**, **the first Friday of July**, or **Three weeks from Friday**. You can also click the scroll-down button (triangle) at the right end of the Due Date text box and choose the date you want from the drop-down calendar.

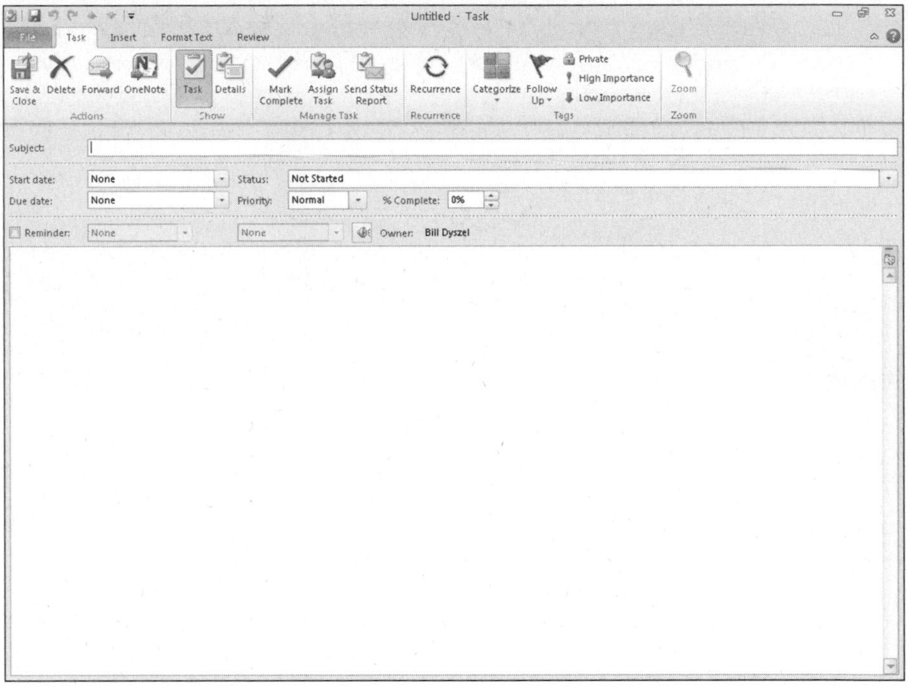

Figure 9-4:
Enter your
new task
in the Task
form.

6. **(Optional) To assign a start date to the task, click the Start Date box and enter the start date.**

   If you haven't started the task, you can skip this step. You can use the same tricks to enter the start date that you use to enter the due date.

   When you're entering information in a dialog box such as the Task form, you can press Tab to move from one text box to the next. You can use the mouse to click each text box before you type, but pressing Tab is a bit faster.

7. **(Optional) Click the Status box to choose the status of the task.**

   If you haven't begun, leave Status set to Not Started. You can also choose In Progress, Completed, Waiting on Someone Else, or Deferred.

8. **(Optional) Click the triangle at the right end of the Priority box to choose the priority.**

   If you don't change anything, the priority stays Normal. You can also choose High or Low.

9. **(Optional) Select the Reminder check box if you want to be reminded before the task is due.**

   If you'd rather forget the task, forget the reminder. But then, why enter the task?

10. **(Optional) Click the date box next to the Reminder check box and enter the date when you want to be reminded.**

If you entered a due date, Outlook has already entered that date in the Reminder box. You can enter any date you want (see Figure 9-5). If you choose a date in the past, Outlook lets you know that it won't be setting a reminder. If you open the scroll-down menu by clicking the triangle on the right of the date box, a calendar appears. You can click the date you desire in the calendar.

There's no reason that the reminder date you enter has to be the same as the due date of the task. You might consider setting a reminder sometime before the task is due. That way you avoid that last-minute angst over things that you forgot until the last minute. Unless you enjoy last-minute anxiety, you should use reminders.

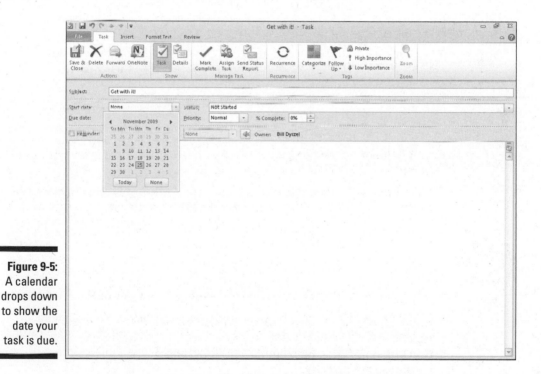

Figure 9-5:
A calendar drops down to show the date your task is due.

11. **(Optional) Enter the time you want to activate the reminder in the Time box.**

The easiest way to set a time is to type the numbers for the time. You don't need colons or anything special. If you want to finish by 2:35 p.m., just type **235**. Outlook assumes that you're not a vampire — it schedules your tasks and appointments during daylight hours unless you say otherwise. (If you *are* a vampire, type **235a**, and Outlook translates that to

2:35 a.m. If you simply *must* use correct punctuation, Outlook can handle that, too.)

12. **(Optional) In the text box, enter miscellaneous notes and information about this task.**

    If you need to keep directions to the appointment, a list of supplies, or whatever, it all fits here.

13. **Click the Save & Close button to finish.**

    Your new task is now included in your Task List, waiting to be done by some fortunate person. Unfortunately, that person is probably you.

Adding an Internet link to a task

If you type the name of a Web page, such as www.outlookfordummies.com, anywhere in the Task form, Outlook changes the text color to blue and underlines the address, turning it into a hyperlink that you can click to jump to a Web site. That makes it easy to save information about an exciting Web site; just type or copy the address into your task. To view the page you entered, just click the text to make your Web browser pop up and open the page.

Editing Your Tasks

No sooner do you enter a new task than it seems that you need to change it. Sometimes I enter a task the quick-and-dirty way and change some of the particulars later — add a due date, a reminder, an added step, or whatever. Fortunately, editing tasks is easy.

The quick-and-dirty way to change a task

For lazy people like me, Outlook offers a quick-and-dirty way to change a task, just as it has a quick-and-dirty way to enter a task. You're limited in the number of details you can change, but the process is fast.

If you can see the name of a task, and if you want to change something about the task you can see, follow the steps I describe in this section. If you can't see the task or the part you want to change, use the regular method, which I describe in the next section of this chapter.

To change a task the quick-and-dirty way, follow these steps:

1. **Click the thing you want to change.**

   You see a blinking line at the end of the text, a triangle at the right end of the box, or a menu with a list of choices.

2. **Select the old information.**

   The old text is highlighted to show it's selected (as shown in Figure 9-6).

Completed items are shown with a line through the text.

The item you've selected for editing

Past-due items are red.

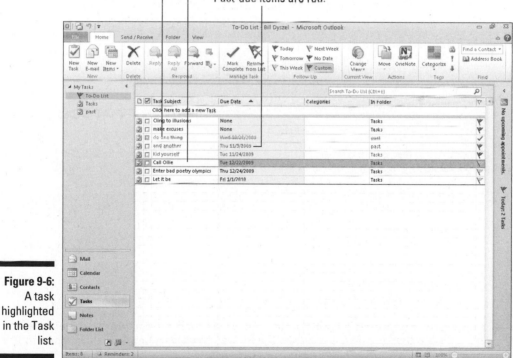

Figure 9-6:
A task
highlighted
in the Task
list.

3. **Type the new information.**

   The new information replaces the old.

4. **Press Enter.**

Isn't that easy? If all you want to change is the name or due date, the quick-and-dirty way will get you there.

The regular way to change a task

If you don't want to be quick and dirty, or if the information you want to change about a task isn't on the list you're looking at, you have to take a slightly longer route.

To make changes to a task the clean-and-long way (also known as the regular way), follow these steps:

1. **Click the Tasks button in the Navigation pane (or press Ctrl+4).**

   The Tasks module opens.

2. **Click the Simple List button in the Current View section of the Ribbon.**

   You can choose a different current view if you know that the view includes the task you want to change. The Simple List view is the most basic view of your tasks; it's sure to include the task you're looking for.

3. **Double-click the name of the task you want to change.**

   The Task form appears. Now you can change anything you can see in the box. Just click the information you want to change, type the new information, and click the Save & Close button (or press Alt+S).

4. **Change the name of the task.**

   The name is your choice. Remember to call the task something that helps you remember the task. There's nothing worse than a computer reminding you to do something that you can't understand.

5. **To change the due date, click the Due Date box.**

6. **Enter the new due date in the Due Date box.**

   Plenty of date styles work here — **7/4/11**, **the first Friday in July**, **Six weeks from now**, whatever. Unfortunately, **the 12th of Never** isn't an option. Sorry.

7. **Click the Start Date box and enter the new start date.**

   If you haven't started the task, you can skip this step. You don't absolutely need a start date; it's just for your own use.

8. **Click the scroll-down button (triangle) at the right end of the Status box to see a menu that enables you to change the status of the task.**

   If you're using Outlook at work and you're hooked up to a network, the Status box entry is one way of keeping your boss informed of your progress. You'll need to check with your boss or system administrator if this is the case.

If you're using Outlook at home, chances are that nobody else will care, but you may feel better if you know how well you're doing. You can't add your own choices to the Status box. (I'd like to add, "Waiting, hoping the task will go away." No such luck.) Figure 9-7 shows the Task box with the Status field highlighted.

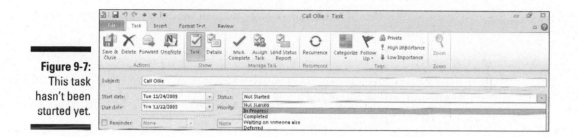

Figure 9-7:
This task
hasn't been
started yet.

9. **Click the scroll-down button (triangle) at the right end of the Priority box to change the priority.**

    Switch the priority to High or Low, if the situation changes (see Figure 9-8).

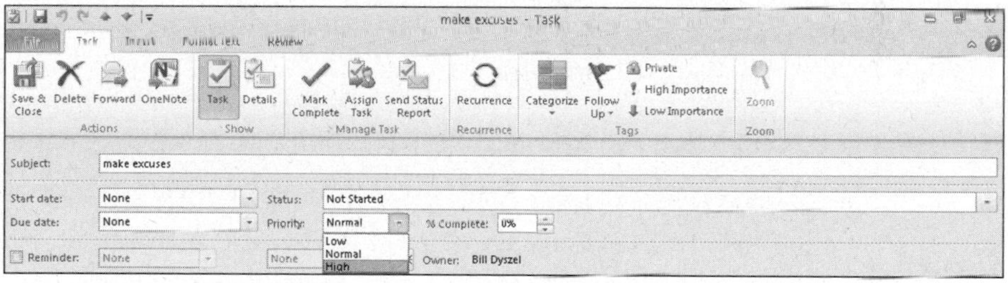

Figure 9-8:
Let's hear it
for a lower
priority.

10. **Select or deselect the Reminder check box if you want to turn the reminder on or off.**

    Reminders are easy and harmless, so why not use them? If you didn't ask for one the first time, do it now.

11. **Click the date box next to the Reminder check box to enter or change the date when you want to be reminded.**

    You can enter any date you want. Your entry doesn't have to be the due date; it can be much earlier, reminding you to get started. You can even set a reminder after the task is due, which isn't very useful. You should make sure that the reminder is before the due date. (The default date for a reminder is the date the task is due.)

12. **Change the time that you want to activate the reminder in the time box.**

    When entering times, keep it simple. The entry **230** does the trick when you want to enter 2:30 p.m. If you make appointments at 2:30 a.m. (I'd rather not know what kind of appointments you make at that hour), you can type **230a**.

13. **Click the text box to add or change miscellaneous notes and information about this task.**

    You can add detailed information here that doesn't really belong anywhere else in the Task form (as shown in Figure 9-9). You see these details only when you open the Task form again; they don't normally show up in your Task list.

14. **Click the Save & Close button to finish.**

    There! You've changed your task.

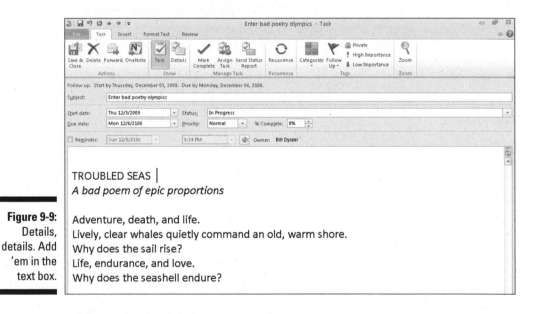

Figure 9-9: Details, details. Add 'em in the text box.

Deleting a task

The really gratifying part about tasks is getting rid of them, preferably by completing the tasks you entered. You may also delete a task you changed your mind about. Of course, nothing is stopping you from deleting tasks you just don't want to bother with; this version of Outlook can't really tell whether you've actually completed your tasks. (Rumor has it that the next version of Outlook will know whether you've finished your tasks and report to Santa. So don't be naughty!)

To delete a task, follow these steps:

1. **Select the task.**

2. **Click the Delete button in the Ribbon.**

    Alternatively, you can press Ctrl+D or press the Delete key on your keyboard. Poof! Your task is gone.

Managing Recurring Tasks

Lots of tasks crop up on a regular basis. You know how it goes — same stuff, different day. To save you the effort of entering a task, such as a monthly sales report or a quarterly tax payment, over and over again, just set it up as a recurring task. Outlook can then remind you whenever it's that time again.

To create a recurring task, follow these steps:

1. **Open the task by double-clicking it.**

    The Task form appears.

2. **Click the Recurrence button on the Task Form toolbar (or press Ctrl+G).**

    The Task Recurrence dialog box appears (see Figure 9-10).

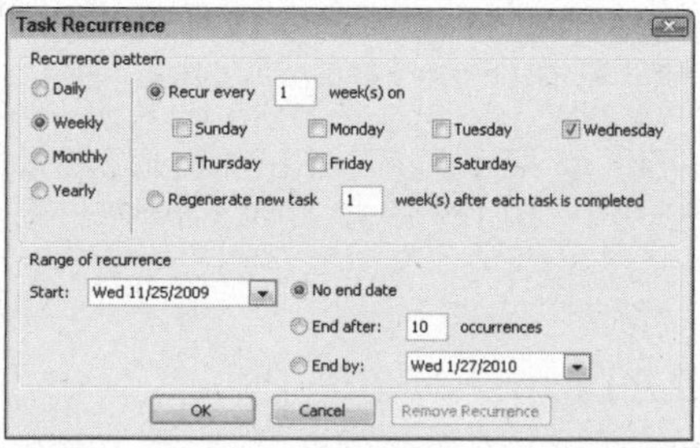

Figure 9-10: How often should this task be done?

3. **Choose the Daily, Weekly, Monthly, or Yearly option to specify how often the appointment occurs.**

   Each option — Daily, Weekly, Monthly or Yearly — offers you choices for when the task recurs. For example, a daily recurring task can be set to recur every day, every five days, or whatever. A monthly recurring task can be set to recur on a certain day of the month, such as the 15th of each month or on the second Friday of every month.

4. **In the Recur Every box, specify how often the appointment recurs, such as every third day or the first Monday of each month.**

   If you choose to create a monthly task, for example, you can click the scroll-down buttons (triangles) to choose First and then choose Monday to schedule a task on the first Monday of each month.

5. **In the Range of Recurrence section, enter the first occurrence in the Start box.**

6. **Choose when you want the appointments to stop (no end date, after a certain number of occurrences, or at a certain date).**

7. **Click the OK button.**

   A banner appears at the top of the Task form describing the recurrence pattern of the task.

8. **Click the Save & Close button.**

Your task appears in the list of tasks once, but it has a different type of icon than nonrecurring tasks so that you can tell at a glance that it's a recurring task.

Creating a regenerating task

A *regenerating task* is like a recurring task, except that it recurs only when a certain amount of time passes after the last time you completed the task. Suppose that you mow the lawn every two weeks. If it rains for a week and one mowing happens a week late, you still want to wait two weeks for the next one. If you schedule your mowings in Outlook, you can use the Regenerating Task feature to enter your lawn-mowing schedule.

Follow these steps to create a regenerating task:

1. **Open the task by double-clicking it.**

   The Task form appears.

2. **Click the Recurrence button in the Ribbon (or press Ctrl+G).**

   The Task Recurrence dialog box appears (see Figure 9-11).

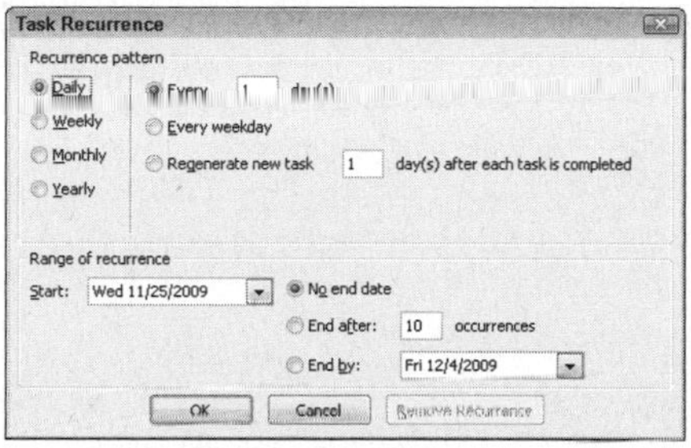

Figure 9-11:
Regenerate
a task in
the Task
Recurrence
dialog box.

Task Recurrence

Recurrence pattern

- Daily
- Weekly
- Monthly
- Yearly

- Every [1] day(s)
- Every weekday
- Regenerate new task [1] day(s) after each task is completed

Range of recurrence

Start: Wed 11/25/2009

- No end date
- End after: [10] occurrences
- End by: Fri 12/4/2009

OK   Cancel   Remove Recurrence

3. **Click the Regenerate New Task option.**

4. **Enter the number of days between regenerating each task.**

5. **Click the OK button.**

   A banner appears in the Task form that describes the regeneration pattern you've set for the task.

6. **Click the Save & Close button.**

Your task appears in the list of tasks once, but it has a different type of icon than nonrecurring tasks have so that you can tell at a glance that it's a regenerating task.

Skipping a recurring task once

When you need to skip a single occurrence of a recurring task, you don't have to change the recurrence pattern of the task forever; just skip the occurrence you want to skip and leave the rest alone.

To skip a recurring task, follow these steps:

1. **Click the Tasks button in the Navigation pane (or press Ctrl+4).**

   Your list of tasks appears.

2. **Click the words *Simple List* in the Current View section of the Ribbon.**

   It doesn't matter which view you use, as long as you can see the name of the task you want to skip. I suggest the Simple list because it's . . . well, simple.

3. **Double-click the name of the task you want to change.**

   The Task form appears.

4. **Click the Skip Occurrence button in the Ribbon.**

   The due date changes to the date of the next scheduled occurrence.

5. **Click the Save & Close button.**

   Your task remains in the list with the new scheduled occurrence date showing.

Marking Tasks Complete

Marking off those completed tasks is even more fun than entering them, and it's much easier. If you can see the task you want to mark complete in either the To-Do bar or your Task list, just right-click the item and choose Mark Complete. Nothing could be simpler.

To mark a task complete, follow these steps:

1. **Click the Tasks button in the Navigation pane (or press Ctrl+4).**

   The Tasks module opens.

2. **Click the words *Simple List* in the Current View section of the Ribbon.**

   Actually, you can choose any view you want, as long as the task you're looking for shows up there. If the task that you want to mark complete isn't in the view you chose, try the Simple list, which contains every task you've entered.

3. **Select the check box next to the name of the task that you want to mark complete.**

   The box in the second column from the left is the one you want to select (see Figure 9-12). When you select the check box, the name of the task changes color and gets a line through it. You're finished.

You can view a list of the tasks that you've marked complete by clicking the words *Completed Tasks* in the Current View section of the Ribbon. All the jobs you've polished off show up there in a nice, neat list. Ah! How satisfying!

Outlook has more than one place for marking tasks complete. You can look at the Task list I just described, as well as certain views of your calendar and also the list of tasks in Outlook Today.

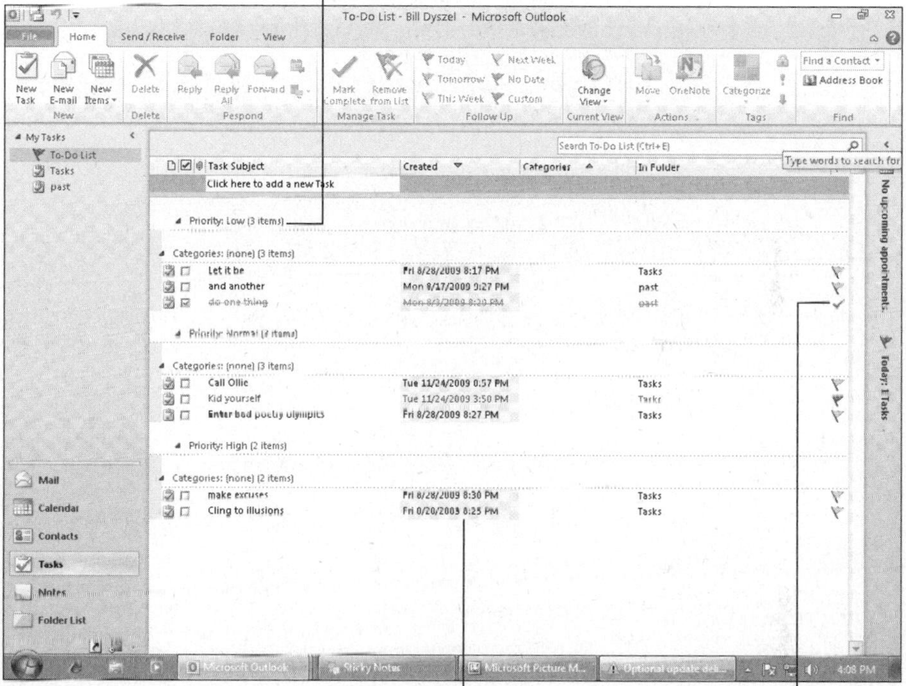

The priority of your tasks is shown at the top of each group.

Figure 9-12:
A check
marks the
task
complete.

The date on which you
entered each task

A check appears next to
tasks you've marked
completed.

Picking a color for completed or overdue tasks

When you complete a task or when it becomes overdue, Outlook changes the color of the text for the completed tasks to gray and the overdue tasks to red, which makes it easy for you to tell at a glance which tasks are done and which tasks remain to be done. If you don't like Outlook's color choices, you can pick different colors.

Here's how to change the color of completed and overdue tasks:

1. **Click the File tab.**

   The Office menu appears.

2. **Click Options.**

   The Outlook Options dialog box appears.

3. **Click Tasks.**

   The Task Options page appears (as shown in Figure 9-13).

When you click inside the Daily Task List,
a special set of tools appears to help you
manage your tasks.

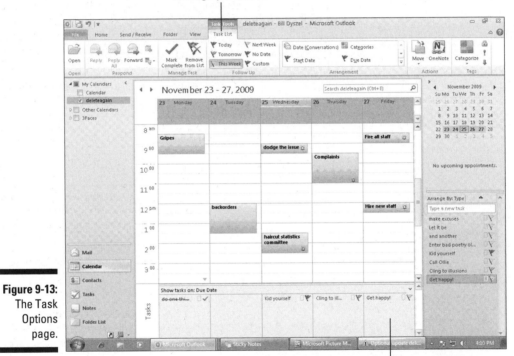

Figure 9-13:
The Task
Options
page.

The Daily Task List lets you display your tasks below
your calendar in a way that makes it easy to associate
tasks with the days when you have time to do them.

4. **Click the Overdue Task Color button.**

   A list of colors drops down.

5. **Choose a color for overdue tasks.**

6. **Click the Completed Task Color button.**

   A list of colors drops down.

7. **Choose a color for completed tasks.**

8. **Click the OK button.**

Your completed and overdue tasks will appear in your list in the colors you chose.

Viewing Your Tasks

Outlook comes with several ways to view your Task list and enables you to invent and save as many custom views as you like. The views that come with Outlook take you a long way when you know how to use them.

To change the view of your tasks, click the name of one of the following views from the Current View list in the Navigation pane:

✔ **Simple List** view presents just the facts — the names you gave each task and the due date you assigned (if you assigned one). The Simple List view makes it easy to add new tasks and mark old ones complete. However, you won't see any extra information. If you want details . . .

✔ **Detailed** view is a little more chock-full of the fiddly bits than the Simple List view. It's really the same information, plus the status of the tasks, the percentage of each task complete, and whatever categories you may have assigned to your tasks.

✔ **Active** view shows you only the tasks you haven't finished yet. After you mark a task complete — zap! Completed tasks vanish from the Active view, which helps keep you focused on the tasks remaining to be done.

✔ **Next Seven Days** view is even more focused than the Active view. The Next Seven Days view shows only uncompleted tasks scheduled to be done within the next seven days. It's just right for those people who like to live in the moment, or at least within the week.

✔ **Overdue Tasks** view means you've been naughty. These are tasks that really *did* need to be "done yesterday" (when it *was* yesterday) but are still hanging around today.

✔ **Assigned** view lists your tasks in order of the name of the person upon whom you dumped, er, I mean *to whom you delegated,* each task.

✔ **Completed** view shows (you guessed it) tasks you've marked complete. You don't need to deal with completed tasks anymore, but looking at the list gives you a warm, fuzzy feeling, doesn't it?

- **To-Do List** view includes all the tasks you've entered as well as any flagged e-mails that show up in the To-Do bar. The other Task List views only show the items you've added directly to the Task list.

- **Prioritized** view groups your tasks according to the priority that you've assigned to each one (see Figure 9-14). That way, you know what's important as well as what's urgent.

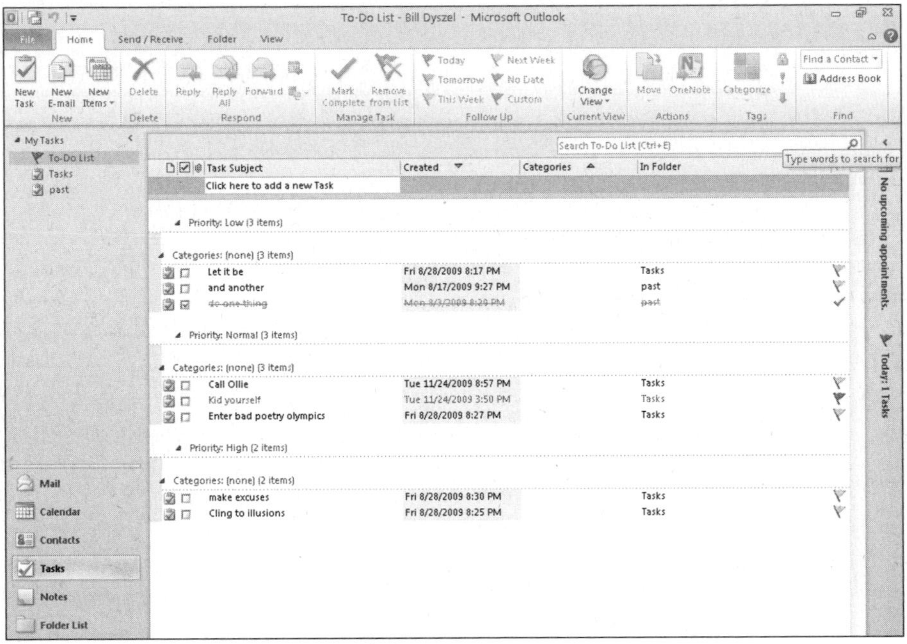

Figure 9-14: The Prioritized view helps you balance your workload.

Tasks in the Calendar

The Task list and the To-Do bar help you track what you need to do. After that, you need to figure out when you have time to do all that stuff. That's why Outlook offers a display of upcoming tasks in the Weekly view of your calendar (see Figure 9-15). In a strip along the bottom of the screen, you see icons that represent tasks whose due dates fall on each of the days displayed. If you find that you've stacked up more to-dos than can be done on a single day, just drag the task to a day when it can be done. You can even drag a task up to a particular hour in the calendar and reserve a specific time to get that thing done.

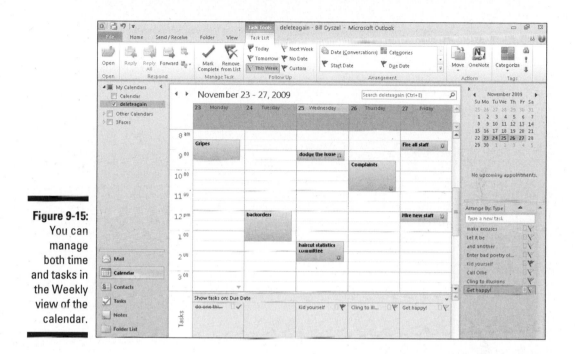

Figure 9-15:
You can
manage
both time
and tasks in
the Weekly
view of the
calendar.

Chapter 10

For the Record: Notes and Journal Entries

*T*he simple, dopey features of a program are often my favorites — the features I end up using all the time such as Outlook Notes and the Outlook Journal. Outlook Notes is my favorite underappreciated feature. There's really nothing earth-shattering about Notes, and certainly nothing difficult. This feature is just there when you need it — ready to record whatever strange, random thoughts are passing through your head while you're doing your work. (As you can tell from my writing, strange, random thoughts are a common occurrence for me. That's why I love using Notes.)

The Journal is Outlook's most underappreciated feature, a place for recording who did what and when they did it. The feature gets so little use that it no longer rates a button in the Navigation pane the way it did when Outlook was a new product. But just because the Journal is easy to overlook doesn't mean that it can't do a lot for you.

Writing a Note

How did we ever live without those little yellow stick-on notes? They're everywhere! The funny thing about stick-on notes is that they came from an inventor's failure. A scientist was trying to invent a new formula for glue, and he came up with a kind of glue that didn't stick very well. Like the computer scientists who came later, he said, "That's not a bug; that's a feature!" Then he figured out how to make a fortune selling little notes that didn't stick too well. It's only natural that an invention like this would be adapted for computers.

A note is the only type of item you can create in Outlook that doesn't use a normal dialog box with menus, ribbons, or toolbars. Notes are easier to use — but somewhat trickier to explain — than other Outlook items; I can only describe the objects you're supposed to click and drag. No name appears on the Note icon, and no name exists for the part of the note you drag when you want to resize it (although you can see what one looks like in Figure 10-1).

Figure 10-1:
Your note
begins as a
nearly blank
box.

11/25/2009 4:12 PM

Tricky notes

Each time you start a program, the Windows taskbar at the bottom of the screen adds an icon. That way, you know how many programs you're running. If you click an icon for a program on the taskbar, you switch to that program. If you start Word and Excel, for example, you see two icons on the taskbar. When you have two or more documents open in Word or Excel, you see one icon for each document.

When you create a new item in Outlook, a second icon remains available on the taskbar for the item you're creating. The icon remains until you close and save the item. It's like having

two or more programs open in Windows simultaneously. The advantage of this arrangement is that you can leave something like a note open for a long time and keep switching to it to add comments. The disadvantage is that if you don't look at the taskbar to see how many notes you have open, you may be creating a clutter of notes when you may prefer just one.

Another advantage is that you can have two notes open at the same time, or a note and an e-mail message, and drag text from one to the other.

Here's the basic scoop on how to take virtual notes while doing your work:

1. **Click the Notes button in the Navigation pane (or press Ctrl+5).**

   The Notes list appears.

   You don't actually have to go to the Notes module to create a new note; you can press Ctrl+Shift+N and go right to Step 3. I suggest going to the Notes module first only so that you can see your note appear in the list of notes when you finish. Otherwise, your note seems to disappear into thin air (even though it doesn't). Outlook automatically files your note in the Notes module unless you make a special effort to send it somewhere else.

2. **Click the New button.**

   The blank Note box appears.

3. **Type what you want to say in your note (as shown in Figure 10-2), and click the Note icon in the upper-left corner of the note.**

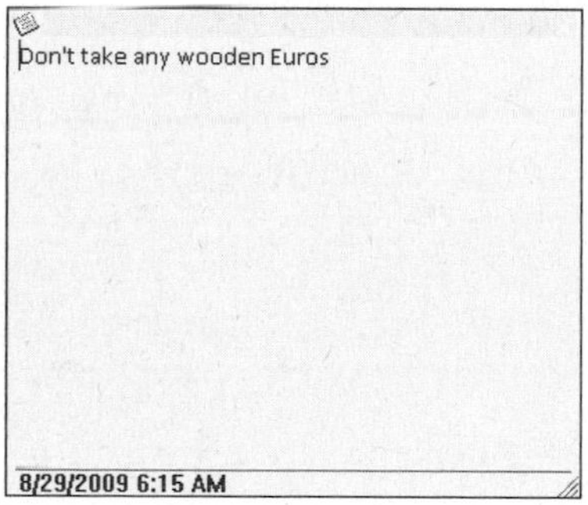

Figure 10-2:
You can write a note to remind yourself of something.

> Don't take any wooden Euros
>
> 8/29/2009 6:15 AM

4. **Press Esc.**

   An even quicker way to create a note is to press Ctrl+Shift+N in any Outlook module. You don't see your note listed with all the other notes until you switch to the Notes module, but you can capture that thought before you drift back to online shopping.

Finding a Note

Unlike paper stick-on notes, Outlook notes stay where you put them so that you can always find them — or at least your computer can find them. As a matter of fact, you can find any item you create in Outlook just by using the Search tool. (I wish I had a Search tool to help me round up all my lost galoshes and umbrellas.)

Here's how to find a misplaced note:

1. **Click the Notes button in the Navigation pane.**

   Your list of notes appears. The Search box appears at the top of the screen; see Figure 10-3.

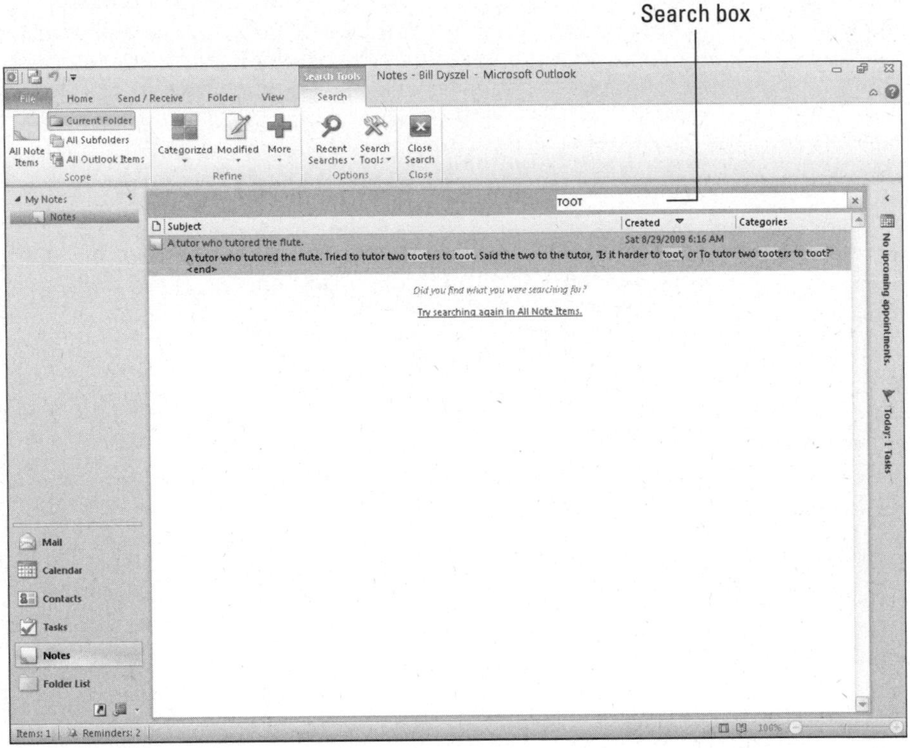

Search box

Figure 10-3:
The Search
Notes box.

2. **In the Search box, type the word or phrase you're looking for.**

   Don't worry about capitalization. Outlook doesn't rely on it.

3. **If the note you're looking for turns up, double-click the Note icon to read what the note says.**

Reading a Note

When you write a note, no doubt you plan to read it sometime. Reading notes is even easier than writing them. To read a note, follow these steps:

1. **Click the Notes button in the Navigation pane.**

   Your list of notes appears.

2. **Double-click the title of the note you want to open.**

   The note appears on-screen (as shown in Figure 10-4). You can close the note when you're done by pressing Esc.

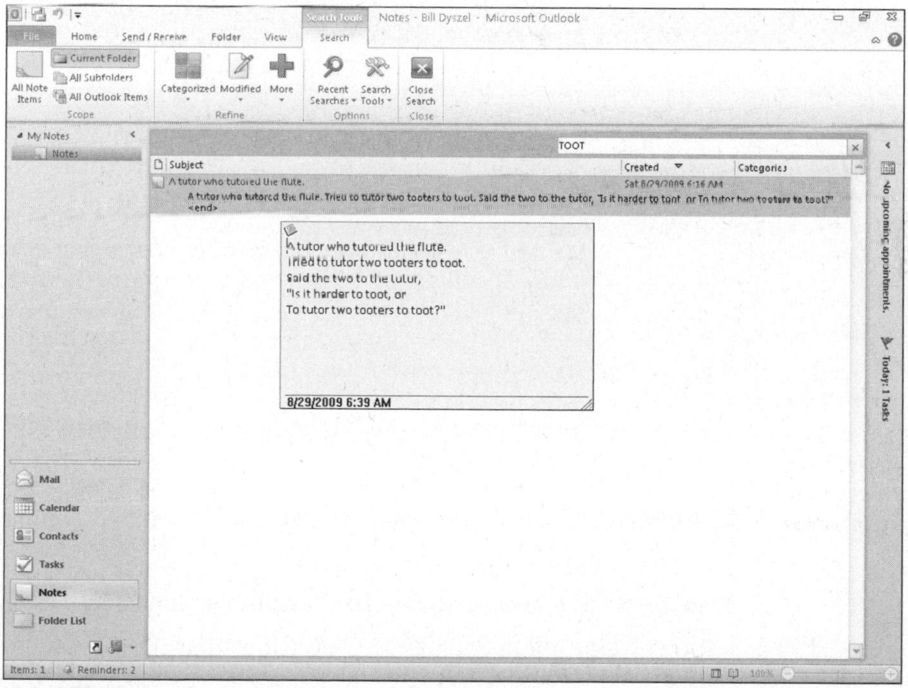

Figure 10-4:
Ah ha! The missing note is found.

Funny how notes look the same when you're reading them as they do when you're writing them.

Deleting a Note

What if you change your mind about what you wrote in a note? Fortunately, notes don't have to stick around forever. You can write one this morning and throw it out this afternoon. What could be easier?

Here's how to delete a note:

1. **Click the Notes button in the Navigation pane.**

   Your list of notes appears.

2. **Click the title of the note you want to delete.**

3. **Click the Delete button in the Ribbon (or simply press Delete).**

   Poof! Your note is gone forever.

Changing a Note's Size

You may be an old hand at moving and resizing boxes in Windows. Notes follow all the rules that other Windows boxes follow, so you'll be okay. If you're new to Windows and dialog boxes, don't worry — notes are as easy to resize as they are to write and read.

To change the size of a note, follow these steps:

1. **Click the Notes button in the Navigation pane (or press Ctrl+5).**

   Your list of notes appears.

2. **Double-click the title of the note you want to open.**

   The note pops up.

3. **Move your mouse pointer to the lower-right corner of the note until the mouse pointer changes into a two-headed arrow pointed on a diagonal.**

   Use this arrow to drag the edges of the note to resize it. Don't be alarmed. Resizing boxes is much easier to do than to read about. After you resize one box, you'll have no trouble resizing another.

4. **Drag with your mouse until the note box is the size you want it to be.**

   As you drag the mouse pointer around, the size of your note box changes (as shown in Figure 10-5). Don't worry if the size doesn't come out right the first time; you can change the note size again by dragging with the mouse again.

Taking your pick: Multiple selections

When you're sorting your notes or assigning them to categories, one way to work a little faster is to select several notes simultaneously. If you want to select a group of notes that you can see one right after another in a list, click the first one and then hold down Shift while clicking the last one. That action selects not only the notes you clicked but also all the notes in between.

If you're selecting several items that aren't arranged next to one another, hold down Ctrl while clicking each item. The notes that you click are highlighted, and the others stay plain. Then you can open, move, delete, or categorize the entire group of notes you selected in a single stroke. To view several notes, right-click any notes you've selected and choose Open.

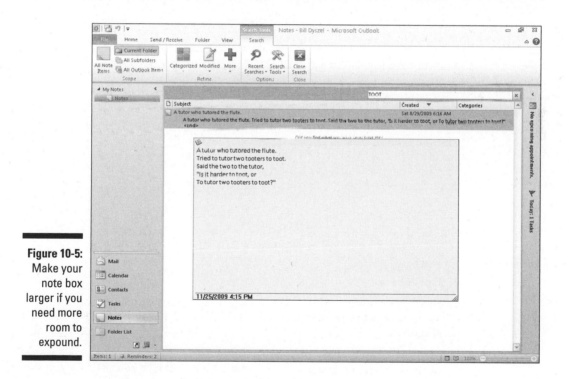

Figure 10-5:
Make your note box larger if you need more room to expound.

Viewing Your Notes

Notes are handy enough to stash tidbits of information any way you want, but what makes notes really useful is what happens when you need to get the stuff back. You can open your notes one by one and see what's in them, but

Outlook's Notes module offers even handier capabilities for arranging, sorting, and viewing your notes in a way that makes sense for you.

Icon view

Some folks like Icon view — just a bunch of notes scattered all over, as they are on my desk. Because I can already see a mess of notes anytime I look at my desk, I prefer organized lists for viewing my notes on my computer, but you may like the more free-form Icon view. To use Icon view, click the Large Icons button in the Current View section of the Navigation pane (shown in Figure 10-6). When you do, the screen fills with a bunch of icons and incredibly long titles for each icon.

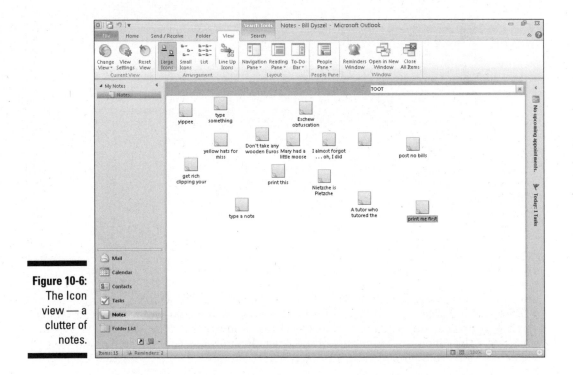

Figure 10-6:
The Icon view — a clutter of notes.

Outlook uses the entire text of your message as the title of the icon, so the screen gets cluttered fast. If you prefer creative clutter, this view is for you. If not, keep reading.

Notes List view

The Notes List view is as basic as basic gets. Just the facts, ma'am. The Notes List view shows the subject and creation date of each note, as well as the first few lines of text. To see the Notes List view, click the words *Notes List* in the Current View section of the Navigation pane to make a listing of your notes appear; see Figure 10-7.

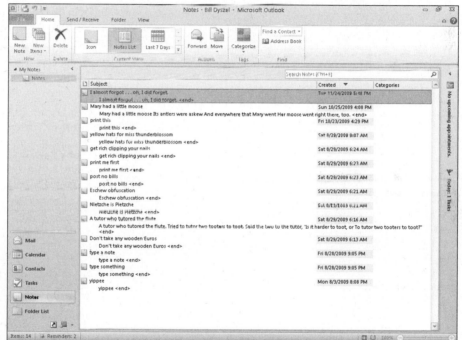

Figure 10-7: Your Notes List view.

 I usually recommend Notes List view for opening, forwarding, reading, and otherwise dealing with notes because it's the most straightforward. Anything you can do to a note in Notes List view, you can do in the other Notes views. The difference is that the other views don't always let you see the note you want to do things to.

Last Seven Days view

The notes you dealt with in the last few days are most likely to be the notes you'll need today. So, Outlook includes a special view of the notes you modified in the last seven days. You're more likely to quickly find what you're looking for in the Last Seven Days view. To see your notes for the last seven days, click the words *Last 7 Days* in the Current View section of the Ribbon. Figure 10-8 shows what you get.

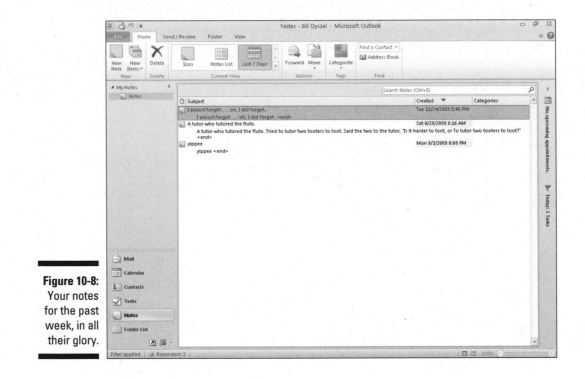

Figure 10-8:
Your notes for the past week, in all their glory.

If you haven't modified any notes in the past seven days, Last Seven Days view will be empty. If having an empty view bothers you, create a note. That'll tide you over for a week.

The Reading pane

Outlook notes aren't all that tough to read — just click the Notes button in the Navigation pane and read away. If you tend to write lengthy notes and need to see the full text of your notes regularly, you can open the Reading pane by clicking the View tab and choosing Reading Pane. When you do that, you'll see any note you select enlarged to fill half the screen.

Printing Your Notes

You can organize and view your notes in so many clever ways that you'll also want to print what you can see, or at least the list of what you can see.

Computer screens are pretty, but there's still nothing like ink on paper. Of course, you can print a note. Remember, though, that if you add color to your notes (as discussed in the next section), the colors don't show when you print them, even if you have a color printer. Colors just provide a way of organizing your notes.

To print a note, follow these steps:

1. **Click the Notes button in the Navigation pane.**

   The Notes list appears.

2. **Click the title of the note you want to print.**

3. **Click the File tab and choose Print.**

   The Print screen appears (see Figure 10-9).

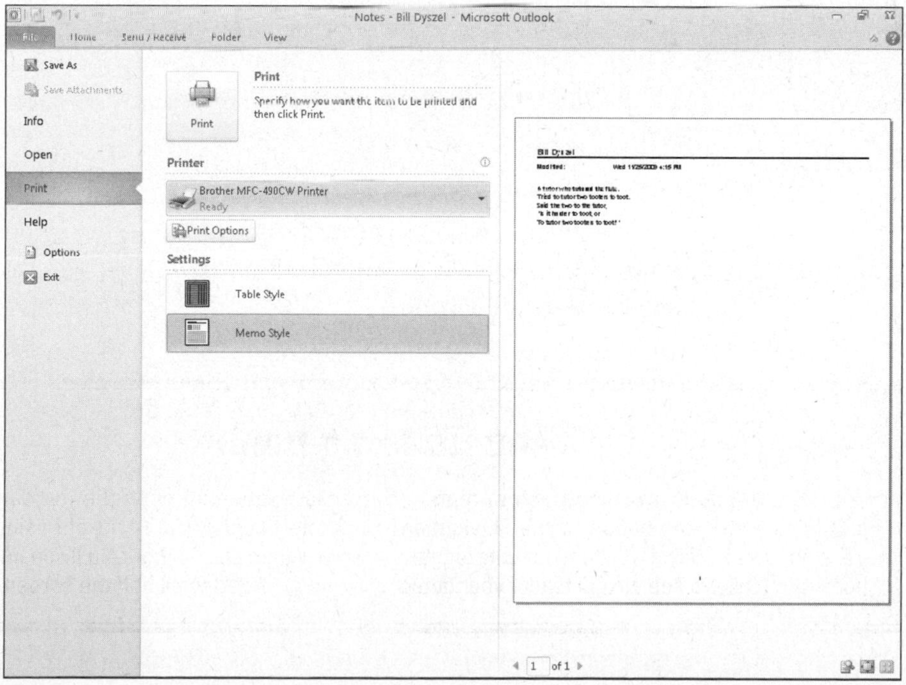

Figure 10-9: The Print screen.

4. Click the Print button.

Outlook prints the contents of your note.

If you want to print some, but not all, of your notes, click the first note you want listed and then hold down Shift while clicking the last note you want to appear in your printout.

Changing Your Default Options for New Notes

Plain old notes are fine; you really don't need to change anything. But if you want to make some changes, the Options dialog box on the File tab gives you lots of . . . well, options. All adjustments you make in the Options dialog box change the size, color, and other qualities of your note when you first create the note. You can also change these qualities after you create the note.

Changing the size and color

To change the color and size of your notes, follow these steps:

1. Click the File tab, and choose Options.

The Options dialog box appears.

2. Choose Notes and Journal.

The Notes and Journal page of the Outlook Options dialog box is where you change the options for the Notes module of Outlook.

3. Click the Default Color box.

A list of colors drops down (as shown in Figure 10-10). Choosing one changes the color of all your notes when you create them. The people at Microsoft seem to like pastels, because blue, green, pink, yellow, and white are the only colors they've offered for Notes since 1996. Perhaps burgundy and off-mauve notes will come into fashion in a century or so for more color-conscious computer users.

4. Choose a color.

5. Click the Default Size box.

You are offered Small, Medium, or Large. Choosing one of these options sets the size of your notes when you create them.

6. Click the OK button.

Your notes appear in the size and color to which you changed them.

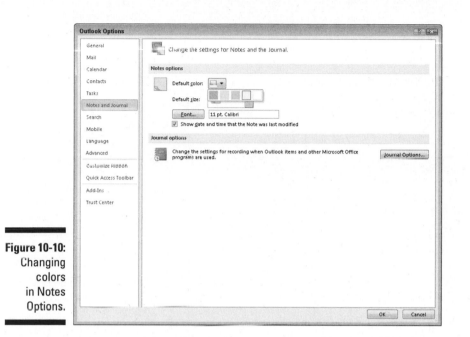

Figure 10-10:
Changing
colors
in Notes
Options.

Turning the date and time display on or off

At the bottom of each note, Outlook displays the date and time when you most recently changed the contents of the note. You may notice that you change a lot of notes on Mondays around 9:45 a.m. You may not want to notice that fact, so you can turn this handy little feature off.

To turn off the date and time display, follow these steps:

1. **Click the File tab, and choose Options.**

   The Options dialog box appears.

2. **Choose Notes and Journal.**

   The Notes and Journal page of the Outlook Options dialog box appears (see Figure 10-11).

3. **Select or deselect the Show Date and Time That the Note Was Last Modified check box.**

A check mark appears in the check box if you click once, and then it disappears if you click a second time. If you want to turn off the time and date display, make sure that the check box is deselected.

4. **Click the OK button.**

The time and date no longer show up on command, unless you follow the same steps you used in turning them off to turn them on again.

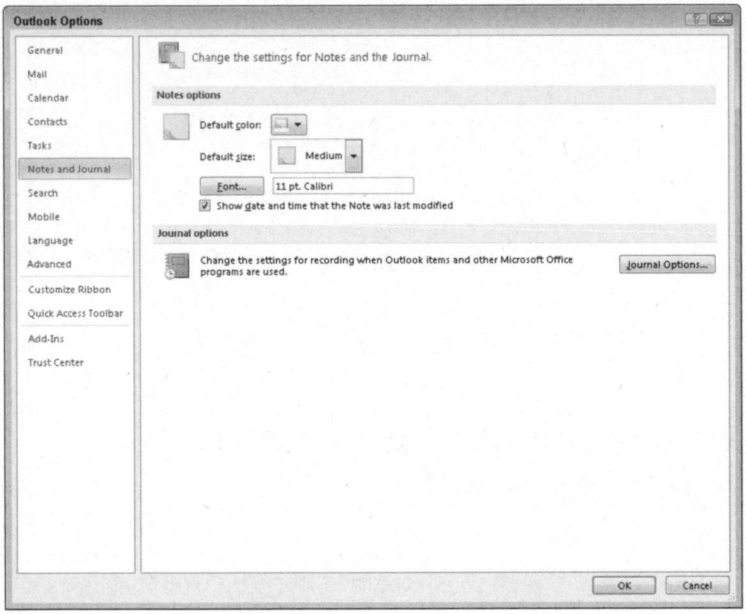

Figure 10-11:
Time for
some
advanced
options.

Forwarding a Note

Forwarding a note really means sending an e-mail message with a note included as an attachment. It's helpful if the person to whom you're forwarding the note uses Outlook, too.

Follow these steps to forward a note:

1. **Click the Notes button in the Navigation pane.**

The Notes list appears.

2. **Click the title of the note you want to forward.**

3. **Click the Forward button on the Ribbon's Home tab.**

The New Message form appears (as shown in Figure 10-12).

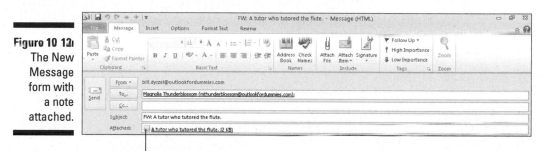

Figure 10-12: The New Message form with a note attached.

Attachment

4. **Click the To text box and type the e-mail address of the person to whom you're sending your note.**

   You can also click the To button to open the e-mail Address Book. Then just look up the name of the person to whom you want to forward your note, click the To button, and then click the OK button.

5. **Type the subject of the note in the Subject box.**

   The subject of your note will already be in the Subject box of the New Message form. You can leave it alone or type something else.

6. **If you want, type the text of a message in the text box.**

   You don't really have to include a message. Your note may say all you want to say, but you can also add regular e-mail message text.

7. **Click the Send button.**

   Your message is sent off to its intended recipient(s).

If your Outlook note includes the address of a page on the World Wide Web (such as www.dummies.com), you can simply click the address to launch your Web browser — just as you can in all the other Outlook modules.

Keeping a Journal for Tidy Recordkeeping

Sometimes, when you want to find a document or a record of a conversation, you don't remember what you called the document or where you stored it, but you do remember *when* you created or received the item. In this case, you can go to the Journal and check the date when you remember dealing with the item and find what you need to know.

To get good use from the Journal, though, you have to use it (details, details . . .). You can set Outlook to make journal entries for nearly everything you do, or you can shut the Journal off entirely and make no entries in it. If you put nothing in the Journal, you get nothing out.

Don't Just Do Something — Stand There!

What's the easiest way to make entries in the Journal? Do nothing. After it's turned on, the Journal automatically records any document you create, edit, or print in any Microsoft Office application. The Journal also automatically tracks e-mail messages, meeting requests and responses, and task requests and responses. A few programs other than the Microsoft Office applications also have the capability to make entries in the Journal, but that feature is most often used with Office programs.

There's a catch: You have to tell Outlook that you *want* automatic Journal recording turned on. (All right, so you *do* have to do something besides just standing there.) Fortunately, if you haven't activated the Journal's automatic recording feature, Outlook asks whether you want to turn the feature on every time you click the Journal icon.

To turn on the Journal's automatic recording feature, follow these steps:

1. **Click the File tab, and choose Options.**

   The Options dialog box appears.

2. **Choose Notes and Journal.**

   The Notes and Journal page of the Outlook Backstage view appears.

3. **Click the Journal Options button.**

   The Journal Options dialog box appears (as shown in Figure 10-13), offering check boxes for all the types of activities you can record automatically — and the names of all the people for whom you can automatically record transactions such as e-mail.

4. **Select the check box for items and files you want to automatically record and for contacts about whom you want information recorded.**

   The list of people in the For These Contacts box is the same as the list of people in your Contact list. You can manually create Journal entries for people who are not in your Contact list; see the following section of this chapter.

5. **Click the OK button.**

   The Journal promptly begins automatically recording the items and files you selected for the contacts you named.

Figure 10-13:
The Journal
Options dia-
log box.

Recording an Outlook item in the Journal manually

If you don't want to clutter your journal by recording everything automatically, you can enter selected items manually — just drag them to the Journal icon. For example, you may not want to record every transaction with a prospective client until you're certain you're doing business with that client. You can drag relevant e-mail messages to the Journal and retain a record of serious inquiries. When you actually start doing business with a new client, you can set up automatic recording.

Follow these steps to manually record items in the Journal:

1. **Click the Folder List button in the Navigation pane (or press Ctrl+6).**

   The Folder list, which includes a small icon for the Journal, appears in the Navigation pane.

2. **Drag the item you want to record (such as an e-mail message) to the Journal icon in the Folder list.**

   The Journal Entry form appears (see Figure 10-14) displaying an icon that represents the item you're recording, along with the item's name.

3. **Fill in any information you want to record.**

   You don't have to record anything. The text box at the bottom of the screen gives you space for making a note to yourself, if you want to use it.

4. **Click the Save & Close button.**

   The item you recorded is entered in the Journal. You can see your new entry when you view your journal, as I describe in the section "Viewing the Journal," later in this chapter.

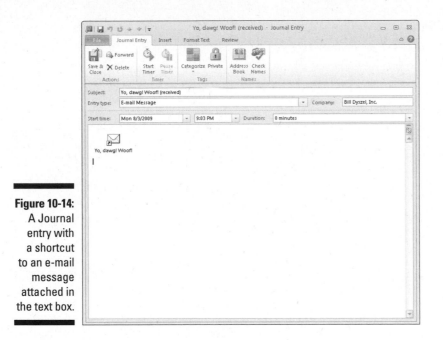

Printing Your Journal

I can't explain why, but I just don't get a complete picture from information on a screen. I still like to print my work on paper to really see what I've done. Printing your journal (or segments of it) enables you to see a printed list of recent or upcoming activities. Stick it on the wall where you can look at it often.

To print your journal, follow these steps:

1. **With the Journal open, select the entries you want to print.**

   If you select nothing, you print the entire list. Also, if you use one of the views I describe later in this chapter (or even create your own view by grouping, sorting, or filtering), what you see is what you print.

2. **Click the File tab and choose Print (or press Ctrl+P).**

   The Print dialog box appears (as shown in Figure 10-15).

3. **Choose Table Style or Memo Style.**

   Table style prints only a list of your journal entries, not the contents of each entry. Memo style prints the contents of your journal entries, with each item appearing as a separate memo.

4. **Click the Print button.**

The list of journal entries you selected prints.

The printed list won't go up on the wall for you, however, unless you put it there.

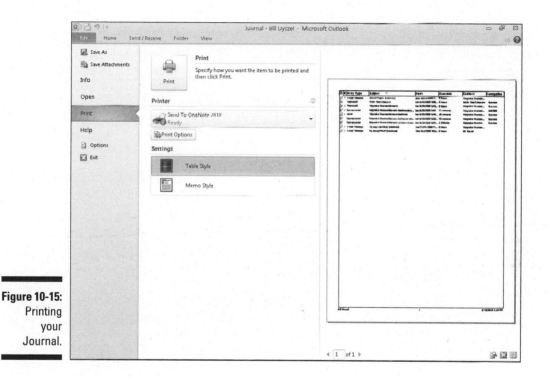

Figure 10-15:
Printing
your
Journal.

Viewing the Journal

As with other Outlook modules, the Journal comes with multiple views that show your entries in different ways, depending on what you want to see — whether that's a record of phone calls or a list organized by the names of the people you've dealt with. The Current view choices in the Ribbon enable you to change quickly from one view to the next.

The Entry List view

The Entry list shows the whole tomato — it's a view that lists all of your journal entries, regardless of whom, what, or when. To call up the Entry list, click the Entry List button in the Current View section of the Ribbon (shown in Figure 10-16).

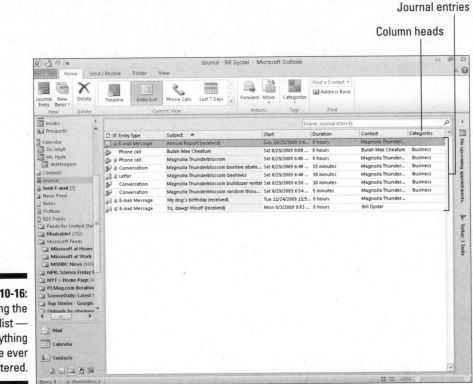

Journal entries

Column heads

Figure 10-16:
Viewing the
Entry list —
everything
you've ever
entered.

You can click the heading at the top of any column to sort the list according to the information in that column. If you want to arrange your list of Journal entries by the type of entry, for example, click the Entry Type header. Your list is sorted alphabetically by type of entry, with conversations before e-mail, e-mail before faxes, and so on.

Last Seven Days view

The items you're likely to need first are the ones you used last. That's why Last Seven Days view offers a quick way to see your most recent activities at a glance. To see a week's worth of Journal entries, click the Last Seven Days button in the Current View section of the Ribbon.

Documents you've created, phone calls, e-mail messages — anything you've done on your computer in the last seven days — can be seen in Last Seven Days view. This view shows anything you've worked on during the last week — including documents that you may have created a long time ago. That's why you may see some pretty old dates in this view.

Phone Calls view

Because you can keep track of your phone calls in the Journal, the Journal enables you to see a list of the calls you've tracked. Simply click the Phone Calls button in the Ribbon. To print a list of your phone calls, switch to Phone Calls view and press Ctrl+P.

Timeline

I've never, ever seen anyone use the Timeline view, an arrangement that shows a strange little chronologically ordered diagram of all your journal entries to show which entries you created first and which you created last. If you keep track of the time you spend on things like phone calls, longer calls take up more space than shorter ones. Clicking the Timeline button in the Ribbon does no harm, but it does very little good either.

It's All in the Journal

The Journal can be helpful whether you choose to use it regularly or rarely. You don't have to limit yourself to recording documents or Outlook items. You can keep track of conversations or customer inquiries or any other transaction in which chronology matters. If you set the Journal for automatic entries, you can ignore it completely until you need to see what was recorded. You can also play starship captain and record everything you do. (I haven't tried Outlook in outer space yet, but I know I would enjoy the view.)

Part IV

Beyond the Basics: Tips and Tricks You Won't Want to Miss

The 5th Wave   By Rich Tennant

"My spam filter checks the recipient address, http links, and any writing that panders to postmodern English romanticism with conceits to 20th-century graphic narrative."

In this part . . .

Many of Outlook's most powerful features aren't obvious. Some Outlook features appear in certain situations and disappear in others. This part shows you the special talents that Outlook can bring to your particular requirements, including the ability to monitor blogs and podcasts, connect from home, and communicate effectively with groups of any size.

Chapter 11

Social Media Magic with Outlook RSS

*E*verybody's doing it — social media that is. You've certainly heard about YouTube, Twitter, LinkedIn, and all the other Web services that seem to have hypnotized everyone. If you have trouble keeping up with social media gibberish, you're not alone; it changes much too quickly for most people to follow. In 2006, for example, MySpace was the number one destination on the Internet. By 2009, every tech conference expert I encountered swore that MySpace had gone out of style; Facebook had become everyone's darling. In just 30 months, MySpace went from tomorrow's hope to yesterday's news.

But social media is important. If you're still in the working world, these new services are no passing fad; social media trends now exert powerful influence on business, culture, and public policy. It doesn't matter which particular service predominates at the moment — you need to keep at least a casual awareness of developments in the world of social media because they could influence your business and your career.

Social Media Basics

It's easy to get confused in a world where social media properties appear and vanish daily. Fortunately, Outlook 2010 can help you keep current by neatly tracking your social media subscriptions along with your e-mail, contacts, appointments, and everything else you need to keep organized (see Figure 11-1).

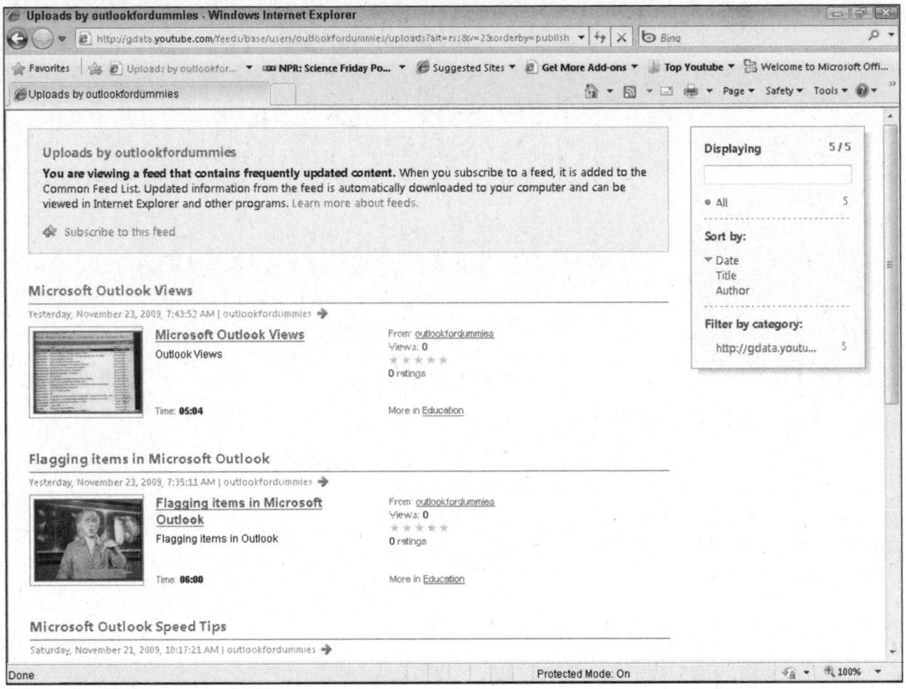

Figure 11-1:
You'll find
blogs and
RSS feeds
on nearly
any topic.

YouTube, blogs, and podcasts are three important segments of the social media world. You can ignore any of them if you want, but chances are that you're reading or viewing many of them already. In case you're new to social media, here's a rundown:

✔ **YouTube:** The big kahuna of Web video sites, YouTube is where 80 percent of Internet visitors go to watch videos. People watch more than a billion YouTube videos every month. You don't have to pay anything to watch YouTube videos; you can just go to www.youtube.com and watch as much as you like. Each person or company that posts videos to YouTube gets a channel in which all their videos are organized. You don't need Outlook to view YouTube videos, but you might want to have Outlook alert you when new videos appear on your favorite channels. YouTube has its own subscription mechanism, but it's strange and flaky — Outlook can give you much more timely notifications of new YouTube videos.

✔ **Podcasts:** Most radio stations — especially news, talk, and information stations such as National Public Radio — offer digital, downloadable editions of the programs they air. Those editions are called *podcasts;* you've probably heard that term mentioned frequently by your favorite radio personalities. While podcasts were originally designed to be played on portable devices, most people listen to podcasts on their computers. If your computer can run Outlook 2010, it can also run Windows Media Player, a program that plays podcasts. Podcasts are typically regular, recurring programs. You can download podcasts one at a time, or you can set up a subscription so that you receive them automatically. Outlook 2010 allows you to receive any podcasts to which you've subscribed and organize them with the same tools you use for organizing e-mail.

✔ **Blogs:** A few years ago, everyone talked about blogs as if they were some big, new, whiz-bang technology, but they're really not. If you surf the Web for news and information like everybody else, you may be reading blogs without even knowing it. Most major news services offer some kind of blog section where reporters and commentators post breaking news and current observations. A blog is really nothing more than a Web page that is designed to allow frequent updates. As with YouTube channels and podcasts, you can use Outlook 2010 to subscribe to your favorite blogs so that you can stay up to date with the newest entries without having to surf all over the Web to find out what's new.

The technique that lets you use Outlook to keep track of all this changing information is called RSS, which stands for *Really Simple Syndication* or *Rich Site Summary* or Rapunzel Sings for Suitors. (Okay, that last one's fake, but if you're a fairy-tale fan you know that she did. It worked pretty well.) RSS technology lets you subscribe to information that changes frequently so that it automatically updates itself. For example, most news organizations such as the *Wall Street Journal* and MSNBC offer RSS feeds of their news stories. When you want to see the latest headlines, you don't need to open a Web site. Just check the RSS feed to look for any headlines that interest you. Every time a new story is posted to the respective Web site, the story shows up on the RSS feed as well.

RSS information is delivered in something called a *feed.* As appetizing as that sounds, it's not very filling. In fact it's not even edible. A feed is just a mechanism for updating information as it changes. Blogs and podcasts usually offer RSS feeds that allow you to keep track of new entries or episodes. Most news services also offer RSS feeds so that you can read the latest news as it becomes available. *The New York Times,* the *Wall Street Journal,* the Associated Press, and lots of other news services include RSS feeds, and there's a good chance that your local newspaper offers one, too. Outlook has a separate folder for receiving RSS feeds so that you can organize the information in a way that you find useful. Generally, you don't need to know how RSS works, but it's good to know it's available when it's useful to you.

Read up

The word *blog* comes from the phrase *Web log,* a kind of open diary in which people post regular entries to a Web site for the whole world to see. Tens of millions of people write blogs these days. Most of those blogs are silly or terrible or totally useless, or all of those things. But even if some of the blogs out there are useless, far more of them are important sources of information you don't want to miss. *Business Week* magazine referred to blogs as "the most explosive outbreak in the information world since the Internet itself. Blogs are not a business elective; they're a prerequisite."

Subscribing to a YouTube Channel in Outlook

Most people watch YouTube videos these days. Some people watch way too many (I won't mention any names). Many of these videos are valuable, but most are a waste of time. How many skateboard face-plants do you really need to watch? (Ouch!)

When you run across a YouTube channel that posts videos that you want to watch regularly, you can subscribe to those channels with a few mouse clicks and you'll be up to date for good. You can often guess the location of a YouTube channel by typing **http://www.youtube.com** in the Internet Explorer address bar, then adding a slash sign and a channel name, as shown in Table 11-1.

Table 11-1	Finding a YouTube Channel
To Find the Channel for This:	*Enter This:*
CBS	www.youtube.com/cbs
PBS	www.youtube.com/pbs
The White House	www.youtube.com/whitehouse
Beyoncé	www.youtube.com/beyonce
Outlook For Dummies	www.youtube.com/outlookfordummies

Yes, this book has a YouTube channel, too. Why should you miss out on the fun? I'll be posting Outlook tips and tricks from time to time, so tune in.

You can also discover new channels by surfing around YouTube and seeing what pops up. Be careful, however — YouTube gets addictive quickly. If you find yourself missing meals or skipping work to watch YouTube, you're hooked. That's when it's time to subscribe to just a few YouTube channels in Outlook and only watch them. Your family will thank you.

Oddly enough, the simplest way to subscribe to YouTube channels in Outlook is to use Internet Explorer. You need Internet Explorer version 7 or later to do that. When you subscribe to a feed in either Outlook or Internet Explorer, that feed becomes available in both programs.

Internet Explorer makes it much easier to subscribe to YouTube channels and other feeds than Outlook does, so if you have a choice, Internet Explorer is the place to go to add a subscription.

To subscribe to a YouTube channel in Internet Explorer, navigate to the channel of your choice and follow these steps:

1. **Click the Feeds button at the top of the screen.**

   A new page opens.

   When you open a YouTube channel or other Web site that offers an RSS feed, the Feeds button at the top of the Internet Explorer screen changes from gray to orange.

2. **Click the Subscribe to This Feed link.**

   The Subscribe to This Feed dialog box appears; see Figure 11-2.

Subscribe to this Feed

Subscribe to this Feed
When you subscribe to a feed, it is automatically added to the Favorites Center and kept up to date.

Name: Uploads by outlookfordummies

Create in: Feeds ▾ New folder

☐ Add to Favorites Bar

What is a Feed?   Subscribe   Cancel

3. **Click the Subscribe button.**

   The Subscribe to This Feed dialog box closes.

Now you can view the feed in either Internet Explorer 7 or 8 or Outlook 2010. Each time that you subscribe to a new YouTube channel, a new folder that displays the channel name appears in the RSS Feeds folder in the Outlook Folder list in the Navigation bar. Just look inside that folder to see what's new. You'll see an entry for each video that looks just like an e-mail message with a picture from that video. When you double-click one of those pictures, the video it represents opens for viewing.

If the subscriptions you choose in Internet Explorer don't show up in Outlook, you may need to check one Outlook setting to make it work. Click the File tab in Outlook, then choose Options, and then choose Advanced. In the RSS section, you'll see the Synchronize RSS Feeds to the Common Feed List (CFL) in Windows check box. Select that check box and you're good to go.

Subscribing to Blogs in Outlook

Blogs work just like YouTube channels as far as Outlook is concerned, and you can subscribe to blogs following exactly the same steps that you use to subscribe to a YouTube channel. Blogs are a little bit easier to understand because they don't usually contain video, just text. In each entry for a blog subscription you'll see a View Article link. Click that link to see the whole blog posting.

Subscribing to Podcasts via Outlook

The term *podcast* is misleading. Lots of people think they can only listen to podcasts with a digital music player. Others don't listen to as many podcasts as they might enjoy because podcasts are a little bit cumbersome to find, download, and play.

You can subscribe to podcasts in Outlook the same way that you subscribe to any other RSS feed. However, you might want to add a few more steps to make it simpler to listen to the podcast after Outlook shows you that it's available.

There's nothing difficult about listening to podcasts, but the process is still somewhat more complex than just clicking the radio button. In the end, it's worthwhile because you get to listen to something that interests you, if you're willing to jump through a few hoops.

To subscribe to a podcast through Outlook, follow along:

1. **Click the File tab, and then choose Account Settings under the Account Settings button.**

   The Account Settings dialog box appears; see Figure 11-3.

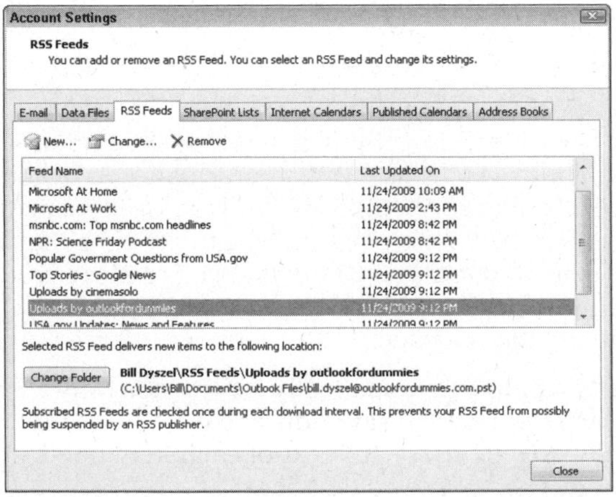

Figure 11-3:
The Account Settings dialog box.

2. Click the RSS Feeds tab.

The RSS sign up page shows the list of feeds to which you've subscribed.

3. Click the New button.

The New RSS Feed dialog box appears; see Figure 11-4.

Figure 11-4:
The New
RSS Feed
dialog box.

New RSS Feed

Enter the location of the RSS Feed you want to add to Outlook:

Example: http://www.example.com/feed/main.xml

Add   Cancel

4. Enter the URL of the RSS feed you want.

This typically looks like an unusually long URL: `http://www.cinema solo.com/atom.xml`. If you enter the address inaccurately, it won't work. Your best bet is to follow these steps:

1. Go to the site where the feed you want is hosted.

2. Right-click the XML, RSS, or Feed button. Different sites use differ-ent names for the same thing, but it's often an orange button.

3. Choose Copy Shortcut.

After you've done that, you can follow the preceding steps and paste the address into the New RSS Feed dialog box.

5. Click the Add button.

The RSS Feed Options dialog box (see Figure 11-5) shows a variety of changes you can make to your subscription:

• **Feed Name:** You can change the name that Outlook displays. Some feeds have long, clumsy names.

• **Delivery Location:** Some feeds generate huge amounts of informa-tion, so you may want to send that information to a special folder or even to a totally separate data file. That can be particularly true for podcasts. If you're on a big corporate network that limits the amount of e-mail messages you're allowed to store, you may want to send your RSS subscriptions to a separate Outlook data file to avoid running out of space.

• **Downloads:** Outlook automatically downloads only a brief sum-mary of each item, which saves disk space but requires you to manually download the full text of each item one by one. When you're subscribing to a podcast, it's best to select the Automatically Download Enclosures for This Feed check box so that you receive the actual podcast file along with the posting that describes it.

- **Update Limit:** Some RSS feed publishers don't let you update your information too frequently. If you try to update too often, they cancel your subscription. If there's a limit assigned to the feed you've chosen, this check box will automatically be selected.

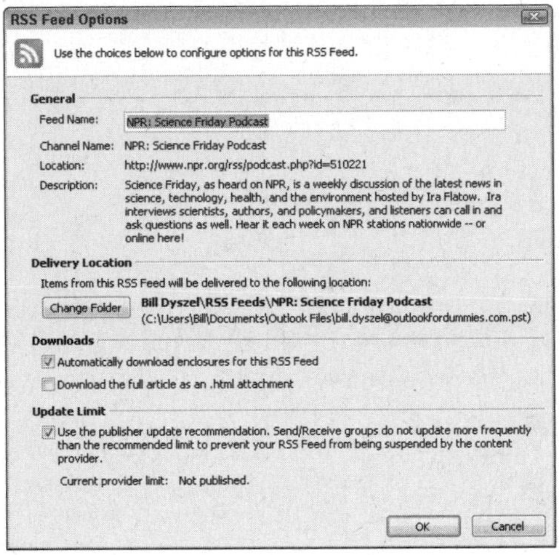

Figure 11-5:
The RSS
Feed
Options dia-
log box.

RSS Feed Options
Use the choices below to configure options for this RSS Feed.
General
Feed Name: NPR: Science Friday Podcast
Channel Name: NPR: Science Friday Podcast
Location: http://www.npr.org/rss/podcast.php?id=510221
Description: Science Friday, as heard on NPR, is a weekly discussion of the latest news in science, technology, health, and the environment hosted by Ira Flatow. Ira interviews scientists, authors, and policymakers, and listeners can call in and ask questions as well. Hear it each week on NPR stations nationwide -- or online here!
Delivery Location
Items from this RSS Feed will be delivered to the following location:
Change Folder   Bill Dyszel\RSS Feeds\NPR: Science Friday Podcast (C:\Users\Bill\Documents\Outlook Files\bill.dyszel@outlookfordummies.com.pst)
Downloads
☑ Automatically download enclosures for this RSS Feed
☐ Download the full article as an .html attachment
Update Limit
☑ Use the publisher update recommendation. Send/Receive groups do not update more frequently than the recommended limit to prevent your RSS Feed from being suspended by the content provider.
Current provider limit: Not published.
OK   Cancel

6. **Click the OK button.**

7. **Click the Close button.**

As you can see, subscribing to a podcast takes a few more steps in Outlook than it does in Internet Explorer, but you get more options. You can also subscribe to a feed through Internet Explorer, then go to Outlook's RSS page, select that feed, and click the Change button to modify your options.

IE versus Outlook

You don't absolutely need to use Outlook for reading RSS feeds. You can sign up for RSS feeds in several popular Web browsers, including Internet Explorer 7 or 8. If you have an earlier version of Internet Explorer, you can download the latest version for free from www. microsoft.com/windows/ie and get started with RSS. Internet Explorer is a good program for reading blogs and news feeds, but it doesn't offer any tools for managing the huge amount of information that RSS can deliver. That's where Outlook comes in. You can also buy a number of specialized programs for managing news feeds, but Outlook does a pretty good job if you're just getting started.

Reading Feeds

After you've subscribed to one or more RSS feeds, they appear in the RSS Feeds folder in the Outlook Folder list. No matter whether you've subscribed to YouTube channels, podcasts, blogs, or anything else, you can read feeds as easily as you read e-mail.

The Navigation pane has no button for RSS feeds, so you have to open the RSS folder to see what's inside. That means it takes a few more steps to read RSS feeds than to read e-mail, but after you find your way to the RSS folder, it's pretty easy.

Follow these instructions to read an RSS feed in Outlook 2010:

1. **Click the Mail button in the Navigation pane.**

   The list of mail folders appears.

2. **Click the plus sign next to the RSS Feeds folder.**

   The folders that contain RSS feeds appear; see Figure 11-6. Each folder contains one feed. If the RSS Feeds folder is accompanied by a triangle and no folders appear below it, no RSS feeds have been set up yet. You have to set up some feeds to make something appear there.

RSS Feeds folder

Figure 11-6:
Each
RSS feed
appears
in its own
folder.

Individual RSS feeds

3. Click the folder that contains the feed you want to read.

You can treat each item in a feed just as you'd treat individual e-mail messages. You can assign categories, move items to folders, and forward messages.

If you've subscribed to one or more podcasts and chosen to download the programs automatically, you'll need to double-click the attachment to the message file to launch Windows Media Player and listen to your podcast.

Sharing Feeds

It's nice to share. People like it when you share your dessert, your table at a restaurant, or especially your lottery winnings. If you run across an RSS feed that you like, Outlook lets you share that too, as long as the person with whom you want to share that feed has Outlook 2007 or later. Outlook 2010 shares feeds nicely with Outlook 2007, but earlier versions can't read RSS feeds.

To share a feed, just start reading an RSS feed you've added to Outlook and then click the Share This Feed button at the top of the screen, in the Ribbon. A specially formatted e-mail message appears, showing the name of the feed you've chosen to share. Just fill in the e-mail address of the person with whom you want to share, and you've done your good deed for the day.

If someone else has chosen to share a feed with you, you'll receive an e-mail message with the words `Subscribe to This Feed` at the top of the message. Just click those words and click Yes in the dialog box that pops up, and you have a new feed to read.

Using the Outlook Social Connector

Outlook 2010 includes a brand-new feature called the Outlook Social Connector or the People pane to help you keep track of the social media activities of your contacts and colleagues.

I know it sounds creepy at first, but in time you'll start to appreciate being able to see your colleagues' other activities, not just what they say in their e-mail message. Of course that may depend on the nature of your colleagues' other activities — sometimes you don't want to know.

The People pane appears in two locations in Outlook — at the bottom of the Reading pane when you're reading an e-mail and at the bottom of a person's contact record in the Contacts module.

The People pane can show you personal and social information that an individual has posted to Microsoft SharePoint, Windows Live, LinkedIn, and possibly other services after Microsoft creates connectors for other services.

If you want to view the People pane while you're reading an e-mail, click the People Pane button in the View tab of the Ribbon.

When you receive an e-mail from a person whose name you've added to your Contacts list, the information you've stored about him or her appears in the People pane. If you've added a picture to the contact record, that appears too. It doesn't matter whether you've added a picture of a pig or a bucket of slop to that person's contact record — whatever's in the contact record shows up in the People pane. It's fun — think of the possibilities!

If you work at a company that uses SharePoint, the information that your colleagues have posted about themselves on SharePoint will turn up in the People pane so that you don't have to go rummaging around the SharePoint server to find out what they've been doing.

Adding a LinkedIn Connection to Outlook

For business purposes, LinkedIn (www.linkedin.com) is the largest and best known social media service. Most of what you find on LinkedIn relates to work and business; you rarely find people describing what they had for breakfast or posting pictures of their kittens there. Many people find LinkedIn to be a valuable resource for finding jobs and discovering people with common business interests.

I've found that Outlook and LinkedIn make a productive pair. LinkedIn invites you to create links with people you know, both business acquaintances and personal friends. However, the people with whom you create connections on LinkedIn need to be LinkedIn members, too. Figuring out which LinkedIn members you might already know can be a time-consuming chore. Connecting LinkedIn with Outlook makes that task simpler and makes both products more valuable and easier to use.

When you add LinkedIn to the Outlook Social Connector, a new contact folder appears in the Navigation pane that displays the full list of people with whom you're connected on LinkedIn, including their pictures and contact information, organized just like your regular collection of Outlook contacts. It also includes a link to that person's LinkedIn profile in the Web site box, which allows you to look up information about that person in case you need to know detailed information.

Adding a LinkedIn connection to Outlook is pretty easy:

1. **To add a LinkedIn connection to Outlook, go to the contact record for that person and open the People Pane by clicking the triangle at the very bottom right corner of the contact record (it's hard to find, I know).**

2. **Click the green plus sign labeled Add on the lower left side of the People Pane.**

   A dialog box appears, from which you can find a list of networks you can add.

3. **Choose LinkedIn and click OK.**

Avoiding Social Mistakes

Microsoft product managers have promised to add connectors that will display information from many other social media services as time goes by. As I write this, Facebook, Twitter, and MySpace are the most popular social media services. You've probably heard of them, and you may even use one or more of them.

Regardless of whether or not you work at a company that uses Outlook 2010, when you send an e-mail to someone who does, it's possible that everything you post to a social media service such as LinkedIn, Twitter, MySpace, or Facebook might show up on their screen automatically. It's true that anyone can discover your social media activities if they look hard enough, but Outlook 2010 can make those activities much more visible to people who matter to your business or career. So be careful with those late-night online confessions. You don't know who'll see them and in what context. Eeek!

Chapter 12

Powering Your Home Office with Outlook

*W*orking at home is different from working in an office (but you knew that). Sure, working in your bunny slippers and bathrobe is pretty unusual in big companies, but telecommuters have to do without the huge network, multiple phone lines, and standing army of computer gurus that many office workers take for granted. That's why Outlook works a bit differently for the home user than it does for the corporate user — and this chapter shows the home user how to get the most from those differences. (If you use Outlook in a large corporation, you may want to skip to Chapter 14, which focuses on using Outlook in big business.)

Investigating an ISP

If you use a computer at home, you probably send and receive e-mail through an outside service. It might be your cable company, your phone company, or a service that your computer dials into over the telephone. The general term for the kind of outfit that provides this service is *Internet service provider,* or *ISP.* ISPs do more than exchange e-mail messages for you. An ISP also provides the Internet connection that enables your browser to access and display pages from the World Wide Web and enables you to do nearly anything that you can do on the Internet.

Keep your e-mail to yourself

Nearly every company that offers Internet connections also offers e-mail service. They often make their e-mail amazingly easy to set up and start using. Don't take the bait. After you set up an address with Verizon or Comcast and send e-mail from that address for a year or more, it gets more and more difficult to change your ISP because you have to notify everyone you know of your new e-mail address. You can get your own e-mail address from lots of different services; many of them are free. You can even set up your name as an e-mail address. For example, if your name is Mordecai Roblevsky, you could get the address `Mordecai@ Roblevsky.com`. If you have a more common name, such as John Smith, it might be too late to grab your name as an e-mail address. You could either choose a variation on your name or change your name to Roblevsky. My favorite service for setting up custom Internet and e-mail addresses is Go Daddy, at `www. godaddy.com`. Go Daddy provides good service overall, no matter how racy their Super Bowl commercials get. Microsoft also offers free e-mail through its Hotmail service (`www. hotmail.com`) as well as from its Windows Live service (`www.windows.live.com`). I like the Windows Live service because it lets you sign up for an e-mail address that ends with `live.com`. I just enjoy having an e-mail address such as *yourname*`@live.com`. It's so optimistic.

Online services, such as America Online and MSN (the Microsoft Network) once served as most people's ISPs, and they still offer that service along with a variety of other features, such as discussion forums and file libraries. If you belong to an online service, you don't need a separate ISP. On the other hand, if you're getting onto the Internet for the first time, it doesn't make sense to seek out a full-featured online service; a basic ISP is probably all you need.

Everything about the Internet and online services can — and does — change quickly. The best way to get and use an online service may change with the introduction of new technologies and services, but what I tell you here is how it is in 2010.

Picking a Provider

If you've never had Internet service, I have a question for you: Where have you been living? On Mars? Even Martians seem to be sending e-mail these days (although they all pretend to be princes from Nigeria). Anyway, you picked a good time to join the party. A fast, easy connection to the Internet is probably just a phone call away. When I moved into my current apartment building, high-speed Internet service was already built right into the walls like telephone service or electricity. I just had to plug one end of a computer network cable into the wall and the other end into my computer, make one phone call, and POOF! I had high-speed Internet service on the spot.

If your home didn't come equipped with Internet connections, check with your phone company or cable company to see what it offers. Maybe you can get the two companies to fight over you and give you a good deal. An extensive list of ISPs can also be found at www.thelist.com, but your local phone and cable providers are usually your best bet.

You may live in an area without high-speed Internet service, which is sad, as well as unlikely in the continental United States. Unless you live 40 miles from Nowhere, some phone or cable company is looking for a way to get high-speed service to you as soon as possible. You have no idea how much time you can waste until you can log on to dozens of useless Web sites every day. There also might be a dialup service in your community that can serve you. But if you have a choice, avoid dialup Internet connections — even if they are cheaper. Most Web sites today are designed for high-speed Internet users. You'll be tearing your hair out after a few hours of surfing most of the popular sites by dialup.

Setting Up Internet E-Mail Accounts

After you've signed up with an ISP, you can set up Outlook to send and receive e-mail from your account. Although any individual Internet e-mail account requires setup only once, you can set up many such accounts if you need them.

One catch with cable modems and DSL

If you have high-speed Internet access from your cable television operator or DSL through a telephone company, congratulations! You'll enjoy zippy Web surfing, and your e-mail will come and go in a flash. You also don't need to deal with a separate ISP, because your cable company or DSL provider does that job for you.

You might run across one catch if you get your Internet connection from one company (such as your cable company) and your e-mail service from another (such as Gmail). In that case, you may need to enter your ISP's mail server name for outgoing e-mail and your e-mail service's server name for incoming e-mail in the steps in the section "Setting Up Internet E-Mail Accounts." That's one method ISPs use to cut down on all that annoying junk e-mail that clutters up the Web. Whether that helps is hard to say, but be ready to deal with that in certain circumstances.

If you're a corporate user, your system administrators may not want you to mess around with account settings — and may have special arrangements and settings that they want you to use when you work from home. Either way, it's best to ask first.

If you're on your own, you should probably call the tech support line from your online service or ISP to get all the proper spellings of the server names and passwords. (Don't forget to ask whether they're case sensitive!)

To set up an Internet e-mail account, follow these steps:

1. **Click the File tab.**

   The Backstage view appears.

2. **Click the Account Settings button and choose Account Settings from the drop-down list.**

   The Account Settings dialog box appears (as shown in Figure 12-1).

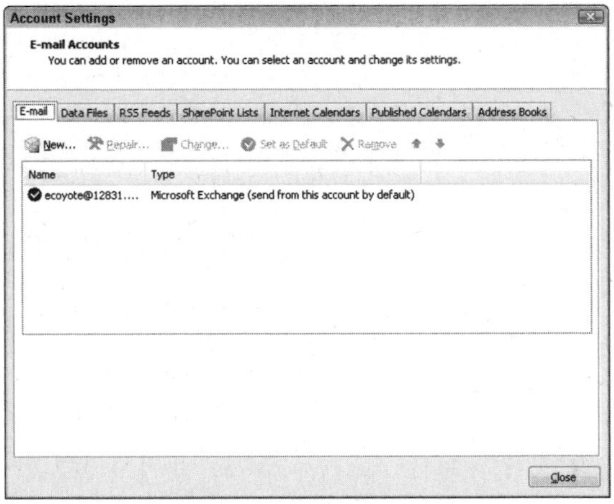

Figure 12-1:
The Account Settings dialog box is where you set up a new e-mail address.

3. **Click the E-mail tab.**

   The E-mail Accounts setup page appears.

4. **Click the New button.**

   The Add New Email Account dialog box appears.

5. **Click Microsoft Exchange, POP3, or IMAP option and then click the Next button.**

   The Add New Account dialog box appears.

6. **Fill in the blanks in the New Account dialog box.**

   Be careful to enter the information accurately — especially your e-mail address and password. Otherwise, your e-mail won't work.

7. **Click the Next button.**

A configuration screen appears, and Outlook begins trying to automatically configure your e-mail account. If it succeeds, the Congratulations screen appears and you can click the Finish button to complete the process.

If the automatic setup fails, check with your e-mail provider to see what settings are recommended. Then you can repeat the previous steps, except you should select the Manually Configure Server Settings check box right before Step 7. That opens the Server Type dialog box, which is where you can enter the settings that your e-mail provider tells you to enter. Each e-mail service differs, but most of them can tell you how to make their e-mail work with Outlook.

If you type one wrong letter in one of your e-mail settings, your messages won't go through. The computers that Outlook has to send messages through (called *servers*) are terribly literal, so it's good to find out whether your setup works while you're still tweaking your settings. The Account Settings dialog box has a button labeled Test Account Settings that you can click to be sure that you've set everything up correctly. If the test fails, try retyping some entries (and then clicking the Test Account Settings button again) until you get a successful test. When the test is successful, the Test Account Settings dialog box says `Congratulations! All tests completed successfully. Click Close to continue.` So that's what you should do.

As I mention earlier in this section, you can set up more than one Internet e-mail account, so each member of the family can have a separate address. You also may want to have different accounts for business use and personal use. Perhaps you just want to set up separate accounts so that you can send yourself messages. Whatever you like to do, the process is pretty much the same.

Your Web site, your e-mail

If you have a Web site, you can probably get a free e-mail account in connection with your site. So, if you have a site called `www.your company.com` (for example), you can also have an e-mail address that looks something like `yourname@yourcompany.com`.

There's an even better chance that the mail service that you get in connection with your Web site is compatible with Outlook. Ask the tech support people from the company that hosts your Web site what you have to do to set up Outlook with their e-mail service.

Dealing with Multiple Mail Accounts

You can use Outlook to exchange e-mail through more than one e-mail address. For example, I have different e-mail addresses for business use and personal use. If you want to create a similar arrangement, just set up a separate account for each address (using the method I describe in the previous section of this chapter).

Telling one Outlook account apart from another isn't too tough. Normally Outlook sends your reply to an e-mail message through the account in which you received the message. When you're replying, you don't have to think about which account you're using. When you're creating a message, however, Outlook sends the message through the account that you marked as the *default account* (the one it must use unless you specify otherwise). If you want to check which account a message will be sent through, click the Accounts button on the Message form's toolbar and look at the Send Message Using box.

If you use only the e-mail address provided by your ISP, you'll get along just fine. But if you want to set up a separate e-mail address for each member of your family, or keep your business e-mail separate from your personal messages, you can open an account with any number of mailbox providers.

Microsoft's Hotmail service is a good place to go for free e-mail accounts. You can either get an account that reads `yourname@hotmail.com` or you can pick other names such as `yourname@live.com`. The `live.com` e-mail addresses are particularly nice because they make people think that you have your own TV show. Mail.com (`www.mail.com`) is another popular provider of electronic mailboxes. You can sign up for an address through Mail.com for free and check your e-mail messages through your Web browser. If you want to take advantage of Outlook's sophisticated mail-management features with your Mail.com account, you can pay an extra $18 per year for what is called a *POP3 account*. (I've been using Mail.com for about ten years, and I think the company does a good job.) Other companies that offer e-mail services include Google (`http://gmail.google.com`) and Yahoo! (`www.yahoo.com`).

Chapter 13

Mail Merge from Outlook to Microsoft Word

*E*ven if you're an old hand at creating form letters and mailing labels in Microsoft Word, the Outlook Mail Merge tool makes it a snap to send letters to people in your Contacts list. It also helps you take advantage of all that precious personal information you've collected in your Contact list.

If you're new to the world of form letters, *mail merge* is the term that computer people use to describe the way you can create a letter on a computer and print umpteen copies, each addressed to a different person. You probably get lots of mail-merged letters every day, but you usually call it junk mail. When you *send* a mass mailing, it's called mail merge. When you *get* a mass mailing, it's called junk mail. But you knew that all along, didn't you?

But seriously, there are many things you might like about sending and receiving mass messages. You're probably glad when your favorite online retailer e-mails you a coupon for a 50 percent discount on all your favorite things. You may need to send a message to a whole group of people to notify them of a party or a meeting or to announce good news. Mass mailings are a part of life now, and often a good part. When you use the Mail Merge feature in Outlook 2010, Microsoft Word really does all the heavy lifting. Outlook just manages the names and addresses and passes them over to Word. If you're not running any version of Microsoft Word, you won't be able to run a Mail Merge from Outlook. I'm told that you can run the Outlook mail merge with any version of Microsoft Word, so if you're sentimental about your old word processors, you don't need to feel left out. As I write this, you can't even buy Outlook 2010 without buying the whole Office 2010 suite, so I assume that you have the latest version of both programs.

You can perform a mail merge without using Outlook, if you like. If you're sending a letter to people who aren't in your contact list (and you don't want to clutter your contact list with unnecessary names), you can use the Mail Merge feature in Microsoft Word. For more about Microsoft Word 2010, take a look at *Word 2010 For Dummies,* by Dan Gookin (published by Wiley).

Mailing Label Magic

You can create a set of mailing labels for everyone in your Address Book in a flash. The Outlook Contact list connects to Word's mail-merge features, so you don't have to mess around with exporting files and figuring out where they went when you want to merge to them. All you have to do is run the Outlook Mail Merge tool.

To create a set of mailing labels, follow these steps:

1. **Click the Contacts button in the Navigation pane.**

   Your list of contacts appears.

2. **Click the Mail Merge button in the Ribbon.**

   The Mail Merge Contacts dialog box appears (see Figure 13-1).

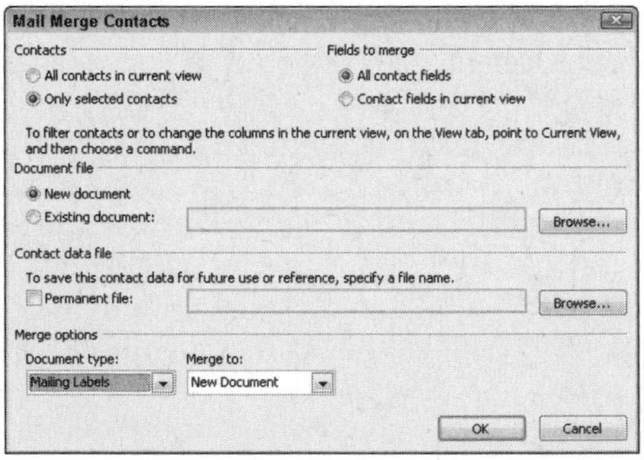

Figure 13-1:
The Mail Merge Contacts dialog box.

3. **Choose Mailing Labels from the Document Type list.**

   The document type list is at the lower-left corner of the Mail Merge Contacts dialog box. The words *Mailing Labels* appear after you make your choice.

4. **Choose New Document from the Merge To list.**

   The Merge To list appears just to the right of the Document Type list at the bottom of the dialog box. Normally, the words *New Document* appear automatically, so you don't have to do anything, but you might want to check to be sure.

5. Click the OK button.

Microsoft Word opens, displaying a dialog box that tells you that Outlook has created a Mail Merge document, but you have to click the Set Up button in the Mail Merge Helper dialog box to set up your document.

6. Click the OK button.

The Mail Merge Helper dialog box appears (see Figure 13-2).

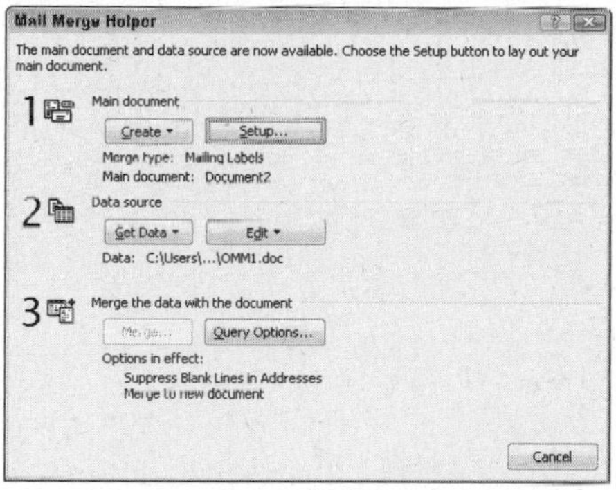

Figure 13-2:
The Mail Merge Helper dialog box.

7. Click the Setup button.

The Label Options dialog box appears (see Figure 13-3).

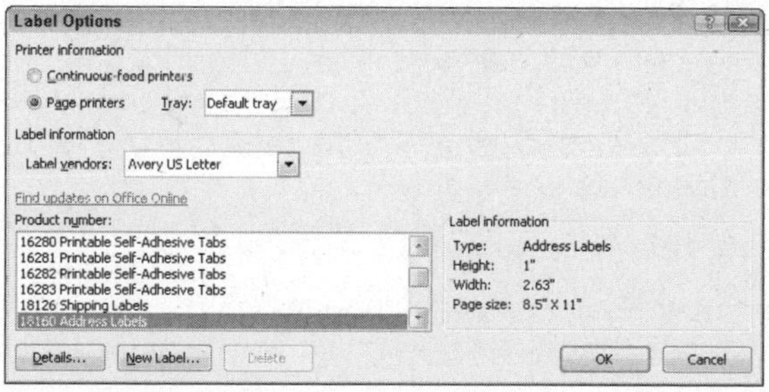

Figure 13-3:
The Label Options dialog box.

8. Choose the label type you want; then click the OK button.

Check the stock number on your label and make sure that it's the same as the one you're choosing. If the stock number isn't available, you can look at the label dimensions in the Label Information section of the Label Options dialog box. When you click OK, the Label Options dialog box closes.

9. Click the Close button in the Mail Merge Helper dialog box.

The Mail Merge Helper dialog box closes.

10. Click the Address Block button in the Microsoft Word Ribbon.

The Insert Address Block dialog box appears (see Figure 13-4) to show you which items of information will appear in the labels you're about to create. In the upper-left corner, you see a list that displays the different ways you might format someone's name, such as Josh Randall or Mr. Joshua Q. Randall. Each time you click a different choice, the results of your choice appear in the Preview box on the right side of the dialog box. You can also select or deselect the check boxes on the left side of the dialog box to include or exclude particular elements of the address. Again, each time you select a check box, the results appear in the Preview box. You don't actually have to do anything in the Insert Address Block dialog box; you can just leave everything alone if you like.

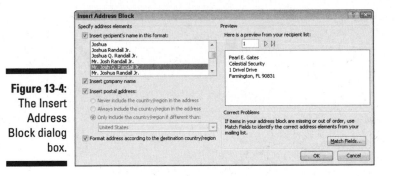

Figure 13-4:
The Insert
Address
Block dialog
box.

11. Click the OK button.

The Insert Address Block dialog box closes. Your document now displays a funny looking code that reads <<AddressBlock>>. That's called a merge code, which is what lets Microsoft Word know which information to place in your document.

12. Click the Update Labels button in the Ribbon.

Now the <<AddressBlock>> code appears many times in your document, to show that Word knows how to fill your page of labels with addresses.

13. Click the Preview Results button in the Ribbon.

Word displays your document the way it will look when you print it. If you like what you see, go to the next step. If you don't like what you see, you can start your merge again and fix whatever you didn't like.

14. Click the Finish & Merge button in the Ribbon.

The Merge to New Document dialog box appears, allowing you to print all the addresses you see in your document, or just part of them. In most cases, you'll choose All to print the whole range.

15. **Click the OK button.**

    You've now created your labels. You can click the File tab and choose Print to send your labels to the printer.

I like to test a mail merge in mailing-label format before doing an actual merge, just to be sure that everything works the way I want it to. You can print labels on regular paper to see what they look like. If you make a mistake setting up the merge, it's faster to find out by printing ten pages of messed-up "labels" on plain paper than by printing 300 messed-up labels.

If you print labels frequently, you can reduce your work by saving the blank label document and using it repeatedly. When you've finished creating your labels, press Alt+Tab a few times until you see a document that looks like your labels, except that it's filled with strange text that looks like this: <<Full_Name>><<Mailing_Address>> and so on. Save that document and name it something you'll remember, such as Blank Labels. The next time you decide to create labels, select the Existing Document check box in the Mail Merge Contacts dialog box. Then click the Browse button and double-click Blank Labels. That eliminates the preceding Steps 7 through 13 and lets you get on to more exciting things, such as stuffing envelopes.

Form Letter Formalities

Today I received a personalized invitation to enter a $250,000 sweepstakes that had my name plastered all over the front of the envelope. How thoughtful and personal! Whenever you get a sweepstakes letter with your name already entered, you're getting a *form letter*. A form letter is a letter with standard text that's printed over and over but with a different name and address printed on each copy. You can send form letters, too, even if you're not holding a sweepstakes. An annual newsletter to family and friends is one form letter you may want to create.

Follow these steps to create a form letter from Outlook 2010:

1. **Click the Contacts icon in the Ribbon.**

   Your list of contacts appears.

2. **Click the Mail Merge button in the Ribbon.**

   The Mail Merge Contacts dialog box appears.

3. **Choose Form Letters from the Document Type list.**

   The document type list is at the lower-left corner of the Mail Merge Contacts dialog box. The words *Form Letters* appear after you make your choice.

4. **Choose New Document from the Merge To list.**

   The Merge To list appears just to the right of the Document Type list at the bottom of the dialog box. Normally, the words *New Document* appear automatically, so you don't have to do anything, but you might want to check to be sure.

5. **Click the OK button.**

   Microsoft Word starts up, displaying a blank document.

6. **Type your form letter, clicking the Insert Merge Field button in the Ribbon to insert merge fields everywhere you want data from your Outlook Address Book to appear in your form letter.**

Now you don't have to settle for sending impersonal, annoying form letters to dozens of people; you can send a personal, annoying form letter to hundreds of people. If you're planning to send an annoying form letter to me, my address is 1600 Pennsylvania Avenue, Washington, D.C.

Merging from Selected Contacts

You probably don't want to send a letter to every person in your contact list. It's easy to end up with thousands of names in your list — the postage alone could cost a fortune. To limit your list of letters or mailing labels to just a handful of contacts, hold down Ctrl and click the names of the people you want to include. After you've selected everyone you want, click the Mail Merge button. The Mail Merge tool creates letters or labels only for the people whose names you select.

Printing Envelopes

You don't have to print to labels if you're planning a mass mailing; you can print directly onto the envelopes that you're sending. With luck, your printer has an envelope feeder. Feeding envelopes one at a time gets old fast.

To print addresses directly onto your envelopes, follow exactly the same steps that I describe in the previous section for creating mailing labels. The only difference you'll notice is that in Step 8, the Envelope Options dialog box appears, with a choice of envelope sizes. Pick the type of envelope you're using (usually number 10, the standard business envelope) and follow the rest of the steps.

If you've never printed multiple envelopes on your printer before, start small. Try printing four or five, just to make sure that your printer feeds envelopes properly. Word and Outlook happily send your printer a command to print hundreds of envelopes in a flash. If your printer chokes on the fourth envelope, however, fixing the problem can take a long time.

If you're printing only one envelope, your best bet is to go right to Microsoft Word and click the Envelopes button in the Ribbon. That opens the Envelopes and Labels dialog box, which has a tiny Address Book icon that lets you pick a name from your Outlook Contact list and add it directly to an envelope or label.

Merging to E-Mail

Another very appealing feature of the Outlook Mail Merge tool is the ability to create merged e-mail. Usually, you don't need to use mail merge for e-mail because you can send a single e-mail message to as many people as you want. But if you want to send an e-mail message to a bunch of people and customize each message, you can do that with a mail merge to e-mail. That way, you won't send your "Dear John" message to George, Paul, or Ringo.

To merge to e-mail, follow the same steps you use to create a form letter, but choose E-Mail instead of New Document from the Merge To list in the Mail Merge Contacts dialog box.

If you're using Outlook on a Microsoft Exchange network, your document goes right to your recipient as soon as you click the Merge button. If you've made a mistake, there's no chance to fix it. I recommend testing your e-mail merge by sending an e-mail to yourself first. Click your own name in the Contact list and then put together your merge message. When you're sure that you've said what you meant to say, select all the people you want to contact and then go ahead with the merge. If you use Outlook at home, you can press Ctrl+Shift+O to switch to your Outbox and see the collection of messages before pressing F9 to send your messages.

Going Pro with Hosted Mailing Services

When your business goals drive you to launch a campaign of mass mailings and e-mail marketing, Outlook's built-in tools are a good enough place to start, but eventually you may want to consider using one of the fine professional services that specialize in e-mail marketing. In addition to making your campaigns look more businesslike, a professional service can help you grow your mailing list and keep track of important information such as who reads each message, how many clicked a link in your message, and how many messages "bounced" back due to an out-of-date e-mail address. Many of the best-known e-mail marketing services can import your contacts from Microsoft Outlook.

Also, your e-mail service provider might cut you off when you try to send too many e-mail messages from Outlook at one time. Many of them do that to reduce the amount of unsolicited "spam" e-mail that goes out from their service. Their purpose is laudable, but they might be preventing you from e-mailing important information to legitimate customers.

A professional e-mail marketing service can also make your whole marketing program more effective with features such as:

- E-mail list cleanup
- Statistics on the success of each campaign
- A/B testing of different versions of e-mail copy to see which is more effective
- Delivery assurance options to make sure your messages don't get blocked as spam.
- Technical support

Each service has particular strengths that may or may not suit your specific needs. There's no doubt, though, that for many businesses, e-mail marketing is the most cost-effective way to improve your business and cultivate long-term relationships with your customers. Some well-known names in the email marketing business include:

- Constant Contact at www.constantcontact.com
- Vertical Response at www.verticalresponse.com
- MailChimp at www.mailchimp.com
- AWeber Communications at www.aweber.com
- iContact at www.icontact.com

You can find even more by going to http://directory.google.com and searching for the phrase "hosted e-mail marketing."

Part V
Outlook at Work

The 5th Wave   By Rich Tennant

"...so if you have a message for someone, you write it on a piece of paper and put it on their refrigerator with these magnets. It's just until we get our e-mail fixed."

In this part . . .

Above all, Outlook is a powerful business tool. Whether you work in a giant organization or in your own home office, Outlook has features that can improve the way you do whatever you do. It also offers unparalleled power to streamline business collaboration. This part reveals the parts of Outlook that are all business.

Chapter 14

Big-Time Collaboration with Outlook

Microsoft is a big company that writes big programs for big companies with big bucks. So, as you'd expect, some parts of Outlook are intended for people at big companies. Big companies that use Outlook usually have a network that's running a program called Microsoft Exchange Server in the background. Exchange Server works as a team with Outlook to let you do what you can't do with Outlook alone. Outlook users on an Exchange Server can look at the calendar of another employee, give someone else the power to answer e-mail messages on that person's behalf, or do any of a host of handy tasks right from a single desktop.

Many features of Microsoft Exchange Server look as if they're just a part of Outlook, so most Exchange Server users have no idea that any program other than Outlook is involved. In practical terms, it really doesn't matter whether you know the technical difference between Outlook and Exchange Server; what's important is that Outlook and Exchange together can tackle a lot of tasks that Outlook can't do as well alone.

Collaborating with Outlook's Help

If your company is like most others, you spend a lot of time in meetings — and even more time figuring out when to hold meetings and agreeing on what to do when you're not having meetings. Outlook has some tools for planning meetings and making decisions that are helpful for people who work in groups. Although some of these features are available to all Outlook users, they work much better when you're using Exchange as well.

Organizing a meeting

Suppose that you want to set up a meeting with three coworkers. You call the first person to suggest a meeting time and then call the second, only to find out that the second person isn't available when the first one wants to meet. So you agree on a time with the second person, only to discover that the third person can't make this new time. You might want to invite a fourth person, but heaven knows how long it'll take to come up with an appropriate time for that one.

If you use Outlook, you can check everyone's schedule, pick a time, and suggest a meeting time that everyone can work with in the first place — with a single message.

To invite several people to a meeting, follow these steps:

1. **Click the Calendar button in the Navigation pane (or press Ctrl+2).**

   Your calendar appears.

2. **Select the Home tab in the Ribbon and click the New Meeting button (or press Ctrl+Shift+Q).**

   The New Meeting form opens.

3. **Click the Scheduling Assistant button.**

   The Attendee Availability page appears (as shown in Figure 14-1). If Outlook does not connect to an Exchange Server, you won't see a Scheduling Assistant button — instead the button will say Scheduling.

4. **Click the Add Attendees button at the bottom of the form.**

   The Select Attendees and Resources dialog box appears.

5. **Click the name of a person you want to invite to the meeting.**

   The name you click is highlighted to show that you've selected it.

6. **Click either the Required or Optional button, depending on how important that person's attendance is to the meeting.**

   The name you select appears in either the Required or Optional box, depending on which button you click.

7. **Repeat Steps 5 and 6 until you've chosen everyone you want to add to the meeting.**

   The names you choose appear in the Select Attendees and Resources: Contacts dialog box (as shown in Figure 14-2).

Scheduling Assistant button

Attendees you've invited   Attendee availability

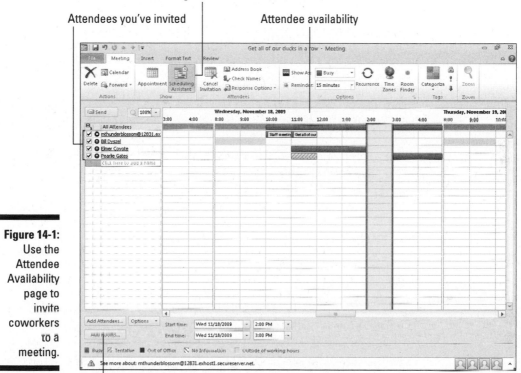

Figure 14-1:
Use the
Attendee
Availability
page to
invite
coworkers
to a
meeting.

Add Attendees button

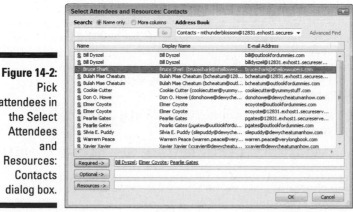

Figure 14-2:
Pick
attendees in
the Select
Attendees
and
Resources:
Contacts
dialog box.

8. **Click the OK button.**

   The Select Attendees and Resources: Contacts dialog box closes, and the names you chose appear on the Attendee Availability page. If Outlook connects with an Exchange server, the Attendee Availability page also shows you a diagram of each person's schedule so that you can see when everyone has free time — depending on how Outlook connects to the Exchange server, it might take a few moments for Outlook to retrieve everyone's schedule. If Outlook does not connect with an Exchange server, Outlook will indicate that it doesn't have information about the attendees' schedules.

9. **On the timeline at the top of the Attendee Availability page, click your preferred meeting time.**

   The time you pick appears in the Start Time box at the bottom of the Attendee Availability page. If you want, you can enter the meeting start and end time in the boxes at the bottom of the Attendee Availability page instead of clicking the timeline. If you don't see a time when everyone you're inviting to your meeting is available, you can select a time that works for everyone from the list of available time slots in the Suggested Times window.

10. **Click the Appointment button.**

    The Appointment page appears, with the names of the people you invited to the meeting in the To box at the top of the form.

11. **Type the subject of the meeting in the Subject box, and add details about where the meeting will be held in the Location box.**

    The subject you enter appears in the Subject box, and the location appears in the Location box.

    Many people also use Outlook to set up times for telephone conference calls. The Location box is a good place to enter the dial-in number and conference code when you set up conference calls. Not only does that make the information easier for your attendees to find, it makes Outlook store the information so that you can just click the drop-down arrow at the right end of the Location box to pull your codes up again the next time you organize a call.

12. **Enter any other information that you want attendees to know about your meeting in the Message box.**

13. **Click the Send button.**

    Your meeting request is sent to the people that you've invited, and the meeting is added to your calendar.

If your system administrators see fit, they can set up Exchange accounts for resources such as conference rooms. If they do, you can figure out a location and its availability for your meeting while you're figuring out who can attend.

Responding to a meeting request

Even if you don't organize meetings and send invitations, you may get invited to meetings now and then, so it's a good idea to know how to respond to a meeting request if you get one. ("Politely" is a good concept to start with.)

When you've been invited to a meeting, you get a special e-mail message that offers buttons labeled Accept, Tentative, Decline, Propose New Time, Respond, or Calendar. When you select either Accept or Tentative, Outlook automatically adds the meeting to your schedule and creates a new e-mail message to the person who organized the meeting, telling that person your decision. You can choose Edit the Response before Sending to include an explanation to the message, or just select Send the Response Now to deliver your message.

When you receive a meeting invitation, the message includes a preview of your calendar for the date and time of the meeting — giving you a quick snapshot of your availability; see Figure 14-3. This preview is only a small slice of your schedule, displaying about an hour or so before the meeting starts and about an hour or so after the meeting's start time. If the meeting is scheduled to last longer than two hours, you can scroll down to see more of your schedule — and if the meeting is scheduled to last longer than two hours, you might also want to pack a lunch.

Calendar preview

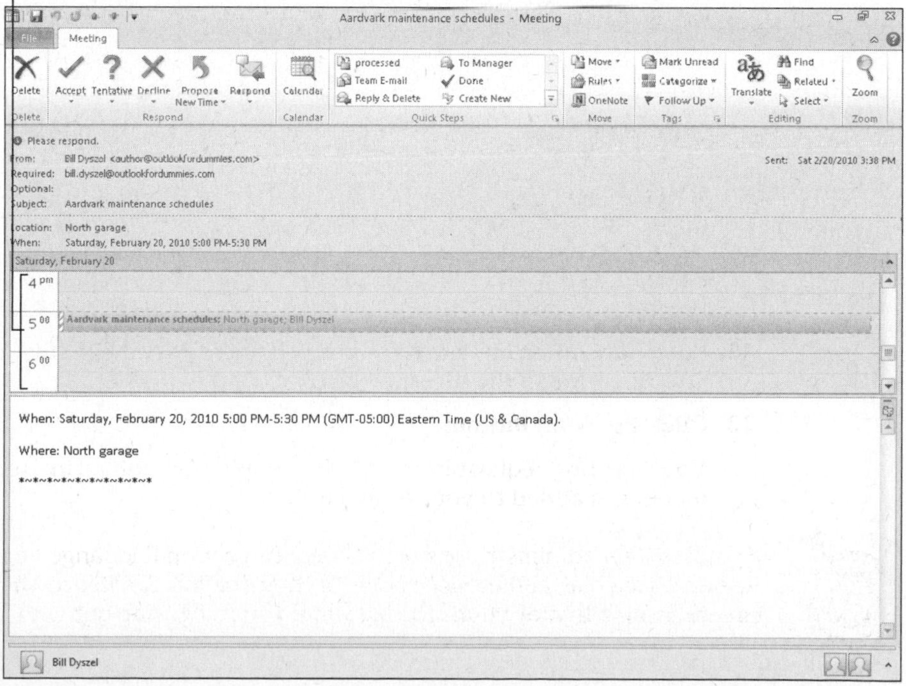

Figure 14-3: Meeting invitations include a preview of your calendar.

If you decline a meeting request, Outlook generates a message to the meeting organizer. (It's good form to add a business reason to explain why you're missing a meeting — "Sorry, I have a deadline," rather than "I have to wash my aardvark" or "Sorry, I plan to be sane that day.") If you click the Calendar button, Outlook displays your complete calendar in a separate window so that you can get a bigger picture of what your schedule looks like.

Checking responses to your meeting request

Each time you organize a meeting with Outlook, you create a small flurry of e-mail messages inviting people to attend, and they respond with a flurry of messages either accepting or declining your invitation. You may have a good enough memory to recall who said Yes and No, but I usually need some help. Fortunately, Outlook keeps track of who said what.

To check the status of responses to your meeting request, follow these steps:

1. **Click the Calendar icon in the Navigation pane.**

   The calendar appears.

2. **Double-click the item you want to check.**

   The meeting opens.

3. **Click the Tracking button.**

   The list of people you invited appears, listing each person's response to your invitation (as shown in Figure 14-4).

Figure 14-4:
See the
RSVPs from
your VIPs.

Name	Attendance	Response
mthunderblossom@12831.exhc	Meeting Organizer	None
Bill Dyszel <bill@outlookfordumi	Required Attendee	None
Bill Dyszel	Required Attendee	None
Bruce Shark (bruceshark@shali	Required Attendee	None
Bulah Mae Cheatum (bcheatum	Required Attendee	None
Bulah Mae Cheatum (bcheatum	Required Attendee	None
Cookie Cutter (cookiecutter@y	Required Attendee	None
Don O. Howe (donohowe@dew	Required Attendee	None
Elmer Coyote <ecoyote@outlo	Required Attendee	Accepted
Elmer Coyote	Required Attendee	Accepted
Pearlie Gates	Required Attendee	None
Pearlie Gates (pgates@outlook	Required Attendee	None
Silvia E. Puddy (silepuddy@dew	Required Attendee	None
Warrern Peace (warren.peace(	Required Attendee	None
Xavier Xavier (xxavier@dewvch	Required Attendee	None
Click here to add a name		

Sad to say, only the meeting organizer can find out who has agreed to attend a certain meeting. If you plan to attend a certain meeting only because that special someone you met in the elevator might also attend, you'll know whether that person accepted only if you organized the meeting yourself. You can tell who was invited to a meeting by checking the names on the meeting request that you got by e-mail.

Taking a vote

Management gurus constantly tell us about the importance of good teamwork and decision making. But how do you get a team to make a decision when you can't find most of the team members most of the time? You can use Outlook as a decision-making tool if you take advantage of the Outlook voting buttons.

Voting is a special feature of Outlook e-mail that adds buttons to an e-mail message sent to a group of people. When they get the message and if they are also using Outlook, recipients can click a button to indicate their response. Outlook automatically tallies the responses so that you can see which way the wind is blowing in your office.

To add voting buttons to an e-mail message you're creating, follow these steps while creating your message. For more about creating messages, see Chapter 4.

1. **With the New Message form open, click the Options tab in the Ribbon and then click the Use Voting Buttons button.**

   A list of suggested voting buttons appears. The suggested choices include the following, as shown in Figure 14-5:

   - Approve;Reject
   - Yes;No
   - Yes;No;Maybe
   - Custom

   If you choose Custom, the Properties dialog box opens. Type your own choices in the Use Voting Buttons text box. Follow the pattern of the suggested choices; just separate your options with a semicolon. If you want to ask people to vote on the lunch menu, for example, include a range of choices such as Pizza;Burgers;Salad.

2. **Click the set of voting buttons that you want to use.**

   The message You have added voting buttons to this message now appears at the top of your message. If you are adding your own custom choices, however, you'll need to click the Close button in the Properties dialog box when you are done to return to your message.

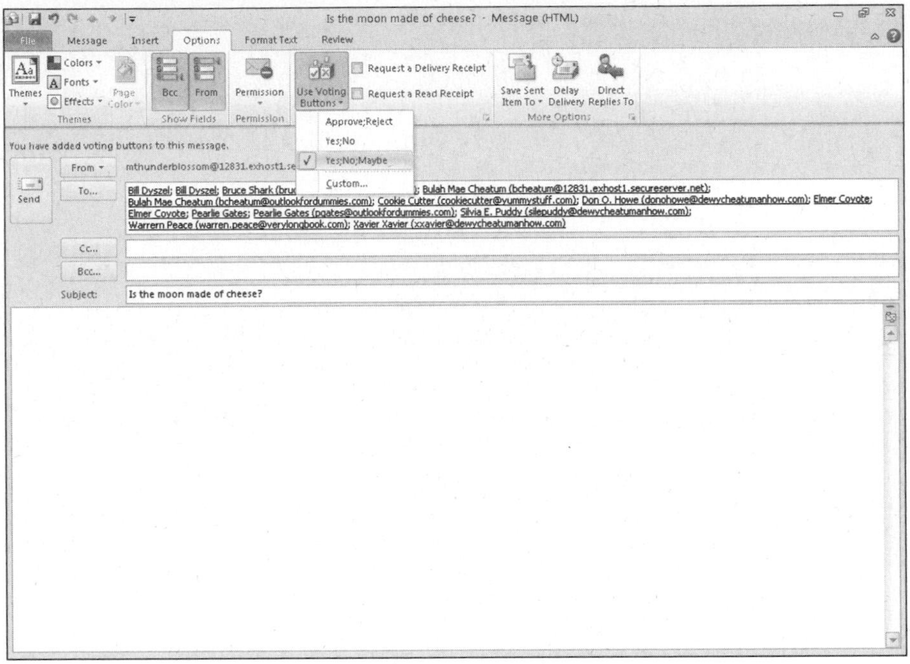

Figure 14-5:
Cast your
vote from
the voting
buttons list.

3. **Click the Send button.**

   And there you are! Democracy in action! Isn't that inspiring? When your recipients get your message, they can click the button of their choice and zoom their preferences off to you.

Tallying votes

When the replies arrive, you'll see who chose what by looking at the subject of the replies. Messages from people who chose Approve, for example, start with the word *Approve;* rejection messages start with the word *Reject.*

You can also get a full tally of your vote by checking the Tracking tab on the copy of the message you send in your Sent Items folder. To do so, follow these steps:

1. **Click the Sent Items icon in the Folder list.**

   Your list of sent messages appears.

2. **Double-click the message you sent to ask for a vote.**

   The message you chose opens.

3. **Click the Tracking button.**

   This shows you the list of people you've asked for a vote — and how they voted. A banner at the top of the Tracking page tallies the votes (as shown in Figure 14-6).

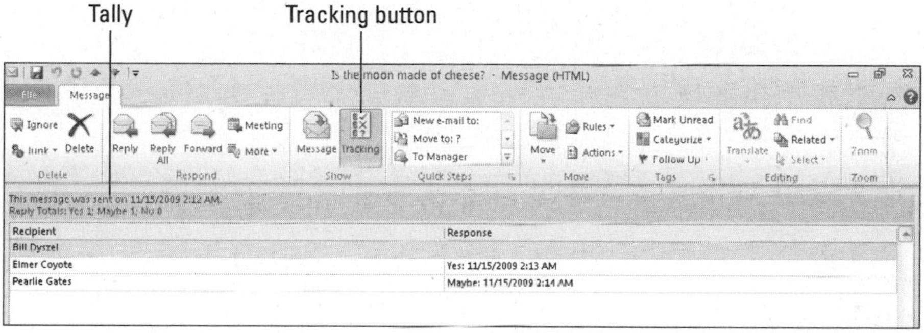

Tally   Tracking button

Figure 14-6: Check the Tracking tab to get a quick tally of how people voted.

Assigning tasks

As Tom Sawyer could tell you, anything worth doing is worth getting someone else to do it for you. Outlook enables you to assign a task to another person and keep track of that person's progress.

To assign a task to someone else, follow these steps:

1. **Right-click an item in your Tasks list.**

   A shortcut menu appears.

2. **Choose Assign Task.**

   A Task form appears.

3. **Type the name of the person to whom you're assigning the task in the To box, just as you would with an e-mail message.**

   The person's name appears in the To box (as shown in Figure 14-7).

4. **Click the Send button.**

   The task is sent to the person to whom you've assigned it.

The person to whom you addressed the task gets an e-mail message with special buttons marked Accept and Decline, much like the special meeting request message that I discuss earlier in this chapter. When the person clicks Accept, the task is automatically added to his or her Task list in Outlook. If the person clicks Decline, that person is fired. Okay, just kidding, the person is not actually fired. Not yet, anyway.

Task button

The person you're assigning to the task

Task dates

The task name

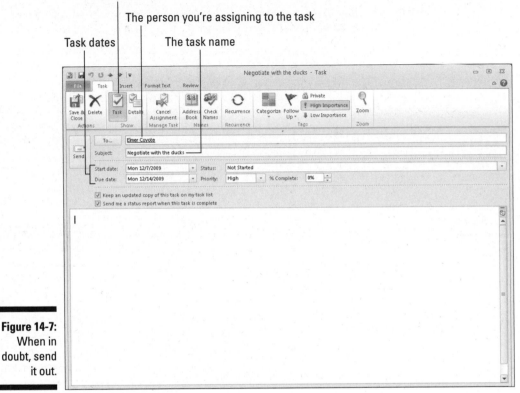

Figure 14-7:
When in
doubt, send
it out.

Sending a status report

People who give out tasks really like the Assign Task feature. People who have to do those tasks are much less enthusiastic. If you're a Task getter more often than you're a Task giver, you have to look at the bright side: Outlook on an Exchange network can also help the boss stay informed about how much you're doing — and doing and doing!

You may have noticed that the Task form has a box called Status and another called % Complete. If you keep the information in those boxes up to date, you can constantly remind the Big Cheese of your valuable contributions by sending status reports.

To send a status report, follow these steps:

1. **Double-click any task.**

   A Task form opens.

2. **Click the Send Status Report button in the Ribbon.**

   A Message window appears, and the name of the person who assigned the task already appears in the To box.

3. **Enter any explanation that you want to send about the task in the text box at the bottom of the form.**

   The text that you type appears in the form.

4. **Click the Send button.**

You can send status reports as often as you like — weekly, daily, hourly. It's probably a good idea to leave enough time between status reports to complete some tasks.

Collaborating with Outlook and Exchange

I focus the rest of this chapter on the features that work only if you have *both* Outlook and Exchange Server. Why confuse non-Exchange users by describing features they can't use?

If you use Outlook at home or in an office without Exchange Server, you won't be able to use the features I describe in the rest of this chapter. But take heart: Little by little, Microsoft is finding ways to make Exchange-only features available to all Outlook users, so you can look over this section as a preview of things to come.

Giving delegate permissions

Good managers delegate authority. (That's what my assistant, Igor, says, anyway.) Extremely busy people sometimes give an assistant the job of managing the boss's calendar, schedule, and (sometimes) even e-mail. That way, the boss can concentrate on the big picture while the assistant dwells on the details.

When you designate a delegate in Outlook on an Exchange network, you give certain rights to the delegate you name — in particular, the right to look at whichever Outlook module you pick.

To name a delegate, follow these steps:

1. **Select the File tab from the Ribbon, click the Info button in the Navigation pane on the left, and click the Account Settings button.**

   A drop-down menu appears with selections for Account Settings, Delegate Access, and Download Address Book.

2. **Click the Delegate Access button.**

   The Delegates dialog box appears.

3. **Click the Add button.**

   The Add Users dialog box appears.

4. **Double-click the name of each delegate you want to name.**

   The names you choose appear in the Add Users dialog box (as shown in Figure 14-8).

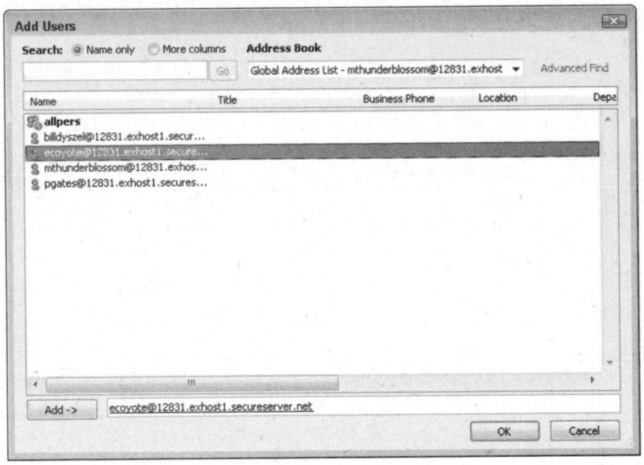

Figure 14-8: Choose those you trust in the Add Users dialog box.

5. **Click the OK button.**

   The Delegate Permissions dialog box appears (as shown in Figure 14-9) so that you can choose exactly which permissions you want to give to your delegate(s).

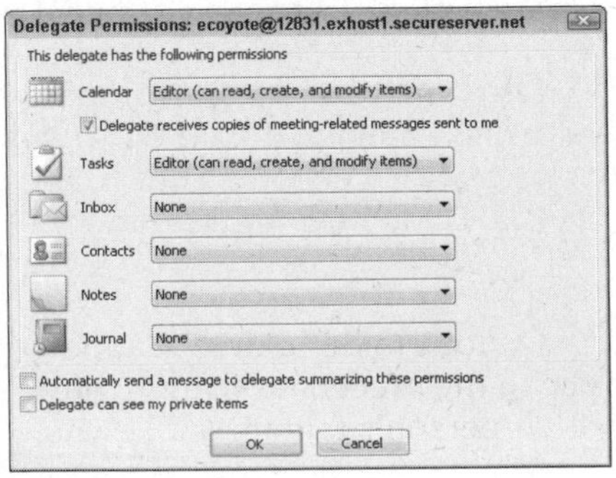

Figure 14-9: Show how much trust you have in the Delegate Permissions dialog box.

6. **Make any changes you want in the Delegate Permissions dialog box.**

   If you make no choices in the Delegate Permissions dialog box, by default your delegate is granted Editor status in your Calendar and Tasks — which means that the delegate can read, create, and change items in those two Outlook modules.

7. **Click the OK button.**

   The Delegate Permissions dialog box closes. The names you chose appear in the Delegates dialog box, as shown in Figure 14-10.

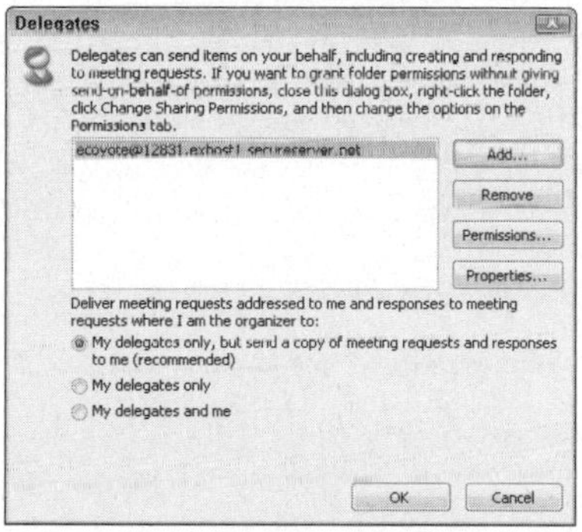

Figure 14-10:
Your designated delegates appear in the Delegates dialog box.

8. **Click the OK button.**

   The Delegates dialog box closes.

Opening someone else's folder

It's fairly common for a team of people who work closely together to share calendars or task lists so that they not only can see what the other people are doing but also enter appointments on behalf of a teammate — for example, if you work in a company that has sales and service people sitting side by side. As a service person, you may find it helpful if your partner on the sales side is allowed to enter appointments with a client in your calendar, while you're out dealing with other clients. To do that, your partner needs to open your Calendar folder.

You can't open another person's Outlook folder unless that person has given you permission first, as I describe in the preceding section. After you have permission, you can open the other person's folder by following these steps:

1. **Select the File tab from the Ribbon, choose the Open button in the Navigation pane on the left, and click the Other User's Folder button.**

   The Open Other User's Folder dialog box appears, as shown in Figure 14-11.

2. **Click the Name button.**

   The Select Name dialog box appears. (It's really the Address Book.)

3. **Double-click the name of the person whose folder you want to open.**

   The Select Name dialog box closes; the name you double-clicked appears in the Open Other User's Folder dialog box.

4. **Click the triangle on the Folder Type box.**

   A list of the folders you can choose appears.

5. **Click the name of the folder you want to view.**

   The name of the folder you choose appears in the Folder Type box.

6. **Click the OK button.**

   The folder you pick is now accessible to you — but it might not be obvious where to find it. If, for instance, you want to see the other person's calendar, click the Calendar button in the Navigation pane, and the other person's calendar appears in the Navigation pane as a shared calendar. If you click the Folder List button in the Navigation pane, the shared calendar will *not* appear.

Viewing Two Calendars Side by Side

It's pretty common for an executive to give an assistant the right to view the executive's calendar. That way, the assistant can maintain the executive's schedule while the executive is busy doing other things. Sometimes, when you're working as someone's assistant, you need to see both the boss's calendar and your own calendar simultaneously. If you have the required rights (permissions), Outlook can display both calendars side by side — and you can compare schedules at a glance.

After you've gone through the steps to open someone else's calendar, you'll see a section labeled Shared Calendars when you click the Calendar button in the Navigation pane. There you'll see the names of people whose calendars you've opened. If you select the check box next to one of those names, that person's calendar appears on-screen right next to yours; see Figure 14-12. (Your screen might look pretty cluttered when you put two busy schedules side by side, so you may need to switch to a one-day view to keep the screen comprehensible.) When you're done viewing two schedules, click the box in the Navigation pane next to the other person's name to go back to viewing one calendar.

Setting access permissions

Many times, a busy executive gives his or her assistant the right to view and even edit the executive's entire Outlook account right from the assistant's desk. That way, the assistant organizes what the executive does and the executive just goes out and does the job. This is known as *granting access permissions,* which is a lot like naming a delegate, as I describe in the section "Giving delegate permissions," earlier in this chapter. When you grant access permissions, however, the power you're giving is broader; you're giving the assistant permission to use the entire account.

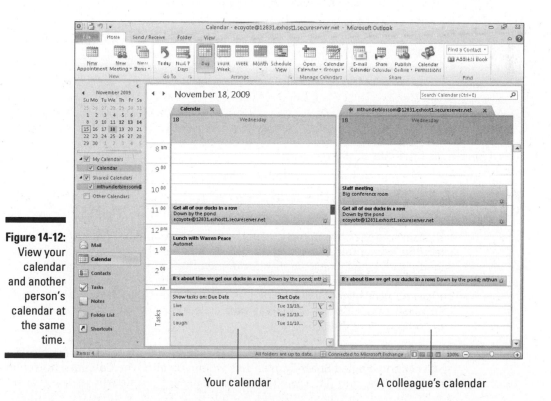

Figure 14-12: View your calendar and another person's calendar at the same time.

Your calendar　　　　A colleague's calendar

Before people can access your account, you have to give them permission by following these steps:

1. **Right-click your account name in the Folder list — your account name is located above the Inbox icon.**

   A shortcut menu appears.

2. **Choose Folder Permissions.**

   The Permissions dialog box appears (as shown in Figure 14-13).

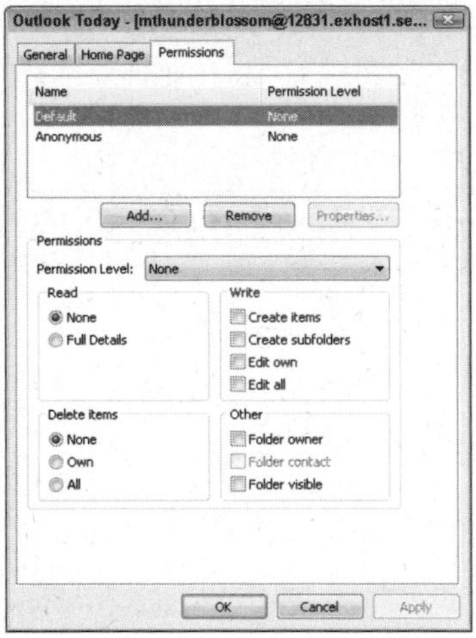

Figure 14-13:
You can grant permission for viewing your folders to anyone on your network.

3. **Click the Add button.**

   The Add Users dialog box, which is really the Global Address list, appears.

4. **Double-click the name of the person to whom you want to give access.**

   The name you double-click appears in the Add box at the bottom of the Add Users dialog box.

5. **Click the OK button.**

   The Add Users dialog box closes, and the name you chose appears in the Name box of the Permissions dialog box.

6. **Click the name that you just added to the Name list in the Properties dialog box.**

   The name you click is highlighted to show that you've selected it.

7. **Click the triangle on the Permission Level box.**

   A list of available permission levels appears. Assigning a permission level gives a specific set of rights to the person to whom the level is

assigned. For example, an editor can add, edit, or remove items from
your Outlook folders, whereas a reviewer can only read items.

8. **Click the OK button.**

Now that you've given a person permission to see your account as a whole,
you must give permission to see each folder in the account individually.
You can grant permission to another person to see almost every folder in
Outlook — even your Deleted Items and Junk E-Mail folders if you want, but
not your Contacts folder. For each folder you want to give a person permission to see, right-click the folder name, choose Properties from the shortcut
menu, select the Permission tab, and then follow Steps 3 though 8. You can
either follow these steps for each icon in the Folder list, or you can read the
section "Giving delegate permissions," earlier in this chapter, to grant access
to another person.

However, you have no way of knowing whether people have given you permission to view their data unless you try to open one of their folders (or
unless they tell you), which prevents nasty hackers from breaking into several people's data by stealing just one password.

Viewing two accounts

If your boss gives you permission to view his or her entire Outlook account,
you can set up your copy of Outlook so that both your folders and the boss's
folders show up in your Outlook Folder list. When you want to see your calendar, click your Calendar folder; when you want to see the boss's calendar,
click the boss's Calendar folder.

To add a second person's account to your view of Outlook, follow these steps:

1. **Right-click your account name in the Folder list — your account name
   is located above the Inbox icon.**

   A shortcut menu appears.

2. **Choose Data File Properties.**

   The Data File Properties dialog box appears, showing the General tab.

3. **Click the Advanced button.**

   The Microsoft Exchange dialog box appears.

4. **Click the Advanced tab.**

   The Advanced dialog box appears (as shown in Figure 14-14).

5. **Click the Add button.**

   The Add Mailbox dialog box appears.

Click the Add button
to open another
person's account.

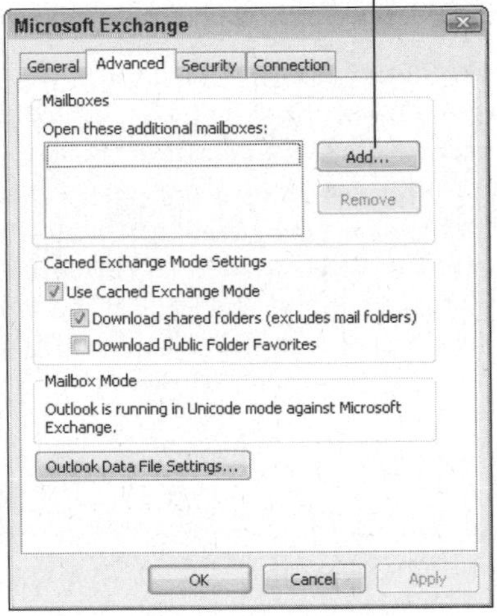

Figure 14-14:
Add some-
one else's
folders to
your Outlook
collection.

6. **Type the name of the person whose account you want to add.**

   You have to type the *username* of the person who you are adding — the
   dialog box does not offer you a list of users to pick from. If you don't type
   the person's username correctly or if the username you typed doesn't
   exist, you get an error message indicating that the name you entered
   couldn't be matched to a name in the Address list. If that happens, make
   sure that you have the exact spelling of the person's username.

7. **Click the OK button.**

   The Add Mailbox dialog box closes, and the person's username appears
   in the Mailboxes window of the Advanced dialog box.

8. **Click the OK button.**

   The Advanced dialog box closes.

9. **Click the OK button.**

   The Data File Properties dialog box closes.

After you add another person's account to Outlook, use the Navigation pane
to see the new person's items. Select Mail from the Navigation pane, and
you'll see a new section in your Folder list called Mailbox, followed by the
new person's username; that's where that person's Mail-related items are
located, such as his or her Inbox. Select Calendar from the Navigation pane
and you'll see a new calendar entry listed in the My Calendars section, followed by the new person's username; that's where that person's calendar is
located. And so it goes for each module that the person has given you permission to view.

MailTips

Wouldn't it be great if Outlook were omniscient and could tell you that the person you want to send a message to is out of the office even before you started writing the message? If you are lucky enough to be working in an office that is using the latest version of Exchange Server, Outlook might have access to a new feature called MailTips. MailTips doesn't give you advice on how to put pithier prose in your e-mails, but it does give you automatic information about your intended recipients as soon as you add their names to the To box. If you want to send a message to John Doe, but John has turned on his Automatic Replies (Out of Office) setting, you will see a MailTip appear at the top of your message displaying John's Out of Office message.

The Automatic Replies (Out of Office) setting is a nifty feature you can use to automatically notify anyone sending you a message when you are not reachable via e-mail, such as when you are on vacation — assuming, of course, that you don't want to be bothered by work e-mails while you are on the beach sipping margaritas. You can get to the Automatic Replies (Out of Office) setting by selecting the File tab in the Ribbon, clicking the Info button in the Navigation pane on the left, and then clicking the Automatic Replies (Out of Office) button.)

MailTips can also notify you of other things, such as when you are addressing a message to a large group of recipients or when an intended recipient's mailbox is full and therefore won't receive the message you want to send. Most of the MailTips you'll see are limited to information about your colleagues within your organization, so don't expect to see a MailTip telling you that your Aunt Petunia is on holiday in the south of France.

About Address Books

Outlook still uses several different Address Books that are really part of Microsoft Exchange Server. The Address Books involve several separate, independent lists of names and e-mail addresses — it's pretty confusing. Microsoft simplified the issue of dealing with Address Books in Outlook 2002 and later versions, but that doesn't help if you use Outlook on a large corporate network. I'll try to help you make sense of it all anyway.

The Outlook Contacts list (what you see when you click on the Contacts button in the Navigation pane) contains all kinds of personal information, whereas an Address Book (what you see when you click the To button in a new message) focuses on just e-mail addresses. An Address Book can also deal with the nitty-gritty details of actually sending your message to people on your corporate e-mail system, especially if that system is Microsoft Exchange Server.

Here's the lowdown on your plethora of Address Books:

- ✓ **The Global Address list:** If you're using Outlook on a corporate network, the Global Address list, which your system administrator maintains, normally contains the names and e-mail addresses of all the people in your company. The Global Address list allows you to address an e-mail message to anybody in your company, without having to look up the e-mail address.

- ✓ **The Contacts Address Book:** The Contacts Address Book is really just the list of e-mail addresses from the Contacts list. Outlook automatically populates the Contacts Address Book so you can easily add people to a message you are sending when you click the To button.

- ✓ **Additional Address Books:** If you create additional folders for Outlook contacts, those folders also become separate Address Books. Your system administrator can also create additional Address Books.

If you're lucky, you'll never see the Address Book. All the addresses of all the people you ever send e-mail to are listed in the Global Address list that somebody else maintains, such as on a corporate network. Under those circumstances, Outlook is a dream. You don't need to know what an Address Book is most of the time — you just type the name of the person you're e-mailing in the To box of a message. Outlook checks the name for spelling and takes care of sending your message. You'd swear that a tiny psychic who knows just what you need lives inside your computer. Unless your Uncle Bob works for your company or is a regular client, however, it is doubtful that his e-mail address will be found in the Global Address list.

Outsourcing Microsoft Exchange

Even if you're allergic to buzzwords, the term *outsourcing* still has its appeal. If you're an entrepreneur or freelancer, you know how distracted you can get with the details of running your business; you simply don't have time to fuss with the details of running an e-mail system such as Microsoft Exchange.

If you think you need the power of Microsoft Exchange but don't have time to deal with the details, plenty of companies are ready to provide Microsoft Exchange services to you at the

drop of the hat. These companies are known as ASPs (application service providers); lots of them are standing by with Microsoft Exchange servers you can log on to for as little as $10.00 per person per month. I used a company called GoDaddy.com for all the examples in this book. I encourage you to check out this company. If you'd like to shop around, you can search the Web for lists of other companies offering *hosted exchange service*.

Under less-than-ideal conditions, when you try to send a message, Outlook either complains that it doesn't know how to send the message or can't figure out whom you're talking about. Then you have to mess with the address. That situation happens only when the address isn't listed in one of the Address Books or isn't in a form that Outlook understands. For these cases, you must either enter the full address manually or add your recipient's name and address to your Contacts list.

Using SharePoint Team Services

Microsoft actually provides more than one method of using Outlook to collaborate with other people. I spend the first part of this chapter describing Microsoft Exchange, the most powerful collaboration tool you can connect to Outlook. But a second product, called SharePoint Team Services, also connects to Outlook and also helps you collaborate.

SharePoint is basically an online-based collaboration tool that helps you coordinate meetings, projects, and activities as well as share documents with other people. But SharePoint can also set up folders in Outlook that enable you to view key information, such as documents, calendars, and tasks from a SharePoint Web site, even when you're not online. SharePoint provides some handy collaboration features that you could use with people outside your organization.

In most cases, you don't have a choice about whether to use Microsoft Exchange or SharePoint Team Services; someone else (such as your system administrator) decides that for you. In fact, you may need to use both products; Outlook connects to Exchange and SharePoint at the same time with no problem. Chances are, if you ever get involved with SharePoint Team Services, you'll do so because someone asks you to join a shared team. If no one ever asks, you don't need to think about it, and you can skip the following sections.

Joining a SharePoint team

The first key to unlocking SharePoint is an e-mail that asks you to join a SharePoint team. The message is simply an ordinary e-mail that contains your username, password, and a link to the SharePoint site. Simply click the link and log in with the name and password you received in the e-mail. When you click the link that comes in the e-mail, your Web browser opens to a site that's devoted to the activities of the team you've been asked to join. Every SharePoint site looks different; click the links on the site to see what it has to offer.

Linking Outlook to SharePoint data

Certain parts of a SharePoint Web site can be tied into Outlook so that the information from the site automatically appears in Outlook. If you see an icon on the SharePoint Web site labeled Connect to Outlook, you can click that icon to send the information from that page straight to Outlook.

Accessing SharePoint data from Outlook

Unlike previous versions of Microsoft Office, Office 2010 is tightly integrated with SharePoint — especially Outlook 2010. If you are granted the proper permissions, Outlook can access virtually any information on the SharePoint site and keep versions of the documents stored on the SharePoint site in sync with the ones stored on your systems — and vice versa.

Information that SharePoint sends to Outlook shows up in its own set of SharePoint folders. If you click the Mail button in the Navigation pane, you see SharePoint includes folders as part of the list. Just click any SharePoint folder to see what's inside. These folders contain shared documents, such as Word, Excel, and PowerPoint files. When you select a document, a preview of it appears in the Reading pane — if you double-click a document, the document opens in its own application, such as Word. If you have the correct permissions, you can edit the document offline and then send the updated document to the SharePoint site with your changes. You can't typically add new items to SharePoint folders directly through Outlook, however. You normally add information to SharePoint through the respective Microsoft Office application, such as Word, or when logged in to the SharePoint site with your Web browser.

You can view shared SharePoint calendars and tasks in Outlook exactly the same way that you view Outlook calendars or tasks information. They appear in the same lists as your own calendars and tasks — you can even view shared calendars side by side with your own calendar, as described earlier in this chapter. If you have the correct permissions, you can make changes to the calendars and tasks, or create new entries.

So when are you most likely to run across SharePoint, and when will you use Exchange? In my opinion, Exchange is best suited for communicating, scheduling, and task setting among people who share the same e-mail system, while SharePoint is better suited for people who need to collaborate with shared documents and information — especially for those who don't share the same e-mail system or company resources.

Chapter 15

Keeping Secrets Safe with Outlook Security

In This Chapter

▶ Obtaining a digital ID

▶ Sending a signed message

▶ Encoding a message

*1*n the movies, computer hackers know everything — your credit card balance, Social Security number, and what you ate for breakfast. There doesn't seem to be a single scrap of personal information that a computer hacker in a movie can't find out.

Are real-life computer hackers just as brilliant and dangerous? Not really. Most crimes involving theft of personal information don't come from hackers sneaking into personal computers. More often than not, these losers dig credit-card slips out of a restaurant dumpster, or they just make a phone call and trick some poor slob into revealing a password.

Even though there isn't some hacker out there who knows what you bought at the Piggly Wiggly (or cares, for that matter), it may be wise to think about security when it comes to your e-mail and personal information. If you work in a corporation, you may be required by law to maintain certain standards of security over the messages you send and receive.

Outlook includes a feature called a Digital ID that enables you to keep your secrets secret, to keep your identity secure, and to be sure that the messages you receive actually came from the people who seem to have sent them. In most cases, you'll need to add some small program to Outlook to enable these advanced security features, but after you've installed these features, you never have to fuss with them again.

If security is a really big deal to you (as it is to people in the finance, law-enforcement, and defense industries), you may want to look into the more sophisticated security systems that are starting to turn up. Several high-tech companies offer systems for confirming identity and ensuring message security using fingerprint readers, eye scanners, and even gizmos that can recognize your face. Although many such systems can hook right into Outlook to make short work of message security, most of them cost quite a bit more than the average person needs to spend.

Getting a Digital ID

You probably receive messages every day from people you've never met. And I'll bet you don't spend much time wondering whether the messages you receive actually come from the people they seem to be — but you might need to think about that from time to time. After all, sneaky hackers can send out e-mail messages that appear to come from someone else. So how can you tell whether the message actually came from the person who appears to have sent it? Of course, if you know the senders personally, you can simply phone them to verify that what you received is what they sent. But a quicker, high-tech approach is to use what's called a *digital signature* — a tiny piece of secret code mixed in with your message to prove three things:

- ✔ That the message really comes from the person who seems to have sent it.
- ✔ That the person who seems to have sent the message really is the person he claims to be.
- ✔ That the person who sent the message sent it intentionally. It's like putting your signature on a check; it shows that you really mean to send a specific message.

If you want to take advantage of Outlook's security features, the first step to take is to get yourself a digital ID. If you work in a large organization, your employer may have obtained that for you — and your local computer gurus may have installed all the software — in which case, you can skip these steps. If you want to get a digital ID for your own use, you can get one from one of the many companies that issue and maintain digital ID services by following these steps:

1. **Click the File tab in the Ribbon.**

   The Backstage view appears.

2. **Click the word *Options*.**

   The Outlook Options screen appears.

3. Click the words *Trust Center*.

The Outlook Options screen appears.

4. Click the Trust Center Settings button.

The Trust Center screen appears.

5. Click the E-Mail Security button.

The E-Mail Security page appears (as shown in Figure 15-1).

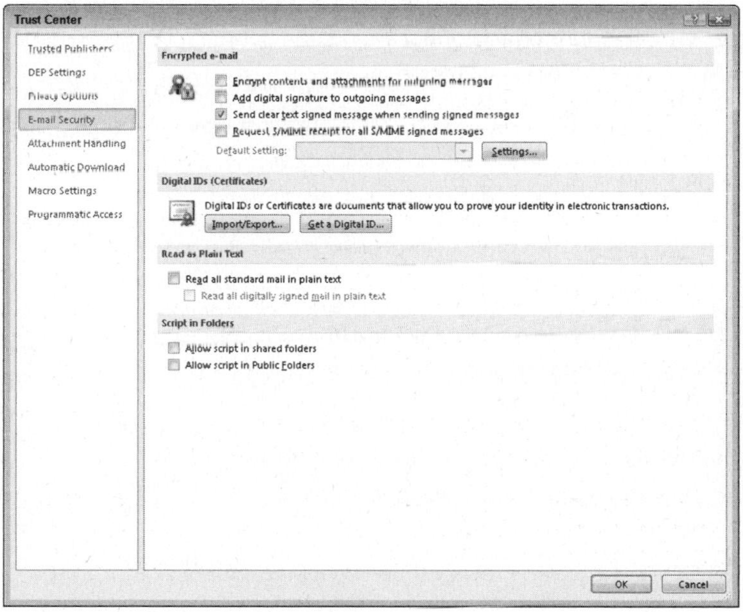

Figure 15-1:
The E-Mail
Security
page is
where you
can start
looking
for your
digital ID.

6. Click the Get a Digital ID button.

A Web site opens, offering a range of choices for obtaining a digital ID.

Quite a few companies offer digital IDs — some for free, but most of them charge a small fee. The range of companies that offer this service varies over time; your best bet is to check the Web sites to see which you prefer. The two best-known vendors of Digital IDs are Thawte (www.thawte.com) and VeriSign (www.verisign.com). After you pick a provider for your digital ID, you fill out a number of forms and pick a password for the ID. You'll also need to exchange several e-mails with a provider of the digital ID; that's how you prove that your e-mail address is really yours.

Sending Digitally Signed Messages

After you have a digital ID, the simplest thing you can do is to send someone a message that contains your digital signature. A digitally signed message does more than simply assure your recipient that you are really yourself — who else would you want to be, after all? Suppose that you want to send an encrypted message that only your recipient can read. To do so, you have to send at least one digitally signed message first so that Outlook can capture details about your digital ID.

After you've obtained a digital ID, you can send a message with a digital signature by following these steps:

1. **While creating a message, click the Options tab at the top of the message screen.**

   The Options Ribbon appears.

2. **Click the icon to the right of the words *More Options*.**

   The Properties dialog box appears (as shown in Figure 15-2).

3. **Click the Security Settings button.**

   The Security Properties dialog box appears.

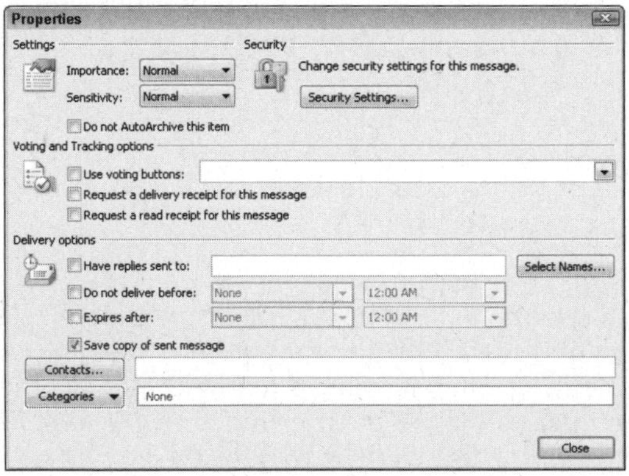

Figure 15-2:
To sign messages one at a time, click the Security Settings button in the Properties dialog box.

4. **Select the Add Digital Signature to This Message check box.**

5. **Click the OK button.**

   The Security Properties dialog box closes.

6. **Click the Close button.**

   Your message is now secure.

Adding a digital signature slows the process of sending a message somewhat because your computer has to check with the computer that issued your digital ID to verify your signature. But because Outlook checks your digital ID, your recipient can be sure that your message really came from you, and that's the whole point of digital signatures.

You can also set up Microsoft Outlook to attach a digital signature to every message you send, if you like. Just go back to the Trust Center, click the E-Mail Security button, and then select the Add Digital Signature to Outgoing Messages check box. In some industries, you may be required to add digital signatures to every outgoing message — but for most people, that's probably overkill.

Receiving Digitally Signed Messages

When you receive a message that contains a digital signature, you see a little icon in the upper-right corner of the message that looks like a little red prize ribbon that you'd win at the county fair for the best peach preserves.

You don't really need to do anything when you get a message like that; the icon itself verifies that the message really came from the person it claims to have come from. But if you're unusually curious, you can find out more about the person who signed the message by clicking the icon and reading the dialog box that appears. What you see should simply confirm what you already know: The person who sent the message is exactly who he says he is — the genuine article, the Real McCoy.

Encrypting Messages

Back in the days of radio, millions of children loved to exchange "secret" messages that they encoded with Little Orphan Annie's Secret Decoder Ring. Outlook does something similar, using a feature called Encryption. Unfortunately, you don't get a colorful plastic ring with Outlook. On the other hand, you don't have to save your box tops to get one — the decoder is built right into Outlook. When you encrypt a message, your system scrambles the contents of your outgoing message so that only your intended recipient can read your message.

Before you can send someone an encrypted message using Outlook's Encryption feature, both you and the person to whom you're sending your encrypted message need to have obtained a digital certificate, as I describe earlier in this chapter. Also, your intended recipient needs to have sent you at least one message with a digital signature, which I also describe earlier, so that Outlook recognizes that person as someone you can trust. Outlook can be pretty suspicious; even your mother can't send you an encrypted message unless you've sent her your digital signature first. Can you imagine? Your own mother! But I digress.

To send an encrypted message to someone who meets all the requirements, follow these steps:

1. **While creating a message, click the Options tab at the top of the message screen.**

   The Options Ribbon appears.

2. **Click the icon to the right of the words *More Options*.**

   The Properties dialog box appears.

3. **Click the Security Settings button.**

   The Security Properties dialog box appears.

4. **Select the Encrypt Message Contents and Attachments check box.**

5. **Click the OK button.**

   The Signing Data with Your Private Exchange Key dialog box appears.

6. **Click the Close button.**

   Your message is encrypted.

When you receive an encrypted message, the contents of the message don't appear in the Reading pane; you have to double-click the message to open it. In fact, if you work in a big organization, your network may deliver the message to you as an attachment to a serious-sounding message warning you that encrypted messages can't be scanned for viruses.

Antivirus Software

One of the biggest risks for every computer owner is a virus infection. You've probably heard news reports about computer viruses that spread across the Internet faster than a wildfire and to much worse effect. Every day new viruses seem to appear, and each new virus gets sneakier about how it wheedles its way into your system. Many viruses come to you through e-mail, often appearing as e-mail messages that seem to come from people you know. Others sneak in through your browser when you're surfing the Web. In most cases viruses only create a mild annoyance, but some are so destructive that they can render your computer permanently useless and destroy all the work you've created and left on that machine, then move on to all your friends' computers and do the same to them.

There's no substitute for effective anti-virus software if you use your computer the way most people do today. Most antivirus programs automatically connect to Outlook, scan incoming message for viruses, and automatically block any message that might be infected.

The tricky thing about antivirus software is that there are fake antivirus programs out there that pretend to protect you, but actually act as viruses themselves, inflicting your machine with alarms and annoyances and forcing you to purchase "updates" that only make the problem worse.

If you don't keep up with the latest developments in antivirus software, your best bet is to buy a well-known brand of antivirus software at your favorite computer store and install it as soon as you can. Some computers come with antivirus software preinstalled, but those packages sometimes want you to buy annual updates. If the software is Norton Antivirus from Symantec, McAfee VirusScan, or Kaspersky Internet Security, you know they're legitimate and you'll do well to buy the updates. You can also go to an antivirus software manufacturer's Web site and buy a downloadable version. The sites for the products I just mentioned are:

✔ Norton Antivirus at www.symantec.com

✔ McAfee VirusScan at www.mcafee.com

✔ Kaspersky Internet Security at www.kaspersky.com

There are also legitimate antivirus titles that you can get for free. Microsoft now offers a free antivirus program called Microsoft Security Essentials (www.microsoft.com/security_essentials), which I haven't yet tested extensively, but it looks good and Heaven knows the price is right. I've relied on a free antivirus program called AVG (http://free.avg.com) for many years, and I've found it to be effective. Bear in mind, however, that if you rely on free antivirus software, you'll have nobody to call when something goes wrong, and antivirus software matters most when something goes wrong, so if you're not comfortable dealing with geeky details yourself, the for-fee antivirus programs are worth what you pay.

Chapter 16

Seeing It Your Way: Customizing Outlook

. . . .

In This Chapter

▶ Customizing Outlook menus and toolbars

▶ Changing columns

▶ Sorting lists

▶ Grouping items in your table

▶ Saving your own views

▶ Using views

. . . .

*U*ser interface is a fancy term for the arrangement of screens, menus, and doodads on your computer. The people who write computer programs spend lots of time and money trying to figure out how best to arrange stuff on the screen to make a program like Outlook easy to use.

But one person's dream screen can be another person's nightmare. Some people like to read words on the screen that say what to do; other people like colorful icons with pictures to click. Other people prefer to see information in neat rows and columns; still others like to see their information arranged more (shall we say) informally.

Outlook enables you to display your information in an endless variety of arrangements and views. There's even a button labeled Organize that shows you what choices are available for slicing and dicing the information you've saved in Outlook. This chapter shows you many of the best steps you can take after you click the Organize button.

Customizing the Quick Access Toolbar

Did you ever notice how about 80 percent of your results come from about 20 percent of the work you do? The famous 80/20 rule applies to more things than you might expect. The Quick Access toolbar takes advantage of that idea by letting you keep a few icons for your favorite functions available at the top of the screen so that you can use them anytime. When Outlook 2010 is freshly installed, only three icons appear on the Quick Access toolbar: Send/Receive, Undo, and Customize Quick Access Toolbar. You can customize the Quick Access toolbar to include commands that you use frequently, such as Print, Delete, and more.

To customize the Quick Access toolbar, follow these steps:

1. **Click the Customize Quick Access Toolbar icon.**

   You'll find the Customize Quick Access Toolbar icon at the right end of the Quick Access toolbar. A drop-down list appears that contains the most popular Outlook functions (see Figure 16-1).

2. **Click the name of the function you want to add.**

   An icon for the function you chose appears on the Quick Access toolbar.

Quick Access toolbar drop-down menu

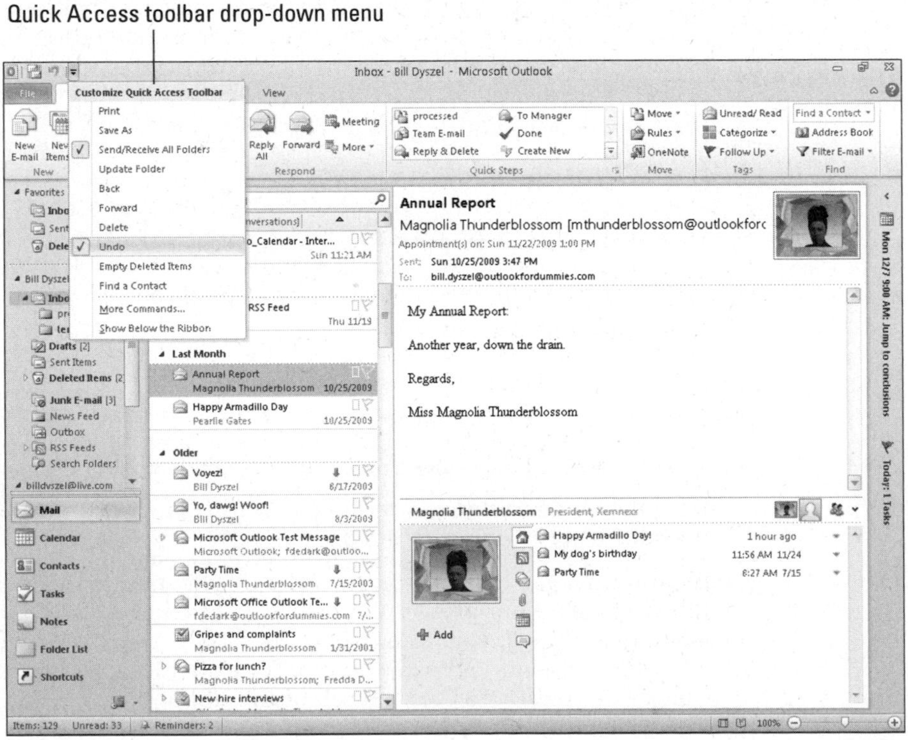

Figure 16-1: Pick your favorite function from the Quick Access toolbar menu.

Wasn't that easy? If you really want to get your hands dirty, you can choose More Commands from the list of commands, which opens the Outlook Options screen, where you'll see about ten more choices on the Popular Commands menu. Those commands include Print, Forward, and Undo. I don't know why those commands are so popular. Eat More Ice Cream would be popular with me, but nobody asked me. You can click the words *Popular Commands* to reveal a list of All Commands. The All Commands list includes hundreds of choices, none of which include Eat More Ice Cream. What a letdown! But just about everything Outlook can do is represented in the All Commands list.

Customizing the Ribbon

Because the Ribbon is the nerve center of Microsoft Office, you have good reasons for wanting to make it your own. On the other hand, the Quick Access toolbar looks the same no matter which Outlook module you're using, so you might consider holding off on customizing the Ribbon until you're sure that you can't get what you're after by customizing the Quick Access toolbar instead. Remember, also, that the Ribbon is made up of several tabs, and each Outlook module has a different Ribbon, each of which has a different set of tabs and a different set of buttons. If you add a button to the wrong part of the Ribbon, you might not be helping yourself.

Follow these steps to customize the Ribbon:

1. **Go to the Outlook module, Ribbon, and tab that you want to modify.**

   The Ribbon you're about to modify appears on the screen.

2. **Right-click any area of the Ribbon.**

   A shortcut menu appears.

3. **Choose Customize the Ribbon.**

   The Outlook Options screen appears (see Figure 16-2).

4. **Drag the command you want to add to or remove from the Ribbon to the spot where you want it to appear.**

   By dragging, you can change the order in which buttons appear on the Ribbon to suit your preference. If you want to add a whole new command to a Ribbon, you need to click the New Group button first, then add the command to the new group. For example, if you want to add a Quick Print button to the View tab of any ribbon, you need to create a new group first.

5. **Click OK.**

Figure 16-2:
The Outlook
Options
screen
offers more
options than
you could
ever need.

The commands on the right side of the screen are the ones that are already in the Ribbon. You can remove them if you want. The commands listed on the left side of the screen are the ones you might be able to add to the Ribbon. Outlook won't let you add just any command anywhere, though. You can only add a command to a particular Ribbon if that command is suitable to the module in which that Ribbon appears. For example, you can't add the Mark Complete command for Tasks to the Calendar Ribbon — that command isn't useful in that location. So the Add button will be grayed out to show that you can't add that command to that location, even if you try.

If you get carried away and customize Outlook beyond recognition, you can undo all your customizations by clicking the Restore Defaults button on the Outlook Options screen. That wipes out all your customizations, but it makes Outlook look normal again.

Enjoying the Views

Choosing a view is like renting a car. You can choose a model with the features you want, regardless of whether the car is a convertible, minivan, or luxury sedan. All cars are equipped with different features — radios, air conditioning, cup holders, and so on — that you can use (or not use) as you please. Some rental car agencies offer unlimited free mileage. Outlook views are much more economical, though. In fact, they're free.

Every Outlook module has its own selection of views, as well as its own set of Ribbons. The calendar has (among others) a view that looks calendar-like. The Contacts module includes a view that looks like an address card. All modules enable you to use at least one type of Table view, which organizes your data in the old-fashioned row-and-column arrangement.

Each type of view is organized to make something about your collection of information obvious at first glance. You can change the way that you view a view by sorting, filtering, or grouping. You can create an endless number of ways to organize and view the information that you save in Outlook. How you decide to view information depends on what kind of information you have and how you plan to use what you have. You can't go too wrong with views, because you can easily create new views if the old ones get messed up. So feel free to experiment.

You don't have to do anything to see a view; Outlook is *always* displaying a view. The *view* is the thing that takes up most of the screen most of the time. The view (or the Information Viewer, in official Microsoftese) is one of only two parts of Outlook that you can't turn off. (You also can't turn off the menu bar.) Most people don't even know that they have a choice of Outlook views; they just use the views that show up the first time they use Outlook. So now you're one step ahead of the game.

Each view has a name, which you can usually find in the Current View section under the Home tab of the Ribbon. If you don't see a Current View section under the Home tab, click the View tab. For some reason, Microsoft doesn't always put the Current View section in the same place on every module's Ribbon.

Table/List view

All modules contain some version of the *Table view* — a rectangle made up of rows and columns. Some Outlook commands also refer to this arrangement as a *List view*. In either case, if you create a new item (by adding a new task to your Tasks list, for example), a new row turns up in the Table view. You see one row for each task in the Table view (as shown in Figure 16-3).

The names of Table views often contain the word *list,* as in Simple list, Phone list, or just list. The word *list* means that they form a plain-vanilla table of items, just like a grocery list. Other Table view names start with the word *By,* which means that items in the view are grouped by a certain type of information, such as entry type or name of contact. I discuss grouped views later in the chapter and show you how to group items your own way.

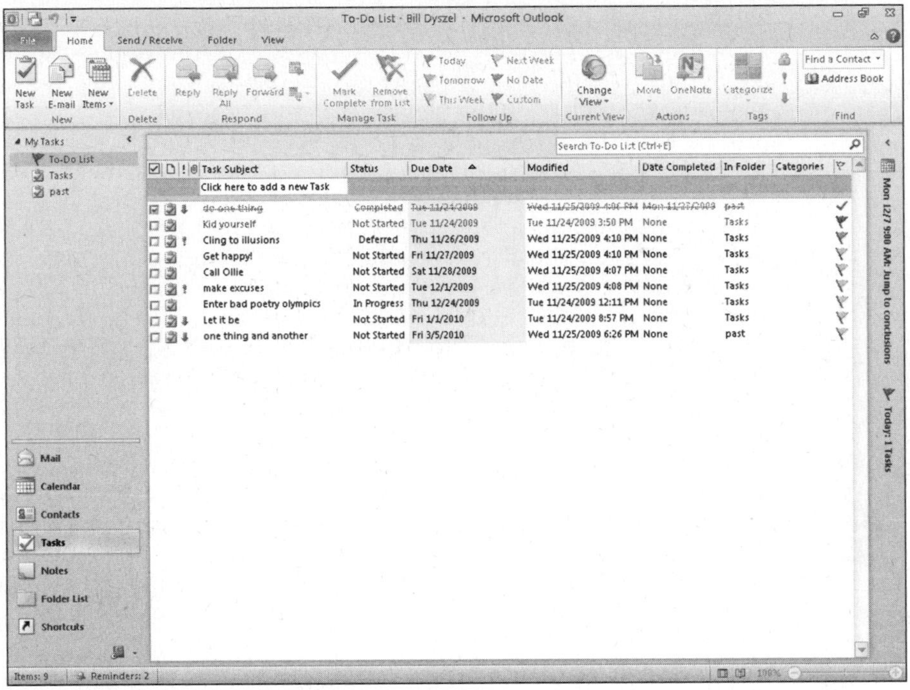

Figure 16-3:
The Tasks module in a Table view.

Icon view

Icon view is the simplest view — it's just a bunch of icons with names thrown together on-screen (as shown in Figure 16-4). The only Icon views that come with Outlook are for viewing notes and file folders. An Icon view doesn't show a great deal of information, and some people like it that way. I like to see more detailed information, so I stay with Table views. There's nothing wrong with using Icon view most of the time; you can easily switch to another view if you ever need to see more.

Card views

Card views are designed for the Contacts module. Each contact item gets its own little block of information; see Figure 16-5. Each little block displays a little or a lot of information about the item, depending on what kind of card it is. (See Chapter 7 for more about the different views in the Contacts module.)

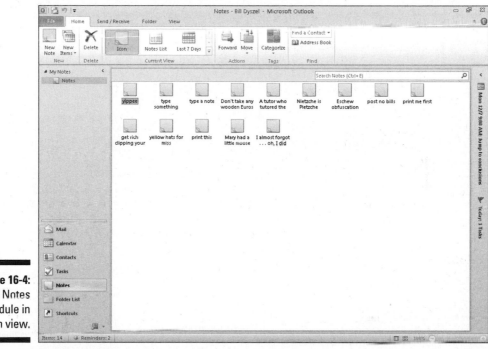

Figure 16-4:
The Notes
module in
Icon view.

Figure 16-5:
See your
contacts in
Card view.

The Card view shows you only a few items at a time because the cards are so big. To make it easier to find a name in your Contacts list, type the first letter of the name that your contact is filed under. Before you know it, you see that person's address card. Also, be consistent with name order: Always put the first name first (or last — whichever you think you might like best) when entering a contact.

Calendar views

The Calendar has a set of views that are particularly suited to viewing dates and setting appointments. This view adds Day, Work Week, Week, Month, and Schedule View buttons to the toolbar, enabling you to switch among views easily. All these views also display a monthly calendar. You can click any date in it to switch your view to that date (as shown in Figure 16-6).

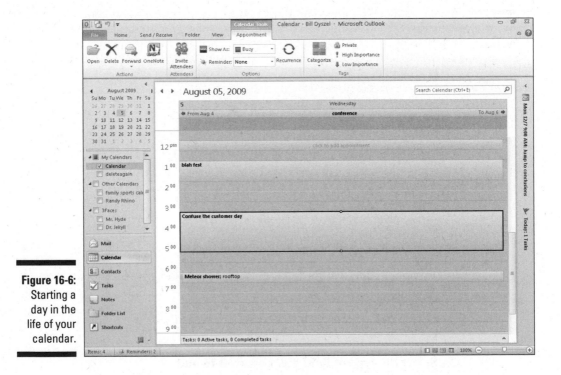

Figure 16-6:
Starting a day in the life of your calendar.

Playing with Columns in Table or List View

Table views (or List views) show you the most detailed information about the items that you've created; these views also enable you to organize the information in the greatest number of ways with the least effort. Okay, Table views look a little dull, but they get you where you need to go.

Table views are organized into columns and rows. Each row displays information for one item — one appointment in your calendar, one task in your Tasks list, or one person in your Contacts list. Adding a row is easy. Just add a new item by pressing Ctrl+N, and then fill in the information you want for that item. Getting rid of a row is easy, too. Just delete the item: Select the item by clicking it with your mouse, and then press Delete.

The columns in a Table view show you pieces of information about each item. Most Outlook modules can store far more data about an item than you can display on-screen in row-and-column format. The Contacts list, for example, holds more than 90 pieces of information about every person in your list. If each person were represented by one row, you would need more than 90 columns to display everything.

Adding a column

Outlook starts you out with a limited number of columns in the Phone view of your Contacts list. If you want more columns, you can easily add some. You can display as many columns as you want in Outlook, but you may have to scroll across the screen to see the information that you want to see.

To add a column in any Table view, follow these steps:

1. **Right-click any column title in the gray header row of the column.**

   A shortcut menu appears.

2. **Select Field Chooser from the shortcut menu.**

   The Field Chooser dialog box appears.

3. **Select the type of field that you want to add.**

   The words *Frequently-Used Fields* appear in the text box at the top of the Field Chooser. Those words mean that the types of fields most people like to add are already listed. If the name of the field you want isn't in one of the gray boxes at the bottom of the Field Chooser dialog box, you can pull down the menu that Frequently-Used Fields is part of and see what's available.

 4. **Drag the field into the table.**

Be sure to drag the new item to the table's top row, where the heading names are (as shown in Figure 16-7).

Notice that the names in the Field Chooser are in the same kind of gray box as the headers of each column. Two red arrows show you where your new field will end up when you drop it off.

Moving a column

Moving columns is even easier than adding columns. Just drag the column heading to where you want it; see Figure 16-8. Two little red arrows appear as you're dragging the heading to show you where the column will end up when you release the mouse button.

1. Click a field type.

2. Drag the field into the table.

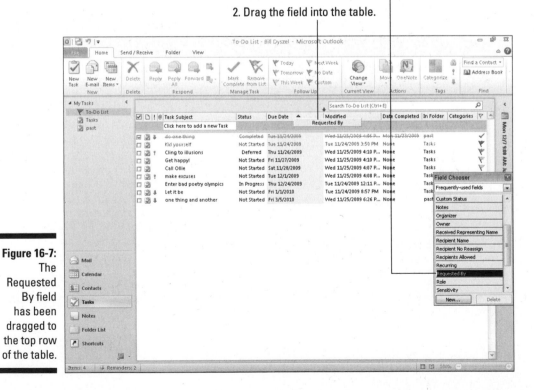

Figure 16-7: The Requested By field has been dragged to the top row of the table.

TIP

Columns = fields

I promised to tell you how to add a column, and now I'm telling you about fields. What gives? Well, columns are fields, see? No? Well, think of it this way: In your checkbook, your check record has a column of the names of the people to whom you wrote checks and another column for the amounts of those checks. When you actually write a check, you write the name of the payee in a certain field on the check; the amount goes in a different field. So you enter tidbits of information as fields on the check, but you show them as columns in the check record. That's exactly how it works in Outlook. You enter somebody's name, address, and phone number in fields when you create a new item, but the Table view shows the same information to you in columns. When you're adding a column, you're adding a field. Same thing.

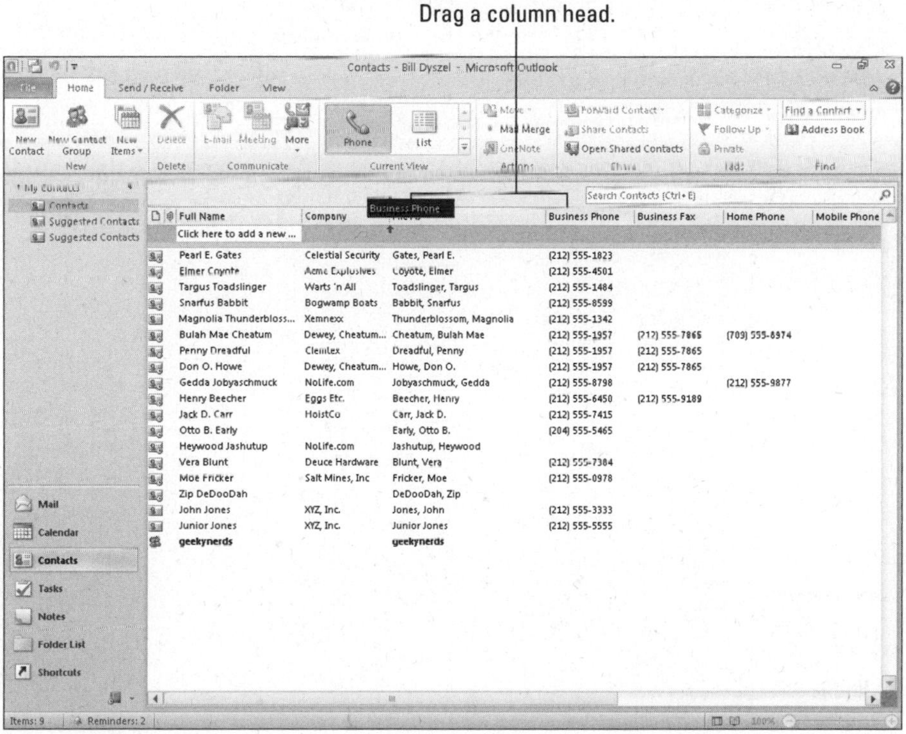

Drag a column head.

Figure 16-8:
Moving the
Business
Phone
column.

Widening or narrowing a column

Widening or narrowing a column is even easier than moving a column. Here's how:

1. **Move the mouse pointer to the right edge of the column that you want to widen or narrow until the pointer becomes a two-headed arrow.**

   Making that mouse pointer turn into a two-headed arrow takes a bit of dexterity. Once you get a little bit of practice, you'll find it fast and easy.

2. **Drag the edge of the column until it's the width that you desire.**

   The two-headed arrow creates a thin line that you can drag to resize the column. (Figure 16-9 shows a column being widened.) What you see is what you get.

If you're not really sure how wide a column needs to be, just double-click the right edge of the column header. When you double-click that spot, Outlook does a trick called *size-to-fit,* which widens or narrows a column to exactly the size of the widest piece of data in the column.

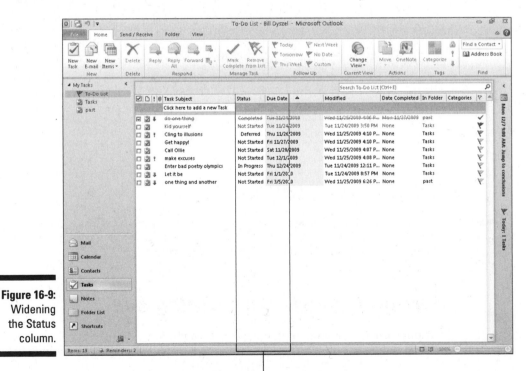

Figure 16-9:
Widening the Status column.

Click and drag to change column width.

Removing a column

You can remove columns that you don't want to look at. To remove a column, follow these steps:

1. **Right-click the heading of the column that you want to remove.**

   A menu appears.

2. **Choose Remove This Column.**

   Zap! It's gone!

Don't worry too much about deleting columns. When you zap a column, the field remains in the item. You can use the column-adding procedure (which I describe earlier in this chapter) to put it back. If you're confused by this whole notion of columns and fields, see the nearby sidebar "Columns = fields."

Sorting Items

Sorting just means putting your list in order. In fact, a list is always in some kind of order. Sorting just changes the order.

You can tell what order your list is sorted in by looking for triangles in headings. A heading with a triangle in it means that the entire list is sorted by the information in that column. If the column has numbers in it, and if the triangle's large side is at the top, the list goes from largest to smallest number. Columns that contain text get sorted in alphabetical order. *A* is the smallest letter, and *Z* is the largest.

Sorting from Table view

This is by far the easiest way: When sorting from Table view, click the heading of a column you want to sort. The entire table is sorted according to the column you clicked — by date, name, or whatever.

Sorting from the Sort dialog box

Although clicking a column is the easiest way to sort, doing so enables you to sort on only one column. You may want to sort on two or more columns.

To sort on two or more columns, follow these steps:

1. **Choose the View tab in the Ribbon and then click the View Settings button.**

   The Customize View dialog box appears.

2. **Click the Sort button.**

   The Sort dialog box appears.

3. **From the Sort Items By menu, choose the first field that you want to sort by.**

   Choose carefully; a much larger list of fields is in the list than is usually in the view. It's confusing.

4. **Choose Ascending or Descending sort order.**

   That means to choose whether to sort from smallest to largest (ascending) or vice versa (descending).

5. **Repeat Steps 3 and 4 for each additional field that you want to sort.**

   As the dialog box implies, the first column that you select is the most important. The entire table is sorted according to that field — and then by the fields you pick later, in the order in which you select them. If you sort your phone list by company first and then by name, for example, your list begins with the names of the people who work for a certain company, displayed alphabetically, followed by the names of the people who work for another company, and so on.

6. **Click the OK button.**

   Your list is sorted.

Grouping Items

Sorting and grouping are similar. Both procedures organize items in your table according to columns. *Grouping* is different from sorting in that it creates bunches of similar items that you can open or close. You can look at only the bunches that interest you and ignore all the other bunches.

For example, when you balance your checkbook, you probably *sort* your checks by check number. At tax time, you *group* your checks: You make a pile of checks for medical expenses, another pile of checks for charitable deductions, and another pile of checks for the money that you invested in *For Dummies* books. Then you can add up the amounts that you spent in each category and enter those figures in your tax return.

The quickest way to group items is to right-click the heading of the column you want to group by and then choose Group by This Field (as shown in Figure 16-10). The Group By box automatically appears, and the name of the field you chose automatically appears in the Group By box. Isn't that slick?

Viewing grouped items

A grouped view shows you the names of the columns that you used to create the grouped view. If you click the Contacts icon and choose the List view (which groups your contacts by company), you see a group of triangular icons on the left side of the list. The word *Company* appears next to each icon because that's the column that the view is grouped on. A company name appears next to the word *Company;* the grouped view includes a separate section for each company in the list.

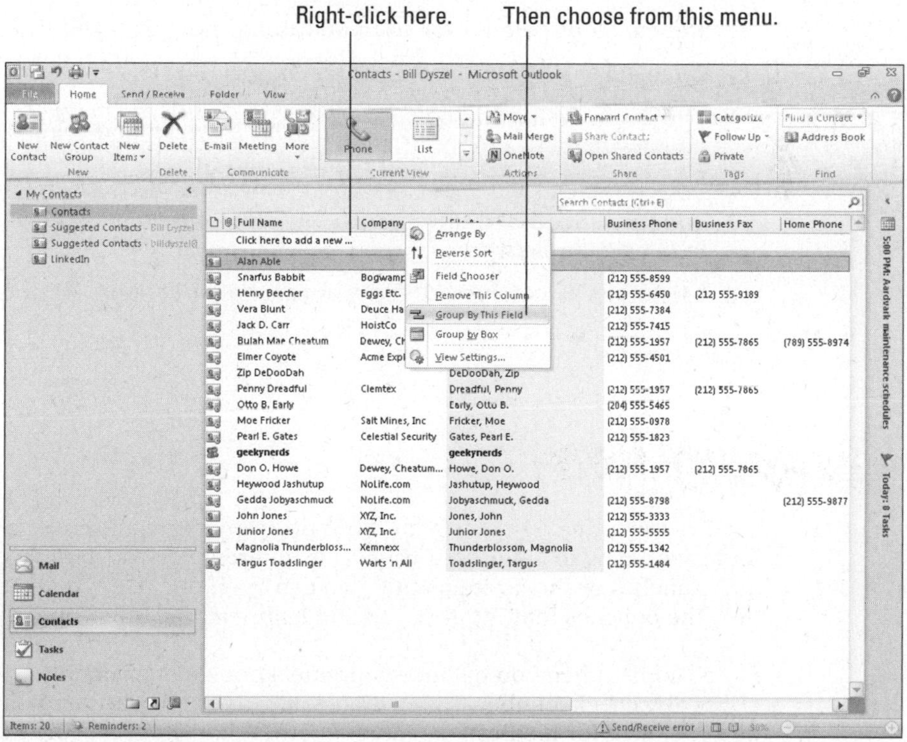

Right-click here.   Then choose from this menu.

Figure 16-10:
You can group items with just a few clicks.

The icon to the left end of the word *Company* either points directly to the right or down and to the right. An icon pointing directly to the right means that there's more to be seen: Click it and the group opens, revealing the other items that belong to the group. A triangle tilted down and to the right means that there's nothing more to see; what you see is what you get in that group.

If you click the name of the company but not the icon, you select the entire group. You can delete the group if you select the company name and press Delete. When a group bar is selected, it's highlighted in blue to distinguish it from the others.

Viewing headings only

You can click each triangle one at a time to open and close individual groups, or you can open or close all the groups simultaneously.

To open or close groups, follow these steps:

1. **Choose the View tab and click the Expand/Collapse button.**

   I think expanding and collapsing are dramatic words for what you're doing with these groups. It's not like Scarlett O'Hara getting the vapors; it's just revealing (expanding) or hiding (collapsing) the contents.

2. **To open a single selected group, choose Collapse This Group or Expand This Group.**

3. **To expand or collapse all the groups, choose Expand All or Collapse All.**

What could be easier?

Saving Custom Views

If you're used to saving documents in your word processor, you're familiar with the idea of saving views. When you make any of the changes to a view that I describe earlier in this chapter, you can save the changes as a new view or make the changes the new way to see the current view. If you plan to use a certain view repeatedly, it's worth saving.

You can save any view you like by using the Define Views dialog box. Choose the View tab, click the Change View button, choose Save Current View as a New View, name your view, and click the OK button. You can do almost anything you want just by changing the views you already have.

Using Categories

There's a lot of value in a good collection of information. However, you can't squeeze full value from a list of contacts or tasks if you can't get a quick handle on which items are important and which aren't. The Categories feature in Outlook is designed to help you distinguish what's urgent from what can wait.

Assigning a category

When you first set up Outlook, you can find out what categories are available by clicking the Categorize button on the Home tab. The Categorize button looks like a small, multicolored tic-tac-toe square; see Figure 16-11. Several other Outlook modules also display the Categorize button; it does the same job wherever you find it. Clicking the Categorize button opens a list of (surprise!) categories, each named after a color. If you simply want to color-code your items from the default, the process is pretty simple.

Categories list

Categorize button

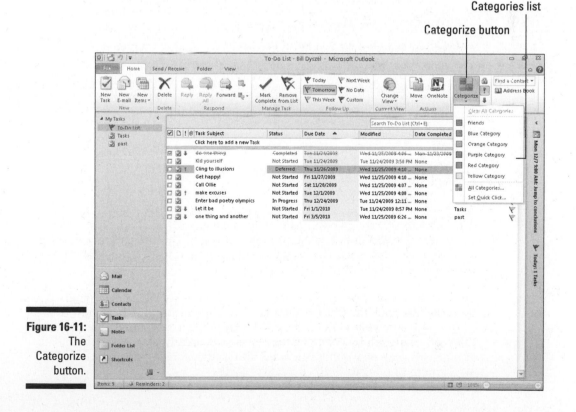

Figure 16-11:
The
Categorize
button.

Follow these steps to assign a category to an item:

1. **Click the item you want to categorize.**

   The item is highlighted.

2. **Click the Categorize button and choose from the list.**

   A colored block appears in the item to indicate which category you chose.

You can assign multiple categories to each item, although putting too many on an item may be more confusing than assigning no categories at all.

Renaming a category

You can memorize what each Outlook category color means if you like, but I would rather have a name associated with each color so that I know why I'm assigning a certain category to a certain item.

To rename a category, follow along:

1. **Click the Categorize button and choose All Categories.**

   The Color Categories dialog box appears.

2. **Click the category you want to rename.**

   The category you select is highlighted.

3. **Click the Rename button.**

   The category you chose is surrounded by a box to show that you can edit it.

4. **Type the new name you want to assign to that category.**

   The name you type appears in place of the old name.

5. **Click the OK button.**

   The Color Categories dialog box closes.

If you change the name of a category that you had already assigned to some Outlook items, that category name changes on those items automatically.

Changing a category color

You can change the color of a category as well as its name. Assigning memorable colors can give important clues about how your work is going or how well you're keeping up with current projects.

Follow these steps to change the color of a category:

1. **Click the Categorize button and choose All Categories.**

   The Color Categories dialog box appears.

2. **Click the category to which you want to assign a new color.**

   The category you select is highlighted.

3. **Click the Color button.**

   A drop-down box appears, showing the colors you can choose.

4. **Click the color you want to assign.**

   The color you chose appears in place of the old color.

5. **Click the OK button.**

   The Color Categories dialog box closes.

You can also choose None and create a colorless category. That's kind of drab, but if it fits your mood, go for it. One possible reason for creating color-less categories is that Outlook only offers 25 colors, and you may have more than 25 categories. But after you get past 25 categories, you might consider cutting down on the number of categories to reduce confusion.

Assigning a category shortcut key

You can give each category a shortcut key, which allows you to assign a category without touching your mouse. That's very handy when you want to zoom through a screen full of e-mail messages or tasks and set everything into some kind of order.

To assign a shortcut key to a category, follow these steps:

1. **Click the Categorize button and choose All Categories.**

   The Color Categories dialog box appears.

2. **Click the category to which you want to assign a shortcut key.**

   The category you select is highlighted to show that you selected it.

3. **Click the Shortcut Key menu.**

   The list of shortcut keys appears.

4. Click the shortcut key you want to assign.

The name of the shortcut key you chose appears to the right of the category.

5. Click the OK button.

You can't assign more than one shortcut key to a category; that would be confusing. However, you can assign more than one category to an item.

Chapter 17

Telecommuting with Outlook Web Access

Virtual work is here! Experts say that in the near future more and more people will telecommute to virtual offices, doing virtual work for virtual companies. You have to hope that these virtual jobs will provide real paychecks. You can't pay real bills with virtual money.

The Web is what makes this brave new world possible, and Outlook works beautifully on the Web, but sometimes you can't tote a full-blown version of Outlook wherever you are. However, Outlook Web Access can help you become super-productive by giving you access to all your Outlook data from any Web-connected computer. If you take advantage of Outlook Web Access, you can turn virtual work into real results.

Understanding Outlook Web Access

Outlook Web Access is part of a program called Microsoft Exchange, which many large and not-so-large organizations run to power advanced Outlook features such as public folders, shared calendars, and assigned tasks. Not every company that uses Microsoft Exchange offers Outlook Web Access, but if yours does, you can log on to Outlook from nearly anywhere: from a computer at your local public library, an Internet café, or any old photocopy parlor. There's nothing difficult about Outlook Web Access; it's really nothing more than a special Web page that looks and acts quite a bit like the version of Outlook you have on your desktop. If your company uses an older version of Microsoft Exchange, Outlook Web Access will look different than what I show in this chapter, but the essential features should be the same.

The desktop version of Outlook is much more powerful than Outlook Web Access, but you many find it enormously convenient to get access to your Outlook data when you find yourself in certain situations, such as

- When you don't want to lug a laptop on a very short business trip just to check your e-mail.

- When you really *do* have to work from home now and then, and you don't want to fuss with getting your home computer connected to the office network.

- When you want to do some simple planning and collaborating with your office colleagues from someone else's computer.

- When you get an e-mail on a mobile device (such as a BlackBerry or smartphone) and want to compose a more detailed response than you'd attempt on the tiny thumb keyboard built into those devices.

- When you need access to your e-mail and other Outlook data from another kind of computer that won't run Outlook. If you own one of those tiny netbooks, you might need to use Outlook Web Access because some netbooks don't run Microsoft Windows, so they can't run the regular version of Outlook.

I like the fact that Outlook Web Access lets me dash off a quick answer to an e-mail or put a task on my To-Do list from nearly anywhere I happen to be. That way, details don't escape me when I'm not sitting at my regular computer.

Also, some organizations only offer Outlook Web Access to certain mobile employees who share a computer. That way the company can keep these people connected to the corporate e-mail system without purchasing a separate computer for every single employee.

Logging on and off

Log on to Outlook Web Access the same way that you sign on to any other Web site: Go to the Internet, enter the address of the page that your organization has set up for logging on to Outlook Web Access, and enter your username and password. The exact steps of the process will differ between organizations, so you'll need to ask your system administrators for the details.

Outlook everywhere

Now that everyone is on the Internet and every-one carries a cell phone (or the like), you can have your Outlook information everywhere at all times. You can access your Outlook information in three main ways:

✔ Outlook on your desktop

✔ Outlook Web Access

✔ A mobile device (such as an iPhone or BlackBerry)

Why would you want three different ways to see the same information? The desktop approach offers more power and flexibility, Outlook Web Access gives you access from other people's computers, and a mobile device gives up-to-the-minute information and allows you to respond on the run.

If you can surf the Web, you can use Outlook Web Access. No special equipment is required. As long as you remember your logon name, password, and the address of your Outlook Web Access page, you're ready to rock. It's just like online shopping, but it costs less.

When you finish your Outlook Web Access session, you should log off by clicking the Log Off icon on the right side of the screen. If you're using a computer in a public place such as an Internet cafe, you don't want the next person using that computer to see your private information.

The Outlook screen

Outlook Web Access looks a lot like the desktop version of Outlook, so you can switch between the two versions without having to figure out a whole new bunch of tricks and techniques. You'll probably notice that the two programs feature a lot of the same icons, designs, and screen parts, including the following:

✔ The **Navigation pane** is an area along the left side of the screen that contains buttons labeled Mail, Calendar, Contacts, Tasks, Public Folders, Rules, and Options; see Figure 17-1. When you click the Mail, Calendar, Contacts, or Tasks button, the main screen reveals the items each of those icons describe: The Mail icon displays e-mail messages, the Calendar icon shows your appointments, and so on. The top half of the Navigation pane displays all the folders you can see in your desktop version of Outlook, including Sent Items, Deleted Items, Tasks, and Notes.

✔ **Toolbars** in Outlook Web Access include fewer tools than the desktop version of Outlook, but they contain all the icons to do what you need to get done. You can get a description of what a toolbar button does by hovering your mouse pointer over the button until a little yellow message box pops up to give you details.

When you're using Outlook Web Access, you see many of the buttons and screens you may recognize from the regular version of Outlook, but you're still really using a Web browser. This means that the menus at the top of the screen, the ones labeled File, Edit, and so on, are part of the browser program, not Outlook. Outlook doesn't have menus anymore. So if you click a menu, you'll get different results than you might expect. For example, if you're reading your e-mail and you choose File➪New, you won't see a New Message form; instead, you automatically open a new window in Internet Explorer. However the screens, toolbars, and buttons do most of the same things in Outlook Web Access that they do in the desktop version of Outlook.

Navigation pane

Folder list

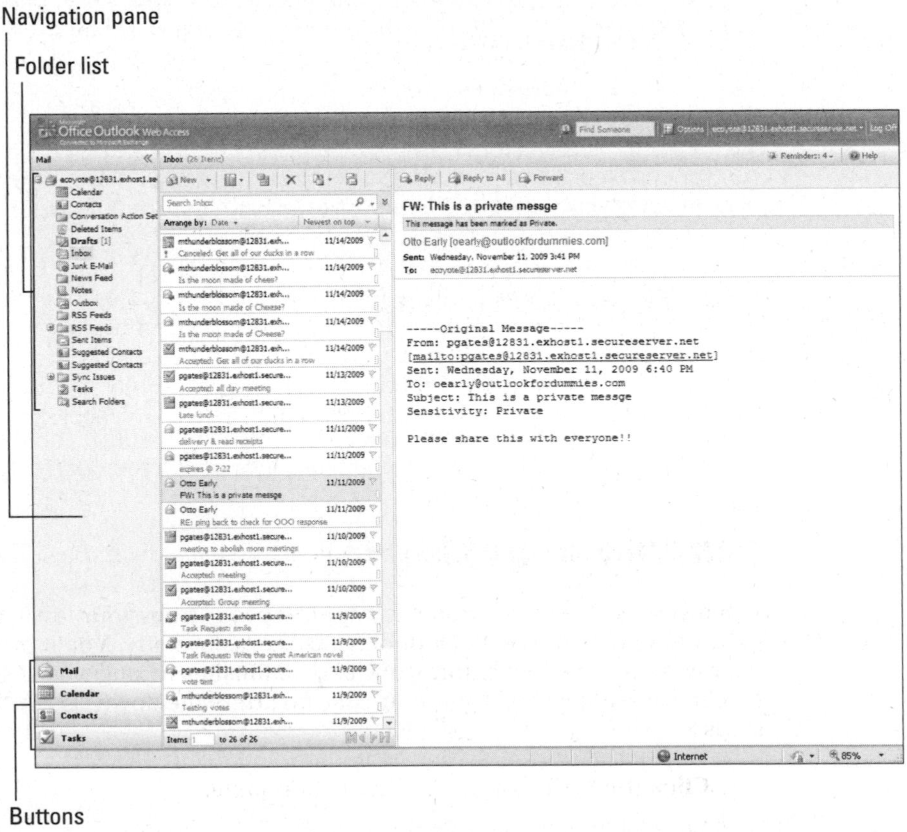

Figure 17-1:
The Outlook
Web
Access
screen
offers tool-
bars and
buttons to
help you get
around.

Buttons

Web E-Mail Basics

Whether you're catching up on juicy office gossip or deleting spam from Nigerian oil tycoons, you can log on to Outlook Web access from any browser to keep yourself in the loop.

Reading messages

If you're stuck out on the road without a company laptop, you still have many ways to catch up on your e-mail, but Outlook Web Access enables you to see the exact collection of messages that you have sitting in your Inbox at the office. Lots of people use the Inbox as a kind of to-do list; Outlook Web Access makes that possible from any computer connected to the Internet.

To read your messages, follow these steps:

1. **Click the Mail icon.**

   Your list of messages appears.

2. **Click the message you want to read.**

   The message text appears in the Reading pane on the right side of the screen. As you click each message in the Message list, the contents show up in the Reading pane.

Just use the arrow keys to move from one e-mail message to the next. An icon near the top of the screen looks like a little message box split in half. Click that icon to see a list of Reading pane options. You can choose to have the pane open on the right or on the bottom, or closed entirely. If you choose to leave the Reading pane closed, you'll need to double-click any message to view its contents in a separate window.

Sending a message

When you feel the urge to dash off a quick e-mail from your favorite Internet cafe, you can do that with Outlook Web Access in a jiffy. You'll probably have your message finished before your barista finishes mixing that High-Octane Mocha Latte Supremo. After your caffeine jitters die down, just follow these steps:

1. **Click the Mail icon in the Navigation pane.**

   Your list of messages appears.

2. **Click the New button on the toolbar.**

   The New Message screen opens (shown in Figure 17-2).

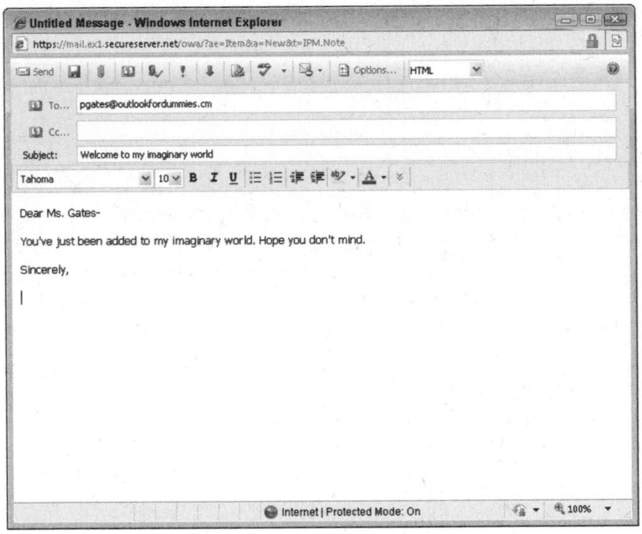

(Screenshot: Untitled Message - Windows Internet Explorer)

To... pgates@outlookfordummies.cm
Cc...
Subject: Welcome to my imaginary world

Tahoma 10 B I U

Dear Ms. Gates-

You've just been added to my imaginary world. Hope you don't mind.

Sincerely,

Figure 17-2:
The New
Message
screen.

3. **Fill out the New Message screen.**

   Put your recipient's address in the To box, a subject in the Subject box, and the message in the main box.

4. **Click the Send button at the top of the New Message screen.**

   Your message is on its way.

TIP

If you're not ready to send your message right away, you can click the Save button and resume work on your message later by clicking the Drafts folder to find your unfinished message. Clicking the message opens it for further editing.

Flagging messages

Outlook Web Access messages have the same flag feature that you know from the desktop version of Outlook. You can even add extra tricks such as dated reminders, which can make you more efficient, no matter whether you do it on the Web or at your desktop. To flag a message in your Inbox, click the little outlined flag to the right of the message title. You can also right-click the outlined flag to open a shortcut menu that offers a variety of flag types as well as the ability to set a reminder date or clear a flag when you don't need it anymore; see Figure 17-3.

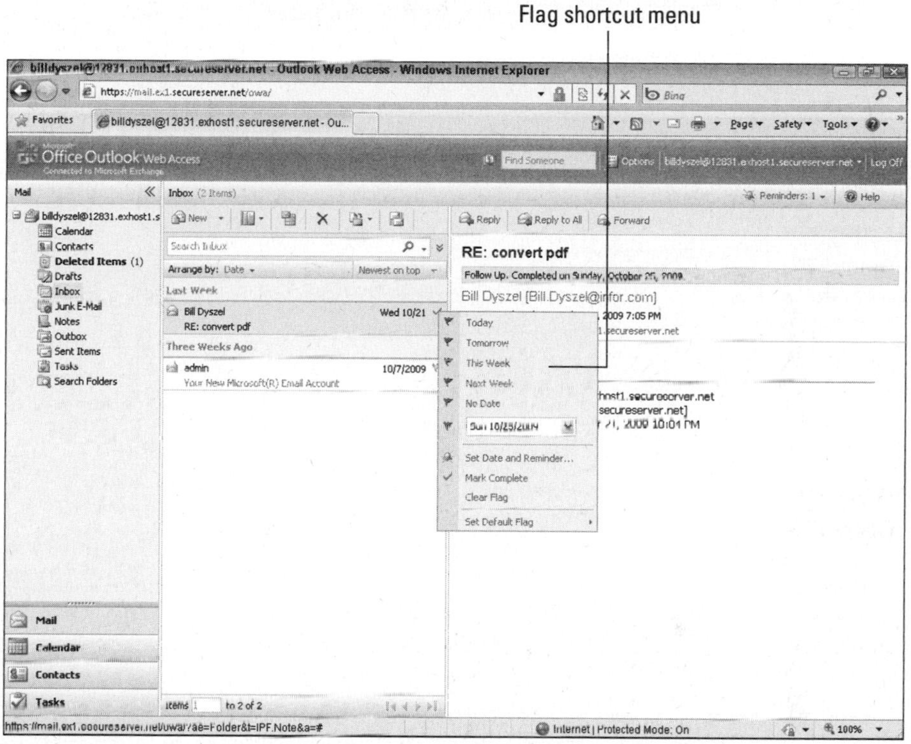

Flag shortcut menu

Figure 17-3:
Choose from
a variety
of flags in
Outlook
Web
Access.

Setting individual message options

You can't set as many options for an individual message in Outlook Web Access as you can in the regular version of Outlook, but you can set priority and sensitivity levels or request delivery notifications and read receipts. Just follow these steps:

1. **Click the Mail icon in the Navigation pane.**

2. **Click the New button on the toolbar.**

3. **Fill out the New Message screen.**

   Put your recipient's address in the To box, a subject in the Subject box, and the message in the main box.

4. **Click the Options button on the toolbar.**

   The Message Options dialog box opens, showing the options you can choose from (as shown in Figure 17-4).

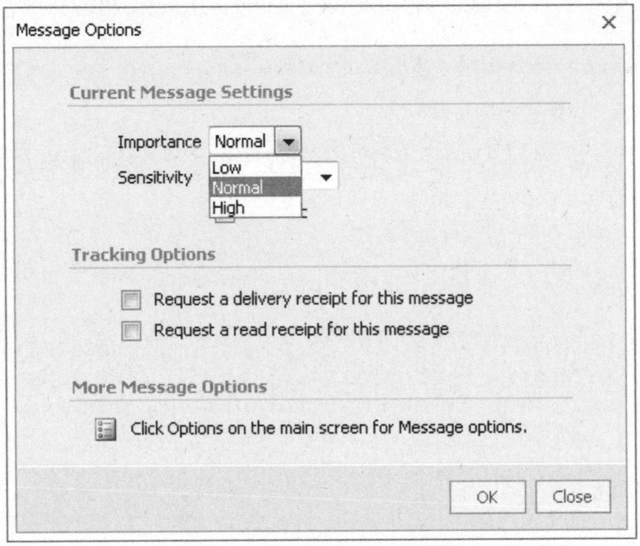

Message Options   ✕

Current Message Settings

Importance Normal ▾
Sensitivity ┌─────────┐ ▾
            │ Low   │
            │ Normal   │
            │ High   │
            └─────────┘

Tracking Options

☐ Request a delivery receipt for this message
☐ Request a read receipt for this message

More Message Options

▤ Click Options on the main screen for Message options.

                                    [OK]   [Close]

Figure 17-4:
Set your
message
to high
priority
on the
Message
Options
dialog box.

5. **Choose the options you want; then click the Close button.**

6. **Click the Send button.**

It's a good idea not to overuse the message options that are available in Outlook Web Access. Setting all your messages to high priority, for example, eventually leads people to ignore your priority markings ("Oh, she thinks everything is urgent; just ignore her."). In fact, sometimes it's wise to mark a message as low priority by clicking the blue, downward-pointing arrow. That tells the person you're contacting that you respect her time, but that you also want to keep her informed. A little courtesy goes a long way. For a full explanation of message options, see Chapter 4.

An easy way to assign high priority to your message is to click the red exclamation point on the Message Form toolbar while you're creating your message.

Tracking Tasks while Traveling

Do you ever have those midnight "Aha!" moments, when you think of something urgent you need to do at work the next day? If you just go back to sleep, you know you'll forget and overlook something really important. That's when the Task module in Outlook Web Access is so valuable. You can log on to your Outlook account from home, enter a task, and then receive a reminder the next morning when you get to work. Everyone at work will think you're a genius, at least until lunch time.

To add a new task through Outlook Web Access, follow these steps:

1. **Click the Tasks icon in the Navigation bar.**

   Your list of tasks appears.

2. **Type the name of your task in the Type a New Task box.**

   The text you type appears.

3. **Press Enter.**

   Your task appears in the task list.

You can't do many of the clever sorting, grouping, and viewing tricks with tasks in Outlook Web Access that you can in regular Outlook. But after you've entered all your tasks, you can work with them in either Outlook or Outlook Web Access.

Organizing Contacts

The whole point of Outlook Web Access is to let you see your collection of information from anywhere — and what's more important than keeping track of the people in your Contact list? Practically nothing, so I show you the basics in the following sections.

Viewing your contacts

Some people see their Contact list as pure gold. They ogle and admire it whenever they're not busy playing Solitaire. If you'd like to sort the contents of your Contact list, click the blue text next to the words *Arrange By* at the top of your Contact list. That reveals a list of ways that you can view your contacts; see Figure 17-5. For your viewing pleasure, you see these options:

- First Name
- Last Name
- Company
- File As
- Department
- Flag Due Date
- Flag Start Date

You can do much more powerful things with your list of contacts in the desktop version of Outlook, but seeing your contacts when you're away from your desk is mighty convenient.

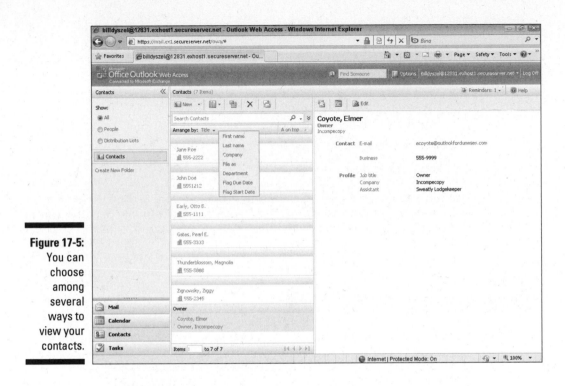

Figure 17-5:
You can
choose
among
several
ways to
view your
contacts.

Adding contacts

A good Contact list is precious; it's even more valuable than that snazzy office chair you covet or even that enviable cubicle near the coffee pot. Outlook Web Access can help you keep your Contact list up to date from wherever you are. For example, if you go to a conference or convention and exchange business cards with lots of people, you probably want to get those names into your Contact list as soon as possible. If your office has Outlook Web Access, you might want to stop at the nearest public library or Internet café, log on to your account remotely, and enter all those new addresses before you go home.

To add a new contact through Outlook Web Access, follow these steps:

1. **Click the Contacts icon in the Navigation pane.**

   Your list of contacts appears.

2. **Click the New button on the toolbar.**

   The Untitled Contact form appears.

3. Fill in the blanks in the Untitled Contact form.

The information you type appears in the Untitled Contact form (as shown in Figure 17-6).

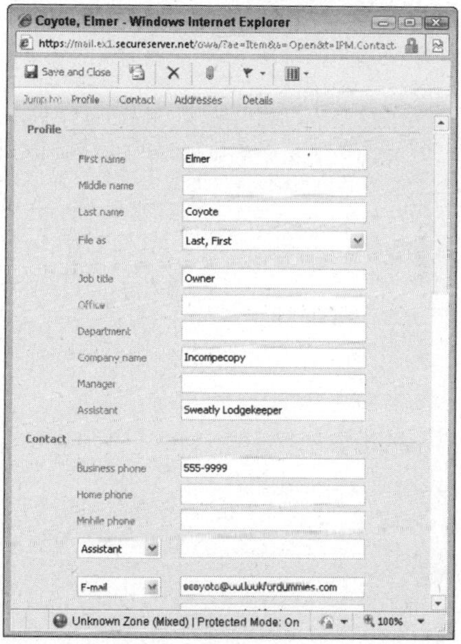

Figure 17-6:
Save information about the people you know on the Contact form.

4. Click the Save and Close button.

The Untitled Contact form closes, and the name you entered appears in your list of contacts.

If you want to edit the contacts you've entered, just open a contact record and follow the same steps you use to enter information about a new contact. (For a fuller explanation of Outlook contact entries, see Chapter 7.)

Using Your Calendar

The beauty (and horror) of using Outlook is that it enables other people to add appointments to your calendar. That means sometimes you won't know what appointments are in your calendar, because you didn't put them there. Some senior executives have assistants to enter Outlook calendar appointments on their behalf.

So a word to the wise: Check your calendar regularly just to be sure that you're in the right place at the right time.

Entering an appointment

If you're a heavy-duty road warrior, you probably keep your calendar on a smartphone for your own reference — but your colleagues often need that information too. It's a good idea to keep your appointments posted in Outlook so that other people at the office know when you're available for meetings, lunches, and random tongue-lashings.

To enter an appointment, follow these steps:

1. **Click the Calendar icon in the Outlook pane.**

   The calendar appears, showing your appointments (as shown in Figure 17-7).

2. **Click the New button on the toolbar at the top of the screen.**

   The Untitled Appointment form appears.

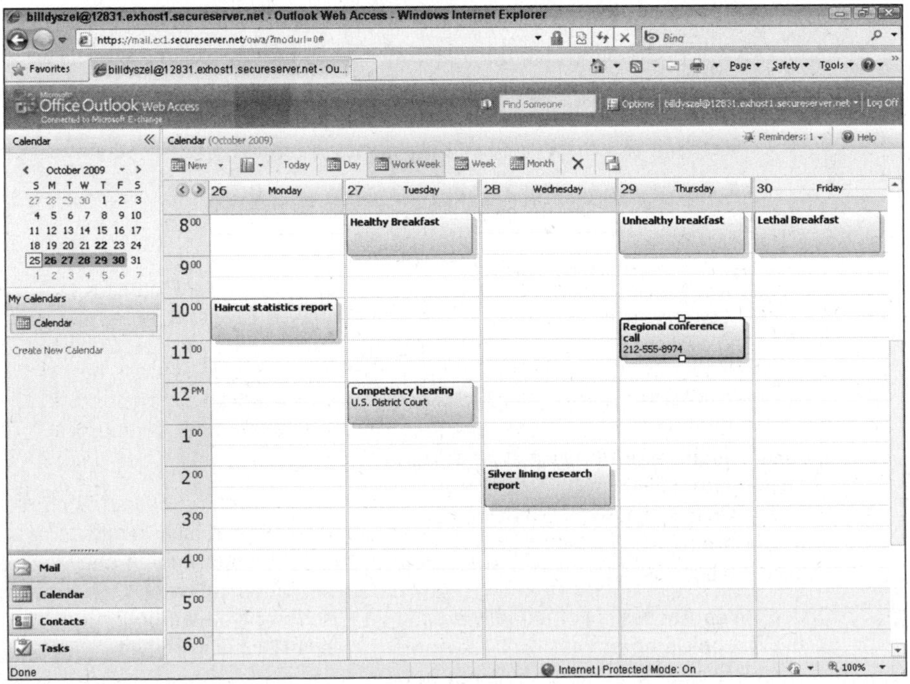

Figure 17-7:
Your calendar displaysyour appointments.

3. **Click the Subject box and enter a name for your appointment.**

   Enter something that describes your appointment, such as "Meeting with Bambi and Godzilla."

4. **Click the triangle next to the Start Time box.**

   A small calendar appears.

5. **Click the date of your appointment.**

   If the pop-up calendar doesn't contain the date you have in mind, click the arrows next to the name of the month in the small calendar until the month you want appears.

6. **Click the triangle in the box to the right of the box where you entered the date; then choose the time of your appointment.**

   The time you entered appears.

7. **Click the Save and Close button.**

While you're entering appointment information, you can enter the location, end time, and other information about your appointment in the appropriately labeled boxes.

An even quicker way to enter an appointment is to click the Day, Work Week, or Week button and then double-click the line that corresponds to the day and hour of your appointment. The New Appointment Form appears, already containing the date and time you chose.

And now for the fine print

Although Outlook Web Access can offer some pretty powerful capabilities to authorized users, it isn't for everybody. Here's why:

✔ Outlook Web Access works best when viewed with Microsoft's own Web browser, Internet Explorer. If you use another browser, such as Firefox or AOL, the program may look quite different from the way I describe it in this chapter. Most of the basic functions are the same, but the exact locations of the buttons differ.

✔ Outlook Web Access is not actually a part of the Outlook program; it's built into the Microsoft Exchange program. You may run across a version that looks and acts quite

differently from the version I describe in this chapter (which is the one most widely available as I write this book).

✔ Outlook Web Access has to be set up by a network administrator through your organization's main computer network. Do-it-yourself setup isn't an option.

✔ If you work for a security-conscious organization that isn't comfortable letting confidential information show up on just any computer anywhere — aw, where's the sense of adventure? — you have to be understanding about that. In that case, stick to using Outlook on your regular desktop computer.

Moving an appointment

You can change the time of your appointment by simply dragging the appointment to the date and time you desire. If you need to change anything other than the date and time of your appointment, double-click the appointment, select the information you want to change, enter the updated information, and then click the Save and Close button. To delete an appointment, click the appointment to select it and then click the black X on the toolbar to zap it. (You can find out more about the power of the Outlook Calendar in Chapter 8.)

Viewing the Calendar

Time-management gurus insist that you manage your schedule for the long term, medium term, and short term. The Outlook Web Access Calendar lets you view your appointments in different ways depending on what you want to see (or avoid seeing). The buttons at the top of the Calendar screen are for changing your view:

- ✔ Today shows today's appointments.
- ✔ Day shows one day.
- ✔ Work Week shows five days.
- ✔ Week shows a week.
- ✔ Month shows a month.

You can't view your schedule in Outlook Web Access at the level of detail that you can with the desktop version of Outlook, but you can add and change items to get the "big picture" and then deal with the details back at your desk.

Mobile Collaboration

If you work in an organization where people hold lots and lots of meetings, you have my sympathy. To help you keep track of all those fascinating confabs, Outlook gives you the tools to stay current on who's meeting when and with whom. Otherwise you might miss that next meeting, and (horrors!) they could be talking about you.

Inviting attendees to a meeting

The only thing that seems to take more time than an office meeting is *planning* one. Although Outlook can't quiet the blowhard who bores everyone at weekly staff meetings (gotta let the boss have *some* fun), it can reduce the time you spend planning them. If you're charged with that duty, you can get a boost from Outlook Web Access by following these steps:

1. **With your calendar open, double-click the appointment to which you want to invite others.**

   The appointment form opens.

2. **Click the Invite Attendees button at the top of the form.**

   Three new fields appear at the top of the form: Required, Optional, and Resources.

3. **Click the Required button.**

   The scheduling screen appears (as shown in Figure 17-8).

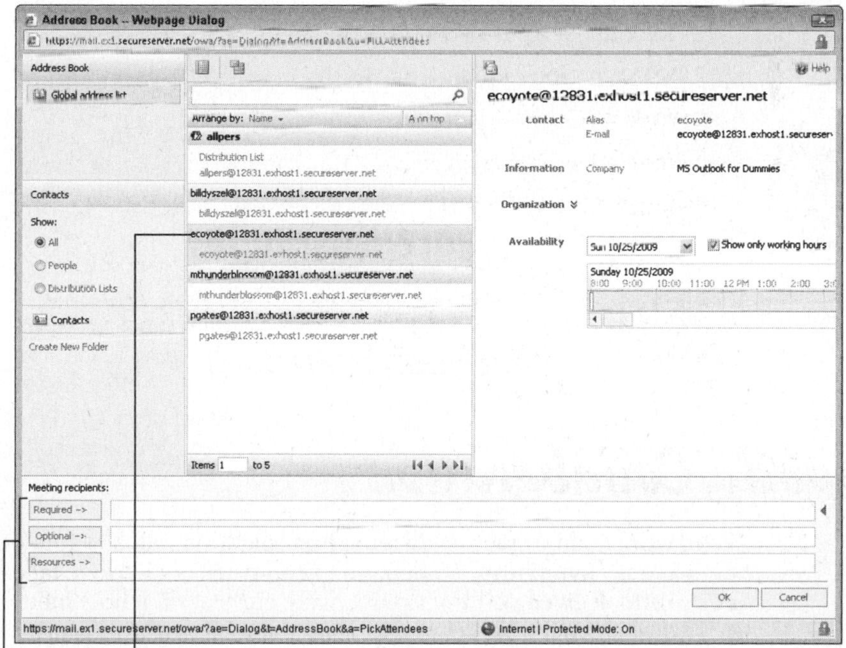

Figure 17-8:
Add your
mates
to your
meeting.

Click a name to select it.

Assign invitees to one of these categories.

4. **Click a name to select it; then click one of the three buttons at the bottom of the screen.**

   You can choose either Required or Optional, depending on how crucial that person's attendance is to the meeting. When you click Required, the name of the person you chose appears as a link in the Find Names dialog box.

   The third choice, Resources, is where you request something you may need for the meeting, such as a conference room or a projector. Some organizations don't set up this option, but the Resources box appears anyway.

5. **Repeat Step 4 until you've chosen everyone you want to add to the meeting.**

   The names you select appear as underlined text on the appointment form.

6. **Click the OK button in the scheduling dialog box.**

   At this point, you can click the Send button to send off your invitation, but you might want to check everyone's availability first. It's no use inviting people to a meeting that they can't attend.

7. **Click the Send button.**

   Your meeting request goes to the people you've invited.

Although the regular version of Outlook offers slicker planning tools than you'll find in Outlook Web Access, the Web version is a big help when you need a quick-and-dirty way to plan a meeting while you're away from the office.

Refresh yourself!

Everyone likes refreshment now and then; Outlook Web Access is no different. I'm not suggesting that you pour a couple of brewskis into your Inbox — you'd rather chug 'em yourself anyway. Because you're viewing Outlook Web Access through a browser, you might need to tell your browser to refresh the display now and then to make sure that you're seeing the latest information that Outlook has to offer. The regular version of Outlook that you use on your desktop always shows you everything it stores, but the Web version sometimes falls behind. You can press F5 to refresh your browser, or you can right-click the screen and choose Refresh from the shortcut menu. After that, feel free to pop a cold one.

Respond to a meeting request

If you travel a lot, you may need to check in frequently to see whether other people in your organization have summoned you to attend meetings when you return. Outlook Web Access enables other people to send you a special e-mail that invites you to a meeting. You can then accept that request to be automatically included in the meeting. To respond to a meeting request, follow these steps:

1. **Click the Mail icon in the Navigation pane.**

   Your list of messages appears.

2. **Click the message that includes a meeting request.**

   The message you click opens, displaying a special toolbar with the Accept, Tentative, and Decline buttons. Meeting requests appear in your Inbox (as with any other e-mail message), but the icon in front of a meeting request looks different from the icon in front of other messages. (Normal e-mail messages have an icon that looks like a tiny envelope; the Meeting Request icon looks like a tiny calendar.)

3. **Click one of the response buttons on the toolbar and then click the Send button.**

   Your response is sent to the meeting organizer.

When you accept a meeting request, the meeting is automatically added to your calendar, and the meeting organizer's calendar reflects the fact that you've agreed to attend the meeting. (To find out more about sending and responding to meeting requests, see Chapter 14.)

Exploring Your Options

You can adjust a limited number of options through Outlook Web Access. To see what options are available, click the Options icon in the Outlook pane. You may want to adjust the e-mail notification options or the way dates are displayed. For the most part, however, you won't miss much if you leave the options alone.

Out of Office message

If you have to call in sick, remember these two important rules:

- ✔ Don't come back from your "sick day" with a glorious new suntan.
- ✔ Turn on your Outlook Out of Office message so that people don't think you're avoiding them (even if you are).

The option you're most likely to use is the Out of Office notice. After all, if you have to take a sick day, you don't want to have to drag yourself into the office to turn on that pesky Out of Office message. Spare yourself the hassle (and your colleagues the germs) by following these steps:

1. **Click the Options button at the top of the screen.**

   The Options page appears.

2. **Click the words *Out of Office Assistant* in the Navigation pane.**

   The Out of Office Assistant screen appears.

3. **Choose the Send Out of Office Auto-Replies option.**

   The circle next to this option darkens to show that you've selected it. You can also add a detailed message, describing all the gory details of why you're absent. (Figure 17-9 shows a typical example.)

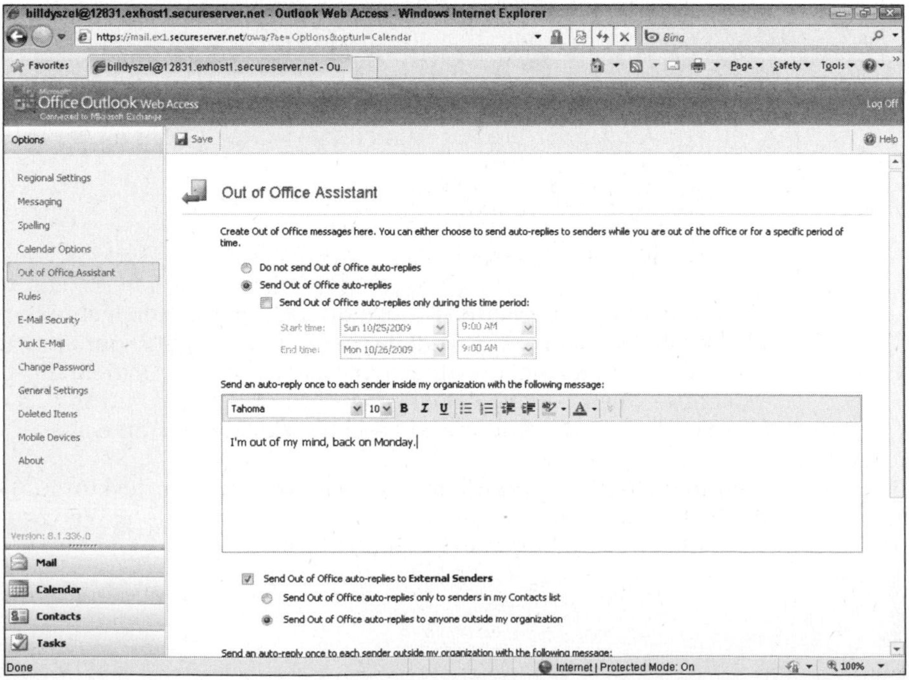

Figure 17-9:
If you're out of the office, let people know.

   4. Click the Save button.

   The Options page closes.

Now you can stop feeling guilty about not coming in. (Well, okay, maybe you'll still feel a teeny bit guilty, but you've done your part.) Try to remember to turn your Out of Office message off when you get back to the office. Otherwise, your coworkers will think that you're still at home lounging around and not at the office lounging around.

Creating a signature

You get to decide when to include the one signature you're allowed to create in Outlook Web Access. Your signature for business might be very grand and official, the better to impress lackeys and sycophants as well as to intimidate rivals. In that case, you might prefer to leave it off the messages you send to your friends — unless, of course, your only friends are lackeys and sycophants. Then, lay it on thick, Your Royal Highness!

Create a signature in Outlook Web Access by following these steps:

   1. Click the Options button at the top of the screen.

   The Options screen appears.

   2. Click in the E-Mail Signature box.

   A blinking cursor appears in the E-Mail Signature box, as shown Figure 17-10.

   3. Type your signature text.

   You can stylize the text using the formatting buttons at the top of the screen.

   4. Click the Save and button.

   The Options screen closes.

If you select the Automatically Include My Signature on Outgoing Messages check box, you can guess what happens. That's right: Your signature is automatically included on all outgoing messages. What a coincidence! If you don't select the check box, you can just click the Signature button at the top of the message form when you want to add the signature to an e-mail.

Bear in mind, the signature that you created on your desktop will not automatically appear when you send messages from Outlook Web access. You have to enter your signature in both places.

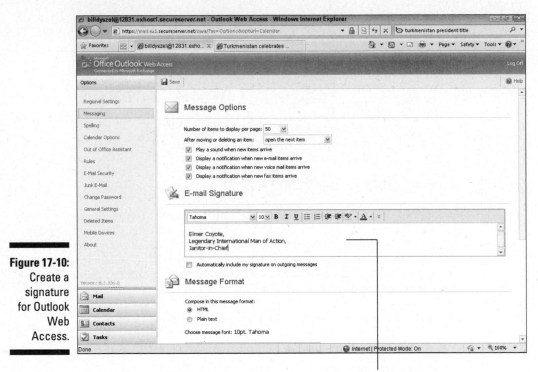

Figure 17-10:
Create a
signature
for Outlook
Web
Access.

Type your signature here.

Part VI
The Part of Tens

In this part . . .

You may ask, "Why do I have a Part of Tens?" Well, why do good things come in small packages? I don't know why, but they do. In this case, I bring you ten good things in ten small packages, and after that, ten more.

Chapter 18

Ten Accessories for Outlook

*O*utlook can do plenty for you without any outside help, but a few well-considered accessories can make your life even easier. Some of my favorite accessories make up for capabilities that Outlook ought to have (in my humble opinion) but doesn't. Some of my other favorite accessories help me use my Outlook data anywhere, anytime.

Smartphones

Smartphones are everywhere today, and they're probably the most powerful "accessory" for Outlook. If you haven't shopped for a new cell phone lately, *smartphones* are cell phones with built-in personal organizing software. The top smartphones at the moment include the iPhone, BlackBerry, and Palm Pre, with the Motorola Droid coming up fast. Although I can enter and manage data in a snap with Outlook, I can carry my most important Outlook info in my pocket on whatever smartphone I'm carrying. I can even read my e-mail on the subway using a smartphone (something I wouldn't try with a laptop).

Microsoft Office

When Outlook was first released, it was a part of the Microsoft Office 97 suite. In certain, special situations, Microsoft offers Outlook as a stand-alone product (or in a package with Internet Explorer), so you may not always have the benefits of using Microsoft Office and Outlook in concert. Office enables you to do all sorts of tricks with outgoing e-mail and graphics, while Outlook makes it a snap to exchange the work you've created in Office via e-mail. I recommend using both, if possible.

A Business-Card Scanner

You can use several brands of business-card scanners to copy contact information into Outlook from the business cards you collect at meetings, conferences, and trade shows. Of course, you *can* enter all the info manually, but if you collect more than a few dozen cards per week, a business-card scanner can save you lots of work.

Mozy Backup

One of the most common questions I hear is, "How do I back up my Outlook data for safekeeping?" I've been using Mozy backup service (www.mozy.com) for a while now, and I'm pretty happy with the simplicity of it. Mozy is a service that automatically backs up the most critical data on your computer and saves it on the Internet where it's safe. If your computer crashes or if, heaven forbid, you should suffer a fire, flood, or other disaster that destroys your computer, you can get your information back and start up where you left off. You'll need a high-speed Internet connection to make use of Mozy. It costs $4.95 per month, and believe me, the peace of mind is worth every penny.

Xobni

Inbox spelled backward is Xobni, an add-in that helps you search, sort, and analyze the information you store in Outlook. It can even tell you what time of day your boss e-mails you most frequently. (Here's a hint: Be available then.) Some of Xobni's better tricks have been added to Outlook already, but you might still give the Xobni free trial version a whirl to see whether you like it.

Microsoft SharePoint

Until now, Microsoft SharePoint was found most frequently in large organizations that needed a way to share information and collaborate smoothly. The program was too cumbersome and expensive for private users and home businesses. Now anybody can buy a service called SharePoint Online, which is what Microsoft is calling the subscription version of SharePoint that it sells for $15 per month. If you have a regular team that collaborates on business projects, you might consider trying SharePoint as a tool for sharing documents and other information.

Microsoft Exchange

Many of the features that appear to be built into Outlook actually require you to run a program called Microsoft Exchange. Exchange lets you share your Outlook information with other people in your office and coordinate meetings and tasks.

You can rent Microsoft Exchange accounts from many different vendors, including Microsoft, for a monthly fee per user. For this book, Go Daddy (www.godaddy.com) provided Exchange hosting. Go Daddy does an excellent job of providing good service and excellent support.

Windows Live

With online giants like Google breathing down its neck, Microsoft is scurrying to create online services that can retain customers. Windows Live is the umbrella under which you can find a whole range of free services that enhance and extend Microsoft Office. From file sharing to calendar publishing, you'll get a lot of value if you sign up for a free account at http://windows.live.com.

Text Messaging Services

Now that everyone has a cell phone, and every cell phone can exchange text messages, it's helpful when you can make Outlook extend itself to any cell phone via text message. Outlook can't do that alone, though — you need to set up a subscription to a service that translates and transmits messages from Outlook to the cell phone you have in mind. To set up text messaging from Outlook, click the File tab in any Outlook module, choose Options, and then choose Mobile and click the Mobile Options button. A screen opens to leads you to a list of providers that can handle that for you.

Dymo LabelWriter

The people who designed Outlook got so excited about e-mail that they completely forgot about that old-fashioned stamp-and-paper system that some people still prefer. (How quaint!) Outlook alone can store zillions of mailing addresses, but it doesn't do a very good job of putting an address on an envelope. I use a Dymo LabelWriter (www.dymo.com) to bridge that gap, printing any address from Outlook to a convenient gummed label that you can stick on a package or envelope faster than you can say "United States Postal Service."

Chapter 19

Ten Things You Can't Do with Outlook

*M*aybe I sound crabby listing the things that Outlook can't do, considering all the things it *can* do. But it takes only a few minutes to find out something that a program can do, and you can spend all day trying to figure out something that a program *can't* do. I could easily list *more* than ten things that Outlook can't do (walk the dog, deflect incoming asteroids — the usual). This chapter lists just the first big ones that I've run into.

Bear in mind that Outlook can't do these ten things when you first get it. Because you can reprogram Outlook with Visual Basic, however, a clever person could make Outlook do many of these things by creating shortcut macros (which is beyond the scope of this book).

Custom-Sort Folders

The most highly organized people I know get even more organized when they use Outlook. They often like to file every e-mail message into just the right folder. They also like to sort their folders in a very particular, highly efficient order, which is not always alphabetical. Unfortunately, the Outlook Folder list automatically sorts itself alphabetically, no exceptions. That drives nit-pickers nutty, but there's no changing it.

Go Back to the Old Menus

Many people like the Ribbon better than Outlook's old menu system. It's bigger and more colorful, no doubt. But if you learned to use computers during the heyday of menus and toolbars, you might long to click the old, familiar menus. Sorry, the Ribbon has it wrapped up for now.

Insert a Phone Number into Your Calendar

When you enter an appointment, it would be nice if Outlook could look up the phone number of the person you're meeting and insert the number into the appointment record. If you have a Palm organizer, you may be used to doing just that with the Address Lookup feature, but you can't get Outlook to follow suit. Maybe some other time.

Open a Message from the Reading Pane

If you're like many people, the list of e-mail messages that you store in Outlook serves as a historical record of everything you do. Maybe you scroll back and forth through your messages from time to time to get a handle on what you've sent to whom, and when you sent it. If your list is relatively long, and you select one message to display in the Reading pane, and then scroll through the list to look at a different message, you can't just right-click the Reading pane to open the message you're viewing. It doesn't seem like it would be terribly difficult for Microsoft to include a right-click command to open the message in the Reading pane, but it isn't there.

Perform Two-Sided Printing

Some people like to print their schedule and keep it in a binder to look just like one of those old-fashioned planner books. I guess they're just sentimental for the good ol' paper-and-pencil days. The only problem with that is that

Outlook doesn't know how to reorganize printed pages according to whether the page is on the left side or the right side of the book when you look at it. This is a very small quibble, but if it's important to you, sorry — you'll have to live with one-sided printing.

Search and Replace Area Codes

It seems like the people at the phone company change area codes more often than they change their socks these days. If you need to change all your 312s to 708s, Outlook can't do that automatically; you'll have to change them one by one. Microsoft did offer a utility for changing Russian area codes, but as for area codes in the United States — nyet!

Embed Pictures in Notes

You can copy and paste a picture, file, or other item into the text box at the bottom of any Outlook record when you open nearly any Outlook form. You can paste a photo of a person in the text box of the person's Contact record, for example, but those little, yellow stick-on notes don't let you do that; they accept only text.

Calculate Expenses with Journal Phone Call Entries

You can keep track of how much time you spend talking to any person, but you can't calculate the total call time or total call cost for billing purposes.

Create a Distribution List from a Single E-Mail

When you get an e-mail message addressed to a whole group of people, it would be nice to be able to create a Distribution list directly from that message. That way, you can send messages to that whole group by sending to a single Distribution list address. You can turn a message from a single person into an individual contact record by dragging the message to the Contact icon, but you can't do that to create a group: You have to add every single person individually to the Distribution list.

Back Up Outlook Data

Many people store their most critical business information in Outlook — information that is so valuable that losing it could practically close a business or end a career. It's no joke. But after more than ten years in the marketplace, Outlook has never been given a decent tool for safeguarding its own data from loss. Yes, everyone knows that you should back up all the data on your computer regularly, and you can make copies of your critical Outlook data (some of those tiny memory keys can do the job, and you can save Outlook data to a handheld computer if need be), but it's a little bit disturbing that no such feature has ever been added to Outlook itself. Some of the online backup services such as Mozy (see Chapter 18) do a good job of backing up your Outlook data.

Ten More Things Outlook Can't Do for You

Alas, Outlook is also deficient in some other ways, though you may prefer to do these things for yourself, anyway.

Outlook can't

- Do the Electric Slide
- Play "Melancholy Baby" for you
- Tattoo the name of you-know-who on your you-know-what
- Catch the Energizer Bunny
- Stop tooth decay
- Take the *Jeopardy!* Challenge
- Refresh your breath while you scream
- Fight City Hall
- Make millions while you sleep
- Find Mr. Right (unless you send e-mail to me)

Oh, well. Aside from all that, it's a pretty neat program. You can save scads of time and work more smoothly by mastering all the things Outlook *can* do for you.

Chapter 20

Ten Things You Can Do after You're Comfy

*I*f Outlook is an iceberg's worth of capabilities, I can only show you the tip in this book. You can already do some formidable tasks with Outlook. Time will tell (and pretty quickly at that) how much more you'll be able to do with future versions of Outlook, Internet Explorer, and all the other powerful technology associated with those applications.

You can't do much to really mess up Outlook, so feel free to experiment. Add new fields, new views, new icons — go wild. This chapter describes a few Outlook adventures to try out.

Customizing the Quick Access Toolbar

Office 2010 features an arrangement of controls (a *user interface,* as geeks like to say) that eliminates menus in favor of big ribbons, tabs, and buttons. The current scheme is much more colorful than the old menu system was, but I have trouble figuring out how to do many of the things I want to do. With an old-fashioned menu system, you know that everything you want to do is on a menu somewhere. In the new arrangement . . . who knows? If you find the new system confusing, don't feel bad; I've been writing books about Outlook for over ten years now, and I'm often baffled by this new scheme.

There is hope, however. After you've found the tool you need, you can right-click the tool and choose Add to Quick Access Toolbar. That adds a tiny icon to that thin strip of icons that sits just above the Ribbon (or below the Ribbon, if you move it there). If you've ever bookmarked a Web site, you know how this works. If you right-click the Quick Access toolbar and choose Show the Quick Access Toolbar below the Ribbon, that's exactly what happens.

Each Outlook form also features its own Quick Access Toolbar as well. That's useful for speeding up tasks that you perform frequently. If you like to print individual e-mail messages from time to time, you can add the Quick Print command when you're reading or composing a message. That way, the Print command is a couple of clicks closer.

Wising Up Your Messages with Smart Art

I don't know whether art makes you smart, but design can make you look smart if you know what you're doing. If you don't know what you're doing, you can fall back on Smart Art, another intriguing feature on the Insert tab of the Ribbon. Smart Art helps you create colorful, annotated designs to add to your e-mail. To get a better picture of what Smart Art can do, click the Insert tab, click the Smart Art button, and try a few designs on for size.

Translating Your E-Mail Messages

If your incoming e-mail messages are so confusing that they seem like they're written in a foreign language, maybe they are. You can translate incoming e-mail messages in Outlook 2010 by selecting some confusing text, right-clicking the text, and choosing Translate from the shortcut menu. If the translations don't even make sense, you can feel better knowing it's not your fault that you can't understand the gibberish people are sending you.

Adding Charts for Impact

Just a few doors down from the Word Art button on the Insert tab of the Ribbon is the Chart tool, which can make the thoughts you express in your e-mail look positively orderly (no matter how disordered your mind may be).

Chart it up with these steps:

1. **Click the Chart tool.**

   You see a two-part gallery: a list of general chart types on the left and specific examples of each type on the right.

2. **Choose a general type from the list on the left.**

3. **Choose a specific type from the list on the right.**

4. **Click the OK button.**

   A grid opens, allowing you to enter numbers.

The mechanics of creating an Outlook chart are very similar to those for creating an Excel chart. If you need more detailed information about creating charts, pick up a copy of *Office 2010 For Dummies* (published by Wiley).

Using Symbols in E-Mail

If you frequently use symbols such as the Euro currency symbol, you can now add those symbols to your e-mail messages by clicking the Symbol button on the Insert tab and choosing the symbol you want. If you choose More Symbols, you can also insert clever things like fractions, arrows, and strange hieroglyphics to baffle your recipients into complying with your wishes.

Opening Multiple Calendars

You can create more than one calendar in Outlook. You might want to do so to track the activities of more than one person, or to keep your business life separate from your personal life (which is always a good idea). The tricky part of keeping multiple calendars is dealing with schedule conflicts between the two. To see two calendars at a time, click the check box next to each calendar name in the Navigation Pane to view both calendars.

Superimposing Calendars

An even slicker way to avoid conflicts on multiple calendars is to superimpose one calendar on top of another. When you have two calendars open, a small arrow appears next to the name of one. When you click that arrow, both calendars appear, one atop the other, with both sets of appointments showing. The appointments in the bottom calendar appear slightly opaque, while the top calendar items look clearer and bolder than the bottom ones. When calendars are superimposed, you can see right away when time is available on both.

Viewing Unusual Numbers of Days

When you're viewing your calendar, you can decide to view only three days or eight days or, for that matter, any number between one and ten days by holding down the Alt key and typing the number of days you want to see. Press Alt+2 for two days, Alt+3 for three days, and so on. Pressing Alt+0 (zero) gives you ten days.

Selecting Dates as a Group

When you're viewing a range of dates, you don't have to limit yourself to fixed days, weeks, or months. Suppose that you want to look at a range of dates from September 25 to October 5. On the To-Do bar, click September 25 and then (while pressing the Shift key) click October 5. All the dates in between are selected, appearing in the Information Viewer.

Pinning a Contact Card

If you want to keep contact information about a person visible on the screen while you do something else, you can hover your mouse pointer over a person's email address until a little rectangle appears containing that person's name, picture, and other info. That's called a Contact card. Near the upper right corner of the contact card there's a tiny picture of a push pin. Click that picture to make the Contact Card float on the screen until you click the picture again to make it go away.

Chapter 21

Ten Shortcuts Worth Taking

*E*ven though computers are supposed to save you time, some days this just doesn't seem to be the case. Juggling buttons, keys, and Ribbons can seem to take all day. Here are some shortcuts that can really save you time and tension as you work.

Using the New Items Tool

To create a new item in whatever module you're in, just click the New Items tool at the far-left end of the Ribbon. The icon changes when you change modules, so it becomes a New Task icon in the Tasks module, a New Contact icon in the Contacts module, and so on. You can also click the arrow next to the New Items tool to pull down the New Items menu.

When you choose an item from the New Items menu (see Figure 21-1), you can create a new item in an Outlook module other than the one you're in without changing modules. If you're answering e-mail, for example, and you want to create a task, click the New Items button, choose Task, create your task, and then go on working with your e-mail.

New Appointment button

New Items menu

New Items button

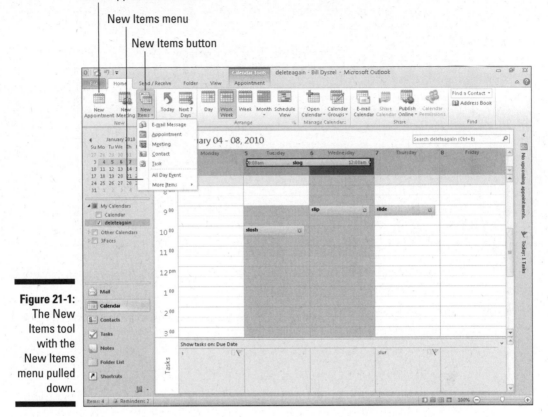

Figure 21-1:
The New
Items tool
with the
New Items
menu pulled
down.

Sending a File to an E-Mail Recipient

You can send a file via Outlook e-mail with only a few mouse clicks, even if
Outlook isn't running. When you're viewing files in Windows Explorer, you
can mark any file to be sent to any e-mail recipient. Here's how:

1. **Right-click the file that you want to send after finding the file with
   Windows Explorer.**

   A menu appears.

2. **Choose Send To.**

   Another menu appears.

3. **Choose Mail Recipient.**

   A New Message form appears. An icon that represents the attached file is in the text box.

4. **Type the subject of the file and the e-mail address of the person to whom you're sending the file.**

   If you want to add comments to your message, type them in the text box where the icon for the file is.

5. **Click the Send button.**

   Your message goes to the Outbox.

Sending a File from a Microsoft Office Application

You can e-mail any Office document from the Office application itself, without using the Outlook e-mail module. Here's how:

1. **With an Office document open in the application that created it, click the File tab.**

2. **Choose Share.**

   The Office Share screen appears.

3. **Choose Attach a Copy of This Document as an E-mail.**

   The New E-Mail Message form appears.

4. **Type the subject of the file and the e-mail address of the person to whom you're sending the file.**

   If you want to add comments to your message, type them in the text box where the icon for the file is.

5. **Click the Send button.**

   Your message goes to the Outbox.

Microsoft Word actually gives you several ways to send someone a file via e-mail. The method I describe in the preceding step list sends the Word file as an attachment to a message. If you choose Send a Link, your recipient just gets a link to the document, which is only useful if you and your recipient both have access to the document, either on the Internet or on your local computer network. You can also send the document as a PDF file, which retains all the formatting so that the document looks the same to your recipient as it does to you, and it also prevents anyone from changing the document. The XPS format has the same benefits as the PDF format, except that more people can read PDF files.

Taking a Note

How often do you need to take a quick note in the course of a busy day? (A lot, I bet.) If Outlook is running, you can take a quick note by pressing Ctrl+Shift+N, typing your note, and pressing Esc. In just a second, your note is stored away for future reference in your Outlook Notes module.

Finding Something

It doesn't take long to amass quite a large collection of items in Outlook — which can then take a long time to browse through when you want to find one specific item. Outlook can search for items at your command if you type the name of what you're seeking in the Search box at the top of every screen. That launches a quick search so that you can get to what you want in a flash.

Undoing Your Mistakes

If you didn't know about the Undo command, it's time you heard the good news: When you make a mistake, you can undo it by pressing Ctrl+Z or by clicking the Undo button on the Quick Access toolbar in the upper-left corner of the screen. So feel free to experiment; the worst you'll have to do is undo! (Of course, it's better if you undo your mistake right away, before you do too many things.)

Using the Go to Date Command

You can use the Go to Date command (as shown in Figure 21-2) in all Calendar views. If you're looking at the Calendar, for example, and you want to skip ahead 60 days, press Ctrl+G and type **60 days from now**. The Calendar advances 60 days from the current date.

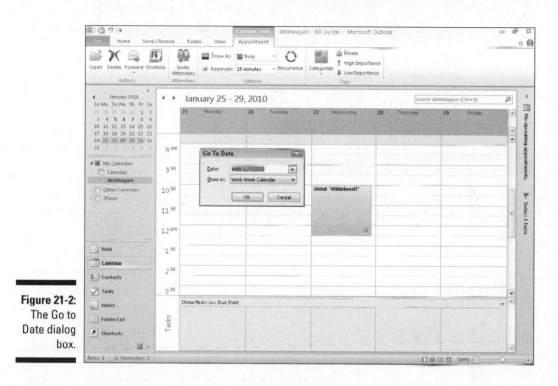

Figure 21-2:
The Go to
Date dialog
box.

Adding Items to List Views

Many Outlook lists have a blank field at the top where you can type an entry and create a new item for that list. When you see the words `Click here to add a new task`, that's exactly what you do. Just click in the field and type your new item.

Sending Repeat Messages

I have one or two messages that I send out repeatedly, so I've stored the text of those messages as Quick Parts to save time. For example, when I'm writing an article about Outlook accessories, I send a message to every company I encounter that makes things for Outlook that says something like this:

> I'm currently writing an article about Microsoft Outlook, and I'd like to evaluate your product, XX, for discussion in the book. Could you send me a press kit?

Because I've saved that message as a Quick Part, when I find a new Outlook accessory vendor on the Web, I just double-click the company's e-mail address in my browser, click the Insert tab, then click the Quick Parts button, and choose the AutoText item that I saved. Then I change the XX to the name of its product and click the Send button. I can have a request out in less than 30 seconds and get on to my next task.

Resending a Message

Sometimes you need to "remind" someone who forgot to do something you asked him or her to do. You could draft a whole new message reminding that person how many times you've reminded him already. But it's faster and easier to go to your Sent Items folder, double-click the message you sent last time, click More Actions, and choose Resend This Message. You might also add a sentence saying "In case this didn't reach you, here's another copy."

Index